Science, Technology and Innovation Studies

Science, technology and innovation (STI) studies are interrelated, as are STI policies and policy studies. This series of books aims to contribute to improved understanding of these interrelations. Their importance has become more widely recognized, as the role of innovation in driving economic development and fostering societal welfare has become almost conventional wisdom. Interdisciplinary in coverage, the series focuses on the links between STI, business, and the broader economy and society. The series includes conceptual and empirical contributions, which aim to extend our theoretical grasp while offering practical relevance. Relevant topics include the economic and social impacts of STI, STI policy design and implementation, technology and innovation management, entrepreneurship (and related policies), foresight studies, and analysis of emerging technologies. The series is addressed to professionals in research and teaching, consultancies and industry, government and international organizations.

More information about this series at http://www.springer.com/series/13398

Ilya Kiriya • Panos Kompatsiaris •
Yannis Mylonas
Editors

The Industrialization of Creativity and Its Limits

Values, Politics and Lifestyles of Contemporary Cultural Economies

Springer

Editors
Ilya Kiriya
National Research University
Higher School of Economics
Moscow, Russia

Panos Kompatsiaris
National Research University
Higher School of Economics
Moscow, Russia

Yannis Mylonas
National Research University
Higher School of Economics
Moscow, Russia

ISSN 2570-1509 ISSN 2570-1517 (electronic)
Science, Technology and Innovation Studies
ISBN 978-3-030-53163-8 ISBN 978-3-030-53164-5 (eBook)
https://doi.org/10.1007/978-3-030-53164-5

This Springer imprint is published by the registered company Springer Nature Switzerland AG.
The registered company address is: Gewerbestrasse 11, 6330 Cham, Switzerland

Acknowledgments

In June 2017, scholars and practitioners from several countries, including Russia, the UK, France, Croatia, Italy, Greece, Switzerland, South Korea, the USA, and Peru, gathered at the Saint Petersburg branch of the National Research University Higher School of Economics (NRU-HSE) to present studies on the contemporary economies, ethics, and aesthetics of creativity. The volume at hand brings together a selection of the conference papers highlighting the constantly developing and multidimensional practices associated with creativity at disparate geographical contexts around the world in the current time. The event was organized by members of the School of Media, NRU-HSE, in Moscow. We would like to warmly thank all the participants of this conference as well as all the contributors who made possible the publication of this volume.

Moscow
March, 2020

Contents

Contributors

Patrick-Yves Badillo University of Geneva, Geneva, Switzerland

Mark Banks CAMEo Research Institute for Cultural and Media Economies, University of Leicester, Leicester, UK

Valerija Barada Department of Sociology, University of Zadar, Zadar, Croatia

Dominique Bourgeois University of Fribourg, Fribourg, Switzerland

Vincent Bullich GRESEC (Groupe de Recherche Sur les Enjeux de la Communication—Research Group on the Challenges of Communication, Université Grenoble Alpes, Grenoble, France

Edgar Buršić Faculty of Interdisciplinary, Italian and Cultural Studies, Juraj Dobrila University of Pula, Pula, Croatia

Evangelos Chrysagis University of Edinburgh, Edinburgh, Scotland, UK

Buršić Edgar Faculty of Interdisciplinary, Italian and Cultural Studies, Juraj Dobrila University of Pula, Pula, Croatia

Nada Endrissat Bern University of Applied Sciences, Bern, Switzerland

Cecilia Ghidotti Institute for Media and Creative Industries, Loughborough University London, London, UK

Ilya Kiriya National Research University Higher School of Economics, Moscow, Russia

Panos Kompatsiaris National Research University Higher School of Economics, Moscow, Russia

Margarita Kuleva National Research University Higher School of Economics, Saint Petersburgh, Russia

Bernard Miège Emeritus, Gresec, University Grenoble Alpes, Saint-Martin-d'Hères, France

Yannis Mylonas National Research University Higher School of Economics, Moscow, Russia

Jaka Primorac Institute for Development and International Relations, Zagreb, Croatia

Tatiana Romashko University of Jyväskylä, Jyväskylä, Finland

Paula Serafini CAMEo Research Institute for Cultural and Media Economies, University of Leicester, Leicester, UK

Chapter 1
The Industrialization of Creativity and Its Limits: Introducing Concepts, Theories, and Themes

Ilya Kiriya, Panos Kompatsiaris, and Yiannis Mylonas

Abstract In this introduction we explore how creativity, loosely referring to activities around the visual arts, music, design, film, and performance, is mobilized by states and governments as a "resource" for economic growth. The creative economy discourse emphasizes individuality, innovation, self-fulfillment, career advancement, and the idea of leading exciting lives as remedies to social alienation. Drawing on the chapters in this volume, this introduction questions this discourse, exploring how political shifts and theoretical frameworks related to creative economy in different parts of the world at a time when the creative industries become more and more "industrialized." We present the interdisciplinary contributions of volume that navigate a variety of geographical contexts, ranging from the United Kingdom, France and Russia to Greece, Argentina, and Italy, and explore issues around art biennials, museums, DIY cultures, technologies, creative writing, copyright laws, ideological formations, craft production, and creative co-ops.

Keywords Creativity · Creative economies · Cultural industries · Cultural economies

1.1 The Industrialization of Creativity and Its Limits: Introducing Concepts, Theories, and Themes

In 2006, Rotterdam art collective BAVO published *Plea for an Uncreative City*, a manifesto-like call for "launching a cultural counterweight against the current launching of Rotterdam as cultural capital of the Netherlands." In its plea, BAVO disputed the ideological underpinnings of the creative economy, the rosy discourse of which promised to regenerate the City of Rotterdam in the context of its status as a European cultural capital. Their critique against creative policy argued that "rather

I. Kiriya · P. Kompatsiaris (✉) · Y. Mylonas
National Research University Higher School of Economics, Moscow, Russia
e-mail: pkompatsiaris@hse.ru

I. Kiriya et al. (eds.), *The Industrialization of Creativity and Its Limits*, Science, Technology and Innovation Studies, https://doi.org/10.1007/978-3-030-53164-5_1

than optimizing the welfare level of the largest possible group," it prioritized "specific groups," including the usual suspects of "artists, designers, ICT-nerds … managers, yuppies, CEOs"; in other words, creative policy was elitist. BAVO's salvo against the creative economy called on citizens to drop their participation in the "creative circus" and instead be "uncreative"; they wanted the city to "embrace its poverty" and cultivate a more inclusive and emancipatory urban imaginary.

BAVO's manifesto summarized critiques against the ideology, agendas, and outcomes of the creative economy as articulated by anti-gentrification activists and critical scholars in response to the British New Labour government's canonization of creative policies in the late 1990s and their subsequent global dissemination. Briefly, the main points of these critiques were that policy foregrounding the seemingly noble concept of creativity as a solution to social ills is exclusionary, generates inequality, enables gentrification, contributes to the myth of the creative genius, and favors the already-haves over the have-nots. More broadly, these critiques said that the creative economy renews capitalist actuality by evoking in it a "new spirit" of openness, participation, and flexibility (Boltanski and Chiapello 2007); essentially, it makes capitalism and structural exploitation look more fun.

Recent critiques against creative economy policy and discourse have come from within its ranks, as even its most enthusiastic and active proponents now question some of their previous beliefs. This is the case of Richard Florida, the sociologist guru of the creative economy, who famously argued in the early 2000s that the economic potential of cities is directly related to their coolness, diversity, and talent as well as their ability to attract hip and unconventional bars and restaurants, festivals celebrating the non-binary, multicultural spaces, and large numbers of entrepreneurs and creatives (Florida 2002: 744–751). While this idea became the dogma and rationale of creative policies during the 2000s, Florida admitted in a more recent book that his insights were wrong in several respects (2017). The cool crowds do not guarantee less inequality and exploitation; on the contrary, they can turn neighborhoods into ghettos for the rich. Who can afford to live in city centers full of hipster cafes designed for tourists and the middle class? Throughout the creative years of the post-2000s, as Florida now suggests, "the less advantaged members of the working and service classes, as well as some artists and musicians, were being priced out" of downtown neighborhoods; urban centers then harvested "a new kind of homogeneity of wealthy people, high-end restaurants, and luxury shops" and "a lopsided, unequal urbanism in which a relative handful of superstar cities, and a few elite neighborhoods within them, benefit while many other places stagnate or fall behind" (2017: iv–v). Even if Florida, the architect of creative cities and the creative economy, has not fully disqualified his earlier thesis, we can conclude that there is now a growing scholarly consensus that an uncritical celebration of creativity is problematic.

In this introduction, we critically assess the present-day industrialization of creativity following its widespread dissemination to different parts of the world. For purposes of clarity and analytical depth, we have divided this book into three parts that correspond to key aspects through which the creative economy and its ramifications can be approached: (1) sustainability in relation to growth and labor,

(2) ideology in relation to self-expression, aesthetics, and politics, and (3) industrialization in relation to the tensions between creativity and market forces. In the first part, the authors problematize the benevolent nature of creative industries in terms of growth paradigms and relationships between employers and employees, focusing on the lived realities that creative economies impose upon different national settings. In their different ways, these contributions ask for whom creative economies are public-spirited, humane, and sustainable. The second part focuses on the ideology of self-expression and aesthetics as drivers of economic configurations in the everyday practices and processes of economic restructuring. Here, the contributors ask how creative policies interpellate and subjectify cultural producers amid economic transformations and how those producers respond. The third part explores the industrial logic of creativity and its implications for capital, financial, and managerial strategies, asking how the fields of technology, innovation, and law interfere with creativity discourse. Overall, the chapters of this volume track and speculate on how larger circumstances, political shifts, and theoretical frameworks may or may not transform creative economy practices and discourses around the world as creative industries become increasingly industrialized. Before we delve into these three parts and the various empirical contexts in which they have developed, we will tackle some key sociological and political-economic approaches that summarize this volume's understanding of creativity.

1.2 Understanding Creativity

First, to ask a recurring question, what is creativity? From a cultural sociology perspective, the term loosely refers to activities that fall under the labels "visual arts," "music," "design," "film," and "performance" and that primarily aim to and are evaluated on their capacity to produce forms of effect and social meaning (Banks 2007; Hesmondhalgh 2007). In policy-orientated engagements, creativity is usually connected with the objectives of economic growth in societies transitioning to a postindustrial model (Hesmondhalgh and Pratt 2005). This model gives rise to state- or market-driven propagation of individuality, the virtues of innovation and self-fulfillment, aspirations for personal and career advancement, unalienating work, and upward social mobility connected to an overarching wish to lead exciting and meaningful lives.

In popular parlance and liberal-positivist literature, "creativity" implies newness, innovation, and originality, promising feelings and emotions of unexpectedness and surprise; to be creative means to be on the right side of things, to be open-minded, innovative, tech savvy, and au courant. Yet, creativity is not an objective condition; its framing depends on the value systems different groups of people employ in the narratives they use to talk about it. Almost any practice in any context can be conceptualized as novel and creative, depending on how and by whom these concepts are framed. To offer an example from conceptual art, Richard Serra's 1968, 3-minute video *Hand Catching Lead* was not considered creative by anyone other than the artist's inner circle. Broader audiences were bored by its depiction of an outstretched hand trying to catch pieces of falling lead and might have even thought it was the work of a madman. Yet, in the years to come, the video rose to fame, as did Serra's reputation as a brilliant conceptual artist. It was showcased in several major international museums and was released on DVD in 2006 by the Centre Pompidou. Serra's works are now celebrated as groundbreaking creative pieces in museums, art schools, and similar venues that define what is creative and what is not.

Likewise, social anthropologists and sociologists have long argued that creativity is a social process rather than an abstract attribution (Bourdieu 1993; Harstup 2007; Hallam and Ingold 2007). Creative producers can never completely transgress the iron cage of social constraint (Friedman 2001); if they do, their works are deemed incomprehensible or even insane. They must draw from "the total matrix of relations in which [they are] embedded and into which [they] extend" (Hallam and Ingold 2007: 9). Within specific fields—the artistic field, for instance—each producer is amenable not only to the history but also what Bourdieu called "the space of possible" that a field offers for recognizing various creations as creative (1993: 176). This was very neatly demonstrated, as Bourdieu put it, by the art of Marcel Duchamp, who showed that "the production of the producer as artist is the precondition for the production of these objects as works of art" (1993: 61). According to this line of thought, creativity is not the work of a single genius but rather that of a collective, social, and cooperative process. Creativity, as any other discursive designation, is primarily a product of power relations.

Although creativity is not an essence, and its semantics shift through time, the designation of a practice or an individual as creative always implies some essentially positive difference over other practices and individuals: for the creatives to exist, there must be a binary opposite, i.e., an uninspired, uncreative mass. This designation prioritizes the idea that creative people utilize exceptional capacities to differentiate themselves from everyone else, whether in art, business, or advertising, and these capacities are always somehow connected to neoliberal market values. Here, a good reference point is Nicholas Garnham's well-known critique of the designation "creative" in neoliberal policy discourse versus the more inclusive and potentially emancipatory "cultural" (2005). Yet, as we will discuss in a later section, this technology—or what Angela McRobbie called the "creativity dispositif" (2016)—has been undergoing its own legitimacy crisis and transformation in recent years as a result of broader political-economic developments. This does not mean that creative economies are a thing of the past; on the contrary, the proliferation of creative activities and clusters in contemporary metropolitan downtowns goes hand in hand with the development of tourist economies, the Airbnb invasion, cheaper flights, the lust for beatified ruins, and the submission of whole urban ecologies to the "imaginary of gentrification" (Lindner 2018: 275).

1.3 The Political Economy of Creativity

In historical terms, creativity as a productive model responded to the broader global sociopolitical and economic shifts of the early 1970s, the traces of which are still visible. In this paradigm, creativity is in tune with what that the Austrian political economist Joseph Schumpeter described as "creative destruction" (1942). Put briefly, for Schumpeter, destruction is intrinsic to capitalism, which requires the periodic erasure of previous structures that define the social relations of production, machinery, and the laws and norms that enable the economy to create new norms that give rise to more efficient, profitable, and innovative processes of production. This occurs as capitalism reaches crises that require the restructuring of the accumulation process. As described by Vincent Miller (2011: 48) and others, there are five waves of innovation during the history of capitalism broadly distinguished by the use of technology and energy: "the first is the so-called Industrial Revolution, based on machines, factories, and canals (initiated in 1771; birthplace: Britain); the second is 'the age of steam,' related to the use of coal, iron and railways (1829; birthplace: Britain); the third is 'the age of steel' connected to the development of heavy engineering (1875; birthplace: Britain, USA, and Germany); the fourth marks the age of the automobile, characterized by the use of oil, petrochemicals, and mass production (1908; birthplace: USA); and the fifth is the 'age of information' defined by communication technology (ICT) (1971; birthplace: USA)" (Perez 2002, in Kostakis 2019: 4). While creativity may be broadly assumed to be part of all these historical waves of creative innovation and destruction, the kind of creativity discussed in this volume relates to developments occurring on a global scale from the early 1970s onward. In this sense, if we follow the five-wave scheme above, creativity, as we know it today, falls into the fifth category, which is characterized by a post-Fordist mode of production that is flexible, decentralized, global, and open (Harvey 1989).

A central historical moment of creativity as a productive model arose during the efforts of capital to overcome the world's early-1970s stagnation of growth, which was triggered by the so-called oil crisis. That moment marked the slowdown of economic growth in the West following the Second World War and was further accompanied by social unrest. According to the standard account by autonomist Marxist theorists (e.g., Berardi 2009) and others (e.g., Harvey 1989), the industrial workforce, which was experiencing rising living standards, demanded fulfilling work and a better share of profits. Western governments and businesses responded to the crisis by attempting to meet both workers' demand for autonomy and capital's demands for innovation and economic restructuring, which meant the progressive dismantling of welfare and protectionist policies established in core Western states after the Second World War (Boltanski and Chiapello 2007; Harvey 2007: 22). Economic restructuring thus occurred by optimizing the creative drives and desires of the workforce as well as the countercultural lifestyles and aspirations of people in the 1960s and 1970s, all the while developing policies that enabled more market freedom. In this context, innovation, technological progress, and creativity are not ahistorical but rather politically driven processes advancing amid conflicting economic interests and social antagonism. The media political economist Nikos Smyrnaios argues that as the globalized capitalist system came to rely mostly on technological innovation, developments such as the Internet, which emerged from the countercultural creative and collaborative spirit of the 1970s, would be monopolized and controlled by multinational corporations, notably Google, Apple, Facebook, Amazon, and Microsoft, the so called GAFAM (Smyrnaios 2018). In effect, however, the monopolization of the Internet also occurs because of the depoliticized character of the so-called Californian Ideology—the spirit of which gave rise to these corporations—that favored distance from party or collective politics and a focus on innovation and entrepreneurship as vehicles of social change (Smyrnaios 2018).

The advocates of the ideological–political doctrine of neoliberalism, for whom the economic crisis of the 1970s was a strategic moment to advance their agendas, held similar views and aspirations with regard to the necessity of innovation and entrepreneurship for social change, stressing the primacy of market mechanisms in all aspects of social life (Slobodian 2018). Neoliberalism meant the effective depoliticization of the economy and, along with it, the de-democratization of politics. Economic and political elites stressed the virtues of the free market and strove for the development of legal frameworks, institutions, and public norms that would conform to their vision of a market-oriented society. In this context, entrepreneurialism, mobility, and innovation became mandatory characteristics in people who wanted to survive and potentially prosper in a highly competitive world. The advent of neoliberalism, the cult of innovation, generalized competition, and the dismantling of welfare resulted in the augmentation of social inequalities, rising levels of exploitation, and the spreading of social insecurity and regimes of exclusion, thereby creating a surplus of people the economy deemed redundant (Bauman 2004). Since then, the national state framework has been crucial in sustaining the free market structure through the organization of institutional and normative regimes mediated by global institutions and rules.

1.4 Part I: Sustainability—Creative Growth, Labor, and Skills

Departing from critical reviews of creativity that situate it within a broader politico-cultural framework, this book's introduction questions the sustainability of the creative economy in terms of its labor and growth models. First, the widespread discourse among activists and critics on the limits of capitalist growth in the context of accelerating climate change and an impending environmental catastrophe (e.g., Malm 2019) can twist the idea that creativity should be mobilized for economic growth, which, as Mark Banks and Paula Serafini note in their contribution to this volume, is a "foundational premise of creative economy thinking." In their chapter,

"Towards Post-Growth Creative Economies? Building Sustainable Cultural Production in Argentina," they debunk the popular belief that the creative industries are "ecologically 'greener,' 'cleaner,' or simply more benign than other, more traditional industries," arguing that they are "highly resource-dependent, energy-intensive, and often seriously polluting." They go on to offer alternative models of cultural collectives working in Argentina that challenge capitalism's growth imperative and commit to horizontal, de-accelerationist, and democratic practices. As their chapter emphasizes, Argentina's alternative economies and post-growth strategies are important, as this is a country that has gone through severe economic crises in recent decades and one in which the neoliberal experiment of unlimited growth has clearly failed.

At the same time, while creative work is generally framed as a win–win scenario in which "one is paid to do what one loves," scholars note that, apart from its potential autonomy, it can also resemble and nurture serfdom practices (Homan 2014: 637). Studies have stressed that decent remuneration in creative sectors is often the exception rather than the rule (Brooke and Wissinger 2017). Nevertheless, the myth of ideal creative work casted in the mold of the creative dispositif overstresses exceptional cases by interweaving the lure of success with the scenario of leading a potentially autonomous life. This dispositif works to both discipline and stimulate creatives in a highly insecure and competitive labor environment (Brooke and Wissinger 2017) in which the "scope of uselessness" (Sennett 2006: 83) broadens and possibilities for upward social mobility are limited.

According to a recent account by Adam Arvidsson (2019), this broadened scope of uselessness and disposability has created a class of "new petty producers" who combine "market orientation with an orientation to alternative values like 'authenticity,' 'impact,' or 'freedom'" (2019: 3). He further wrote:

> The disappearance of stable industrial jobs in the West (and increasingly also in Asia as factories automate), and the transformation of the countryside in Africa and South America due to new enclosures along with climate change, is creating a new generation of outcasts without much to expect from traditional life forms. Increasingly they are joined by middle-class university graduates, who are forced into freelance careers. Together these new "masterless men" have given rise to a new sector of commons-based petty production (17).

The ambivalence of creativity regarding its vocational, career-orientated, and life-fulfilling prospects is highlighted by creative labor's political economy and its supposedly positive nature. Crucially, in their chapter "Creative Workers in Permanent Crisis: Labor in Croatia's Contemporary Arts and Culture," Jaka Primorac, Valerija Barad, and Edgar Buršić raise the significant question of who can afford to work in this sector. The authors argue that the flexibility and work precarity that creative professions in Croatia entail are ultimately a matter of luxury: "in order to work precariously in this sector, workers must have middle-class backgrounds, otherwise they cannot afford to work precariously." In other words, a middle-class identity and aspirations of self-fulfillment set the stage for creative labor before becoming an iron cage in which more and more project work is required so producers are able to continue working.

Likewise, Margarita Kuleva's contribution "The Only Place Where One Can Feel Connected to an International Context and Still Speak Russian: Hybrid Creative Work in Post-Soviet Contemporary Art Institutions" is an effort to "de-Westernize" critical labor studies by focusing on what she calls the "hybrid creative work" of full-time employees in Russian nongovernmental art centers. According to Kuleva, workers in these institutions, which aim to express a post-Soviet and meritocratic ethos in Russia's cultural field, contend on an "ideological battlefield" shaped by the combination of "neoliberal creative entrepreneurialism and the Soviet heroization of work." Creative work in these institutions emerges as a labor-intensive activity in which workers are expected to be permanently available. Therefore, creative work, as with any other type of labor, needs to be understood as inherently ambivalent and embedded within the broader work frameworks of capitalism rather than those of exceptional activities.

Regarding creativity's conceptualization as either a commonly acquired skill or an elitist and exceptional mind-set acquired by talented individuals, Cecilia Ghidotti's "Creative Writing Courses are Useless: Creative Writing Programs and the Italian Literary System" focuses on the recent rise of creative writing degrees and their public perception in Italy while drawing on the example of the Turin-based Holden School. As a recent academic discipline that differentiates itself from other literary studies, creative writing aims to develop a specific field of training meant to cultivate the skills and imaginations of aspiring writers. Ghidotti argues that learning to write literature (e.g., poetry) is generally seen as impossible because it is connected to the elitist idea of a culture of modernist tastemakers and is further marked by underlining beliefs about talent and charisma, i.e., qualities usually attributed to geniuses. However, according to Ghidotti, this view fails to grasp the political economy dimension of these ventures. Instead, critics must focus on the development of skills to produce popular content, connecting creative writing degrees with the broader creative labor market, and assessing the criteria and processes of inclusion or exclusion from the literary field.

1.5 Part II: Ideology—Creative Self-Expression and Aesthetics

Ideology is closely related to the supposedly inherently positive nature of creative economies. How are cultural producers and the general public influenced by the creative discourse and its aesthetic economies to believe that creativity is good, and how do these agents react? In their chapter, "The Art Biennial's Dilemma: Political Activism and Spectacle in Aesthetic Capitalism," Panos Kompatsiaris and Nada Endrissat discuss how the rising number of art biennials, which are de facto markers of creative and intellectual coolness in any cityscape, relates to neoliberal policy agendas of opening locales to international visibility and tourism. For them, "the high aesthetics" of aesthetic capitalism "are supposed to antagonize market relations and incorporate the low aesthetics of social media, marketing, and everyday culture to provide the experience of a mega-event." Highbrow, post-conceptual art and branding techniques are brought together to attract eyeballs in an age of accelerated commodification of attention (Bueno 2016). The proclaimed social engagement of these events is itself ideological, as it needs to be packaged in a specific way to appear radical to art audiences and beyond.

While focusing on the case of Greece's prolonged economic and political crisis (2009–2018), Yiannis Mylonas's chapter "Creativity in the Service of Economic Recovery and National Salvation: Dispatches from the Greek Crisis Social Factory" shows how the term "creativity" was publicly mobilized during the crisis years to promote a model of economic restructuring based on self-reliance, individualism, and entrepreneurialism. Mylonas shows how a "creativity cult" emerged during these years and has been developing through the reformed policy programs of neoliberal restructuring and the "spectacles of entrepreneurial success stories" about start-ups, gastronomical revolution, and local authenticity to beautify the misery of the crisis and produce entrepreneurial subjectivities and individualistic worldviews. At the same time, creativity in the Greek context is promoted in parallel with notions such as meritocracy and sustainability, which form both conservative and progressivist touchstones in a neoliberal and governmental discursive repertoire.

Concurrently, the configuration of entrepreneurialism in conservative political morals and projects goes hand in hand with the emergence of new forms of social conservativism that entail the frequent mobilization of creativity and culture for nationalist projects. For example, theorist Ilya Budraitskis (2017) argued that the Russian government has begun operationalizing cultural production to express a timeless and eternal idea of Russianness that is somehow markedly different from the identity of the West. Here, as Budraitskis notes, cultural conservativism is an instrument of neoliberalism for domestically legitimizing Vladimir Putin's government. Similarly, in Tatiana Romashko's contribution to this volume, "The Production of Cultural Policy in Russia: Authority and Intellectual Leadership," she traces the transformation of this governmental discourse from the period of 1990s liberal decentralization to the "conservative centralization" that began in 2011 and continues as of this writing. For Romashko, this instrumentalization of culture attempts several things at once, namely to "legitimize the federal government," "establish cultural borders between Russia and [European Union] countries," and "reduce 'Russian society to a single national identity." The conservativeness of Russia's new right appears in tandem with the broader global rise of the strongman, forcing us to further question our previously unbridled optimism that views globalization as a liberating force, both economically and socially.

However, ideological interpellations can be negotiated and replayed. With his chapter "Do-it-Yourself Manifestos: Ethics and the Quest for Authenticity," Evangelos Chrysagis examines the manifestos of do-it-yourself (DiY) practitioners in the United Kingdom, where recurring quests for self-expression and authenticity constantly emerge in a "surplus" form amid efforts to capture, tap, and commodify creative energy. Following a literature review on manifesto writing, Chrysagis explains how the recent increase in manifesto formats in cultural production has been accompanied by the promotion of ethical values that overshadow the more instrumental understandings of art and music that policy makers and leading industries pursue. In an era where creativity has come to signify an economic asset framing market-oriented discourses, the three manifestos Chrysagis studies demonstrate that DiY practices and culture, despite the all-pervasiveness of capitalism (or maybe because of it), stand as a useful example of an ethical mode of self-expression. In this regard, the manifestos that Chrysagis explores denote an intention to oppose dominant meanings and cultural forms, seek alternatives, and resist established aesthetics, practices, and their recuperation by the mainstream, despite the risks and pitfalls of co-optation that this quest may entail.

1.6 Part III: Industrialization—Creative Markets and Technologies

The last part of this volume explores how tensions around industrialization occur from the general development of technologies and the market in relation to creative policies and discourses. In Bernard Miège's chapter, "Creative Industries: A Large, Ongoing Project, Still Inaccurate and Always Uncertain," the author taps his pioneering studies on cultural and informational industries to provide us with an overview of their historical development and the mutations they underwent when policy makers began to emphasize creativity. Here, the rise of the creative industries is understood as a global politico-economic project for a generation of economic growth with great heterogeneity, spatially, and in terms of productivity. Miège presents a typology for understanding the distinctions between informational, cultural, and creative industrial production, drawing on a political economy perspective. Creative work is often slower and more artisan-based than informational work, and may not always rely on digital technologies. Such features define the reproducibility and the predictability of informational, cultural, and creative products. These are also connected to the allocation of revenues created through processes of production, circulation, and consumption. Further, there are macroeconomic differences between the cultural and creative industries (e.g., between filmmaking and craftsmanship). Given this, various challenges regarding the development of the creative and cultural industries arise and are connected to issues related to the rise of monopolies (such as the aforementioned GAFAM), the effects of competition on smaller producers, the impact of industrialization on content production, and the rise of amateur/audience users and informal production.

In line with the work of the "French school" on cultural industries, Ilya Kiriya's chapter, "From Craft to Industry: Industrializing the Marginal Domains of Cultural Industries," argues that certain aspects of what was considered craft production have become increasingly industrialized as business models have begun to adjust to new demands for audiences and funding. Kiriya explores cultural domains, such as theater and performing arts, that exist on the margins of industrialization due to difficulties in their technical reproducibility. Digital technologies are changing this by allowing the standardization and reproduction of such cultural forms of production on a mass scale, making them more like the content industries. In effect, this development leads to the financialization of such sectors due to the potential revenues industrialization promises. Kiriya examines different understudied crafts sectors, such as performing arts (e.g., musicals), comedy, and educational practices, and he discusses the changes that their industrialization brings in their reproducibility as well as the division of labor and business model they use. Of crucial importance are processes of aggregation and mediatization, which enable the industrialization of previously marginal crafts mainly through digital technologies and social media.

The monetization of content production as a key feature of the creative and cultural industries model is the main topic of Vincent Bullich's chapter, "Intellectual Property Rights and the Production of Value in a Creative Economy." Indeed, intellectual property rights provide a legal framework for the commodification of creative ideas and the production and sustainability of creative services and products as singularities that can generate profit in a competitive and globalized market environment. The valorization of the creative product emerges from the identity of the producer, which is often what makes a given product attractive to buyers (as we saw above with Serra and Duchamp). The production of singular commodities out of creative ideas is organized by the law, which safeguards the identity of the creative object and regulates the conditions of its ownership. However, intellectual property rights are not a necessary precondition for the development of creative production. The law is meant to protect the product's authenticity from counterfeiting strategies through a monopolistic framework in the market. Here, Bullich notes the importance of the state in maintaining the free market edifice that manifests in the deeply political character of what is usually understood as the neutral site of economy.

Finally, in Patrick-Yves Badillo and Dominique Bourgeois's contribution, "Innovation and Media: Googlization and Limited Creativity," the authors examine the current processes of innovation that occur in the media industries. By empirically focusing on the Swiss media, the main innovations they observe are connected to what they call "Googlization," which is understood as a digital management process with the objective of attracting more online traffic and gathering more data to generate more profits. While examining relevant literature on innovation and by using Schumpeter's creative destruction model to examine how innovation occurs, they conclude that innovation in the media industries has been more destructive to the old model of media production and less innovative and creative to the potential production of more high-quality informational and cultural content. Therefore, this volume's last section on creative industrialization as a process that involves tensions around markets and technological developments follows from the previous two sections, which question the dominant logic of creativity as a supposedly self-generating, neutral, and value-free concept.

References

Arvidsson A (2019) Capitalism and the commons. Theory Cult Soc. https://doi.org/10.1177/0263276419868838

Banks M (2007) The politics of cultural work. Palgrave Macmillan, Basingstoke

Bauman Z (2004) Wasted lives: modernity and its outcasts. Polity, Cambridge

BAVO (2006) A plea for an uncreative city. BAVO Website Online. bavo.biz/plea-for-an-uncreative-city. Last Accessed 2 Dec 2019

Berardi F (2009) The soul at work: from alienation to autonomy. Semiotext(e), Los Angeles

Boltanski L, Eve Chiapello E (2007) The new spirit of capitalism. Verso, London

Bourdieu P (1993) The field of cultural production: essays on art and literature. Polity Press, Cambridge

Brooke ED, Wissinger E (2017) Mythologies of creative work in the social media age: fun, free, and "just being me". Int J Commun 11:4652–4671

Budraitskis I (2017) Contradictions in Russian cultural politics: conservatism as an instrument of neoliberalism. In: Dietachmair P, Gielen P (eds) The art of civil action. Valiz, Amsterdam. http://www.criticatac.ro/lefteast/russian-contradiction/. Accessed 30 Nov 2019

Bueno C (2016) The attention economy: labour, time and power in cognitive capitalism. Rowman and Littlefield International, London

Florida R (2002) The economic geography of talent. Ann Assoc Am Geogr 92(4):743–755

Florida R (2017) The new urban crisis: how our cities are increasing inequality, deepening segregation, and failing the middle class-and what we can do about it. Basic Books, New York

Friedman J (2001) The Iron cage of creativity: an exploration. In: Liep J (ed) Locating cultural creativity. Pluto Press, London, pp 46–61

Garnham N (2005) From cultural to creative industries: an analysis of the implications of the "creative industries" approach to arts and media policymaking in the United Kingdom. Int J Cult Policy 11(1):15–29

Hallam E, Ingold T (2007) Creativity and cultural improvisation. Berg, Oxford

Harstup K (2007) Performing the world: agency, anticipation and creativity. In: Ingold T, Hallam E (eds) Creativity and cultural improvisation. Berg, Oxford, pp 193–206

Harvey D (1989) The condition of postmodernity: an inquiry into the conditions of cultural change. Blackwell, Oxford

Harvey D (2007) Neoliberalism as creative destruction. Ann Am Acad Pol Soc Sci 610:21–44

Hesmondhalgh D (2007) The cultural industries. Sage, Thousand Oaks, CA

Hesmondhalgh D, Pratt AC (2005) Cultural Industries and Cultural Policy. Int J Cult Policy 11 (1):1–13

Homan S (2014) Creative labour: media work in three cultural industries. Int J Cult Policy 20 (5):637–638

Kostakis V (2019) How to reap the benefits of the "digital revolution"? Modularity and the commons. Halduskultuur Estonian J Admin Cult Dig Gov 20(1):4–19

Lindner C (2018) Brutalism, ruins, and the urban imaginary of gentrification. In: Lindner C, Meissner M (eds) The Routledge companion to urban imaginaries. Routledge, London, pp 275–287

Malm A (2019) The progress of this storm: nature and society in a warming world. Verso, London

McRobbie A (2016) Be creative: making a living in the new culture industries. Wiley, New York

Miller V (2011) Understanding digital culture. Sage, London

Sennett R (2006) The culture of new capitalism. Yale University Press, New Haven and London

Slobodian Q (2018) Globalists: the end of empire and the birth of neoliberalism. Harvard University Press, Cambridge

Smyrnaios N (2018) Internet oligopoly: the corporate takeover of our digital world. Emerald, Bingley

Ilya Kiriya holds a PhD in journalism from Moscow State University and PhD in communication studies from Grenoble University (France). He was an assistant professor at the Moscow State University (Faculty of Journalism). Since 2007, he is a full professor at the National research university "Higher School of Economics" where he is a chair of the School of Media. Ilya Kiriya's main scientific interests are in the field of political economy of communication and media in post-soviet countries. His works are published in the *International Journal of Communication, Russian Politics, Hermes Communication Journal.*

Panos Kompatsiaris is an assistant professor of Art and Media at the National Research University Higher School of Economics in Moscow. He holds a PhD in art theory from the University of Edinburgh (2015). He has published on art, culture, and politics in journals including the *European Journal of Cultural Studies, Communication, Culture & Critique, Journal of Visual Art Practice and Social Identities*. His monograph *The Politics of Contemporary Art Biennials: Spectacles of Critique, Art and Theory* (Routledge, 2017) looks at the politics of art biennials in the context of neoliberalism and its crisis. He is currently co-editing a special journal issue on art and value (*Journal of Cultural Economy*).

Yiannis Mylonas is an assistant professor in Media Sociology and Cultural Studies in the School of Media, at the National Research University, Higher School of Economics in Moscow. He is the author of "The 'Greek Crisis" in Europe: Race, Class and Politics" (Brill, 2019), and has previously published articles in journals such as *Critical Discourse Studies, tripleC*; *The Journal of Language and Politics, Continuum, Subjectivity, Race and Class*; *The Journal of Political Ideologies, Javnost/ the Public*, among others.

Part I
Sustainability: Creative Growth, Labor, and Skills

Chapter 2
Towards Post-Growth Creative Economies? Building Sustainable Cultural Production in Argentina

Mark Banks and Paula Serafini

Abstract The ecological crisis and the continued downturn in capitalist economies mean that there is now an urgent need for the creative and cultural industries to offer more genuinely alternative and sustainable models of organising and production. In this chapter, we highlight the existence and emergence of some incipient 'ecological', 'alternative' or 'post-growth' forms of cultural industries production that appear to offer different ways of thinking and doing the creative economy. First, we discuss the current state of cultural policy in relation to the ecological crisis, and argue for 'post-growth' as an avenue for rethinking and restructuring cultural economies. We then draw on empirical work undertaken by one of us (Serafini) in Argentina, to illustrate how in a post-crisis context, post-growth or post-extractivist and ecological imaginaries are already underpinning new forms of socially aggregating and sustainable cultural production. We conclude by arguing that the creative economy must be made more genuinely sustainable in *all* locations in order to help counter any further intensification of an already established set of economic and ecological problems and crises.

Keywords Post-growth · Extractivism · Creative economy · Cultural production · Sustainability · Cooperatives

2.1 Introduction

In the light of ecological crisis and the continued downturn in capitalist economies, there is now an urgent need for the creative and cultural industries to offer more genuinely alternative and sustainable models of organising and production. By this we mean ways of making cultural goods that do not rest on assumptions of (neoliberal) capitalist economy or champion the virtues of expansive and unchecked

M. Banks (✉) · P. Serafini
CAMEo Research Institute for Cultural and Media Economies, University of Leicester, Leicester, UK
e-mail: mark.banks@glasgow.ac.uk; paula.serafini@leicester.ac.uk

I. Kiriya et al. (eds.), *The Industrialization of Creativity and Its Limits*, Science, Technology and Innovation Studies, https://doi.org/10.1007/978-3-030-53164-5_2

'growth', but seek instead to challenge these conventional (and now increasingly failing) understandings, norms and practices. Therefore, in this chapter, we wish to highlight the existence and emergence of some incipient forms of cultural industries production that appear to offer different ways of 'thinking and doing' the creative economy.[1] We will draw on our own shared theoretical interests in 'post-growth' thinking and on the particular empirical work undertaken by one of us (Serafini) in Argentina, to provide a case illustration of how post-growth, or more precisely post-extractivist and ecological imaginaries are productively combining to effect new forms of socially aggregating and sustainable cultural production. Our broader point, however, is that the creative economy must be made more genuinely sustainable in *all* locations in order to help counter any further intensification of an already established set of economic and ecological problems and crises.

2.2 Creativity Economy and Ecological Crisis

For us, the ecological crisis (by which we mean the total and integrated set of economic, social and environmental challenges now faced by global populations) means that some of the foundational assumptions that underpin the creative economy must be brought into question. This includes the widespread belief that the cultural and creative industries are somehow ecologically 'greener', 'cleaner' or simply more benign than other, more traditional industries (see Maxwell and Miller 2017). Compared to 'smokestack' industries or primary extraction or manufacturing, the cultural and creative industries tend to be presented as better by nature. This, however, is a dangerous and damaging assumption—for a number of reasons:

- Firstly, the creative and cultural industries are highly resource-dependent, energy-intensive and often seriously polluting. This includes many of the world's leading digital media technology companies, the global film and television industries, publishing, music and the transport, circulation and logistical systems that sustain them (see Banks 2018; Devine, 2019; Maxwell and Miller 2017; Murdock 2018 for examples).
- Secondly, while the creative economy still tends to be favoured as a 'positive' solution to problems of economic restructuring, often through cultural and 'creative class' regeneration of urban space, research has consistently revealed the creative economy to be also associated with destructive and highly contested forms of gentrification, displacement and valuable resource-use (Novy and Colomb 2013; Oakley and O'Connor 2015).

[1]Broadly defined as the aggregate of all cultural and creative industries, arts, media and technology-led industrial sectors. More specifically it tends to be defined (in the United Kingdom at least) as all the people employed in the officially designated 'creative industries' (whether these people have creative jobs or not) plus all the people working in creative occupations employed in 'non-creative' industries.

- Thirdly, it has become apparent that many hundreds of thousands of low-paid and poorly treated workers are working in degraded or unsafe environments, involved in the global extraction and supply chain of raw materials, and in processes of manufacture producing the creative economy goods that Global North countries most avidly consume (Chan et al. 2016; Qiu 2016). Additionally, the global trade and circulation of waste, e-waste and detritus of the creative economy create problems of disposal, disassembly, toxic hazard, ill-health and death—especially in the most impoverished nations of the Global South (Cubitt 2015; Lepawsky 2018).
- Finally, the optimistic idea that growth can be progressively 'decoupled' from environmental impacts is becoming increasingly regarded as a comforting—but highly dangerous—delusion (D'Alisa et al. 2015; Jackson 2009; Kallis 2018). For example, in the creative economy context, we already have evidence of how the rapidly expanding volume and demand for electronic communications devices (phones, tablets, etc.) will generate environmental costs that will likely outstrip any savings made by efficiency improvements in the design, manufacture and usage of individual devices themselves (Caraway 2017; Maxwell and Miller 2017).

The creative economy is not the solution to, nor separated from, ecological crisis, but is intrinsically *part of* a wider capitalist–expansionist system now facing some serious (and potentially catastrophic) social, economic and environmental challenges. That the future-oriented (but resource hungry) creative economy has thus far failed to consider these challenges in any significant way is deeply troubling, and demands an urgent and combined intellectual, industry and policy response.

2.3 Challenging the Growth Imperative

We want to suggest that one of the key barriers to progressive change in late-capitalist economies (and the creative economy sectors within them), is the relentless and uncritical pursuit of *economic growth*. We note there is almost nothing in the economic policies of advanced capitalist nations that seek to question growth as the primary socio-economic objective, or that considers the potentially damaging consequences of a commitment to unlimited economic expansion. Yet growth, as an idea, is in trouble. Firstly, the global financial crisis of 2007 has not only further curtailed (already falling) rates of growth, but brought to light that per capita GDP across the OECD nations, as well as labour productivity, has been declining for almost half a century (Jackson 2018). Many mainstream economists are arguing that advanced capitalist economies have entered a phase of long term 'secular stagnation'—sustained low, flat or zero real growth rates over time (Krugman 2014; Summers 2014). Secondly, in social terms, while *some* kind of economic growth might initially be as vital and necessary (especially in so-called 'developing' nations), as economies become more 'advanced' the question of what kind (and what level) of economic growth might need to be sustained becomes more contested. There is some evidence to show measures of human happiness, well-being, life expectancy and life satisfaction have stalled (or reversed) in the Global North even as economic output has increased (Jackson 2009; Wilkinson and Pickett 2013). Growth is also problematic in that—where it residually occurs—it seems increasingly to be benefitting the more privileged members of societies at the expense of ordinary populations, as wealth has consistently failed to 'trickle-down' and social inequalities and injustices become more deeply entrenched (Piketty 2014). Finally, in environmental terms, the pursuit of growth is arguably having some catastrophic consequences in terms of accelerated global warming and climate change, and a whole host of destructive and damaging subsystemic effects—such as unsustainable resource extraction, land clearances, pollution, waste, population displacements and species extinctions. The mantra of growth sweeps all before it—yet the disastrous consequences of endlessly seeking to produce more, and produce more quickly, are barely registered in the state (and creative economy) policy context.

Indeed, the pursuit of growth remains a foundational premise of creative economy thinking. In the policies of advanced capitalist economies such as Australia, Canada, France, Germany and the United Kingdom[2] and in cross-national initiatives such *Creative Europe* 2014–2020 the dominant theme is investment in culture and creativity significantly boosts national output. Similarly, there are routine (but unfounded) claims that the creative economy is more socially inclusive, open and egalitarian than other industrial sectors (see Banks 2017 for a strong refutation) and that the innovations and affordances offered up by new media, VR, AI, advanced computing and technology will ensure the creative economy can be expanded within safe and sustainable environmental limits. Indeed, much creative economy policy and advocacy takes for granted the ongoing security and integrity of the natural environment and neglects any consideration of how creative economy production might negatively impact on sustainment of systems of global ecology. For example, prominent interventions such as the United Kingdom's *Culture is Digital* (DDCMS 2018), *Creative Industries Sector Deal* (HM Government 2018) and the *Independent Review of the Creative Industries* (Bazalgette 2017), the *Creative Canada Policy Framework* (Canada Heritage 2017) and *France Créative* (2013) make no reference to environmental or ecological issues, at all. The EU's *Creative Europe* 2014–2020 Programme has no explicitly environmental or ecological objectives beyond promoting 'sustainable' (in this case meaning 'continuous') growth. Similarly, in emerging economies, and in the Global South, for example in Latin America (Avogadro 2016; Kon 2016; WEF 2016) and countries of Africa, the creative economy is commonly tied to pro-growth (and not just pro-development) agendas that tend to talk-up the economic growth potential of creative industries, but mostly neglect to consider the wider ecological dimensions, in either economic, social or environmental terms (e.g. British Council 2016; Hruby 2018).

[2]See, for example Government of Australia (2013), France Créative (2013), Canada Heritage (2017).

This is not to say that 'alternative' or wider ecological concerns are *entirely* absent from mainstream creative economy policy discourse. Beyond the Global North we find some preliminary attempts to theorise and promote more sustainable and ecologically sensitive creative economies in 'developing' nations, for example as presented in the UNESCO/UNITAD *Creative Economy Report* (2013). While such interventions appear to strongly favour more sustainable and ecologically sensitive modes of creative economy development, a common fall-back position is to support the conventional 'sustainable development' paradigm which has always been primarily GDP and growth-led (see Martinez Alier 2009; Demaria et al. 2013). While it might be argued that some initial growth is required in creative economies of the Global South (see Sternberg 2017), we would argue that the ultimate goal should not be a replication of growth imperatives nor the pursuit of the (unsustainable) 'sustainable development' model of advanced capitalist nations, over time.

Yet, we should also note that outside of the creative economy mainstream *other* possible worlds are already being conceived of and formed—ones that reject core assumptions of capitalist economy and disavow any easy and unproblematic commitment to creative economy growth in an assumed world of stable and unlimited abundance.

2.4 Alternative Models to Growth

In recent years, precipitated by intensifying global crisis, a literature on 'post-growth' 'anti-growth' or 'degrowth' has emerged, concerned with highlighting the limits and failures of the capitalist economy, and proposing alternatives that seek ways to maintain the means of life for world populations within a more shared and collective, as well as ecologically balanced, set of socio-economic structures and frameworks (e.g. Daly 2018; Demaria et al. 2013; Gibson-Graham 2006; Jackson 2018; Kallis 2018; Roth 2017). Creative economy theorists have recently started to make connections to this literature—but the potential for further productive engagement is now significant (see Banks 2018; Oakley and Ward 2018). Additionally, in the creative economy context, there is a growing literature on alternative models of economic organising, including work on community provisioning, subsistence and mutual aid (e.g. see de Peuter and Cohen 2015). Researches on cultural and creative co-operatives, non-profits and different kinds of sharing or social economy are also emerging (Boyle and Oakley 2018; Sandoval 2017). New theorisations that challenge existing models of 'creative cities' by proposing more ecologically sound and sustainable urban cultural production are further evolving (Grodach et al. 2017; Kagan and Hahn 2011).

The value of such work is not simply to foreground the possibility of different (and generally more equitable and sustainable) ways of acting and organising economically in the creative sectors, but to fundamentally question the salience of foregrounding the 'economic' as the primary concern of creative and cultural production at all. For many who work in the cultural or creative industries, while there is an economic need to make, distribute and consume various goods and resources, there is a simultaneous need and desire to do so in ways that contribute to the sense of a *life worth living* (Banks 2018; O'Connor 2018). In this way, the creative economy might be seen as a site for 'growth' of a different kind—as an investment in an expansion of sociability, collective togetherness and flourishing, and sets of moral and ethical values that might assume no subordinate status to economic growth and pursuit of the profit-motive. Exponents of such creative economies can be found in all locations, but—as we will now discuss—seem, especially to arise in emergent circumstances of capitalist crisis.

2.5 Alternative Cultural Production in Argentina

In order to think further about what 'post-growth' cultural production might look like, one that seeks to progressively and sustainably combine economic, social and environmental concerns, we turn to recent evidence and experiences from Argentina. Here, as in some other Latin American countries, there is currently a growing promotion of the creative economy on behalf of the state, which coexists with other 'popular'[3] and alternative cultural economies. In this context, the paradigm of 'post-growth' or 'degrowth' as articulated and developed in the Global North is not widely circulated, but there are, however, other parallel paradigms, perspectives and praxes that cultural practitioners draw from which are compatible with post-growth and ecological thinking, such as *post-extractivism, horizontalism,* and *Buen Vivir* (see, for instance, Acosta 2008; Gudynas 2011). We have chosen Argentina as a suggestive setting for highlighting forms of cultural production that can help us think about a post-growth cultural economy, not least because of the socio-economic transformations the country has undergone in the last 20 years, and the responses and strategies this has elicited from different social actors, including social movements and cultural producers. Following the economic crisis that began in the late 1990s, and the popular rebellion of 2001, Argentina offers a recent example of a context in which the neoliberal growth model has visibly failed, and its failure given place to new and alternative forms of surviving, producing, sharing and living. In our exploration, we draw from secondary data on cultural production in the early 2000s, as well as primary interview data from more recent cases.

[3]Here we use the term 'popular' to describe practices and cultural forms that are non-institutional or informal, and constitutive of working class or other socially marginalised cultures.

2.6 Recuperated Businesses and the Rise of Cooperatives

In the late 1990s and early 2000s, Argentina underwent a profound economic crisis, a result of neoliberal policies in the 1990s that led to mass unemployment, the degradation of social services and a drastic increase in poverty levels (Svampa 2011: 19). This generated widespread social unrest, the political mobilisation of both working and middle classes, and eventually, the resignation of President De la Rúa in December 2001 to the chant of '*¡Que se vayan todos!*' (Let them all leave!), words that marked a deep desire for radical, systemic change. Faced with mass unemployment, Argentinians had to devise strategies for survival. This led to a range of formal and informal economic practices that changed not only the economic but also the social fabric; practices like bartering and structures such as cooperatives gave rise to new forms of relating to others, what became known as 'horizontalism' and '*autogestión*'. *Autogestión*, explains Marina Sitrin, does not translate directly into English, but is closest to the anarchist concept of self-management. *Autogestión* is about 'the relationships among people that create a particular project, not simply the project itself'. It refers to 'an autonomous and collective practice' that involves direct 'democratic decision-making processes and the creation of new subjectivities along the way' (Sitrin 2006: vii).

The recuperation of closed-down factories by their workers, and subsequent transformation of these into cooperatives, began with a dozen or so cases in 2001 and rose into the hundreds in the span of two years (Sitrin 2006: 14). These initiatives for survival, be that in the creative sector or elsewhere, emerged from a new understanding of the economy that deliberatively moved away from individual forms of profit gaining towards more horizontal and equitable structures. Horizontal forms of working like cooperatives subscribed to a particular way of governing and democratically thinking, but also to a different understanding of the economic, questioning the position of profit and growth as primary objectives.

An exemplary case of cooperative cultural production in the aftermath of the 2001 crisis is Eloísa Cartonera. Eloísa is a publishing project that emerged in Buenos Aires in 2003, and publishes hand-made books with cardboard covers. In their words, they are 'a group of people who came together to work in a different way, to learn new things through work, to build up a cooperative, to learn how to subsist and manage ourselves, to work towards a common good'.[4] The project responded to the situation of the moment. As a result of mass unemployment, a new figure had emerged in the cities: the *cartonero*. *Cartonero* is the term used to describe people who collect material such as cardboard (*cartón*) and metal, and sell this to individuals or recycling companies. The founders of Eloísa, who were artists and writers themselves, began to buy the cardboard from the *cartoneros* at five times the usual rate and used it to make covers of books. They also began to work with groups of *cartoneros* who would gain training in hand-making books and paint the book covers (Zimmer 2014: 105). The texts were donated either by famous authors or

[4] See http://www.eloisacartonera.com.ar/ENGversion.html

by young, unpublished ones. This non-profit publisher was established as a cooperative, at the beginning selling their productions as art books, and soon after shifting towards a model of affordable literature for all. This model travelled through the continent and now there are *cartonera* publishers all over Latin America.

Cartonera publishers can be read as agents of change on multiple levels. Firstly, they provide a source of income and, on occasion, training for a sector of the 'informal' creative economy. Secondly, they generate a new use for waste materials, contributing, albeit at a small scale, to the process of recycling in countries were often there is a lack of systematic recycling programmes (Bell 2017: 82) and increasing the value (both economic and aesthetic) of the waste material. Thirdly, by making their books affordable and accessible to new audiences, they contribute to a putative democratisation of literature. *Cartonera* publishing can be seen as the 'realization of literature as a social movement [. . .] to intervene directly in urban life' (Zimmer 2014: 105). Lucy Bell argues that this is an "instance of literary production in which the so-called 'three pillars of sustainability' – the environmental, the social and the economic – are invoked, intermeshed and transformed" (Bell 2017: 76–77). But, she adds, because of the way in which these aspects of the project are strongly interconnected, *cartonera* publishers challenge the idea of differentiated forms of sustainability 'pillars' by putting forward a more integrated and dynamic vision of sustainability. Here, for example we must consider how recycling is not only an environmental issue but also a social and economic one.

These practices must also be read in a contextualised manner, acknowledging the range of drivers behind what we could frame as the 'environmentalism of the poor' (Martinez Alier 2002). Indeed, as Bell suggests, the form of sustainability put forward by these publishers stems from the struggle for survival; while Eloísa Cartonera can be understood to be generative of sustainable processes, socialities and uses of waste, it still emerged from a perspective of the world as resource, a resource for the mere act of survival (Bell 2017: 94). Nonetheless, the *cartonera* movement could be said to be a fully ecologically oriented creative economy in the sense that it takes a holistic and total view of the economic, social and environmental impacts of creative economy production, measured against an evaluation of the collective needs of producers and consumers. As such, it offers a suggestive way of rethinking what a 'post-growth' (or genuinely sustainable) creative economy might look like or aspire to be, both practically and philosophically.

2.7 Cultural Production and Alternatives to Extractivism

By way of further example, here we look at how horizontalism and *autogestión* in cultural production are further integrated with environmental and wider ecological concerns in the context of more recent cultural production linked to the movement against 'extractivism'. Extractivism can be described as a model of intensive and extensive extraction of common goods ('natural resources') mostly destined for export, and championed as the only path towards development (Svampa and Viale 2014).

The extractivist model in Argentina takes the form of activities such as mega-mining, certain forms of monocrop agriculture, and fossil fuel extraction, including new and expanding fracking sites. This model has not only led to grave instances of environmental degradation, but also a series of health crises, the displacement of communities, the demise of regional economies and the increased repression of protest. The contemporary stage of extractivism in Argentina, or what some call 'neoextractivism', can be traced back to the mid-1990s, with the growth of monocrop agriculture, and the development of legislation that prepared the way for transnational mega-mining. The expansion of the extractive industries in Argentina has continued throughout the following two decades, first under a series of progressive governments (coinciding with the commodity boom of the early 2000s), and more recently under a market-oriented government (Svampa 2019). As in the rest of Latin America, movements against extractivism in Argentina argue that societies need to work towards alternatives to development that safeguard human and non-human life, enhance democratic participation in decisions over the use of the commons that are horizontal and inclusive, and reject conventional capitalist indicators of wellbeing, such as GDP and other measures of economic growth (Delgado Ramos 2013; Escobar 2014).

In the movement against extractivism, a critical and creative economy of community radio producers has emerged. This has been crucial to subsistence, information sharing and strengthening bonds and identities within the struggle (Serafini 2019). An example of this is the radio station El Brote, based in an alternative community called Semilla del Sur. Semilla del Sur is located in the central province of Córdoba, and is known for its promotion of permaculture and bioconstruction. Córdoba, in turn, is a province that has been heavily impacted by deforestation and by the use of toxic pesticides in monocrop agriculture. El Brote emerged in 2015 as a community-centred, popular and alternative radio station that is part of the ecology of the community of Semilla del Sur. Through its programming, which addresses social, political and environmental issues, it is also integral to the environmental, anti-extractivist movement at the local and regional levels.

Carolina is a media practitioner, and one of the people behind El Brote. After visiting Calamuchita and becoming involved with Semilla del Sur, she decided to leave the city and start a new life in this community. In an interview, she explained how the project for the radio station emerged:

> We began to build the idea of a communications work cooperative, always thinking about other ways of relating to each other, other forms of work, of payment and other economies as well, with an understanding that we cannot have bosses and we cannot be bosses to others either, because this really conditions communication.

El Brote is an important element in the social and cultural life of Semilla del Sur. Neighbours have found a space of 'social contention' in the radio; the radio acts as a medium for them to share their stories and their perspectives on the world. Furthermore, as is often the case for community radio, El Brote offers training and upskilling for community members who take part in it, acknowledging how these skills can contribute to people's future employment. The radio is both materially and culturally embedded within the alternative community of Semilla del Sur. It has a kind of social legitimacy that is territorial, which allows people to come to the radio when they are facing a particular issue, even if they are not regular participants. It is sustained through reciprocal relationships between those who run it and the audience, who have various levels of involvement. The site where the radio is based, for instance, was collaboratively built by the community, following principles of bioconstruction. For the practitioners at El Brote, radio is part of a prefigurative project. In Carolina's words, 'we believe that we really are generating and making possible another reality, always visibilising it from the field of communication'.

El Brote sustains itself through a variety of channels designed to cover basic operational and economic needs. This includes a small degree of commercial activity, such as advertising spots for local businesses, and selling *yerba mate* (a local infusion) from a cooperative in the province of Misiones from within the radio studio. In addition, they have a series of agreements with other local cooperatives (e.g. in water and energy), which allow them to exchange advertisements for the provision of services. They also receive support from neighbours, who have donated items like doors and windows for the renovation of the studio. Finally, El Brote is part of the network FARCO, which is the Argentine Forum of Community Radio. Through FARCO they have access to training and support with material issues, such as the opportunity to receive second-hand equipment from other radios, which they describe as a 'solidary bond' that is paramount to the subsistence of community media in Argentina.

The ethos, processes and programming of El Brote, as well as its position in the wider ecology and economy of Semilla del Sur and the regional environmental movement, correspond with the principles of *autogestión* and horizontality discussed earlier, but also align with what we could call a post-extractivist ethic of care, one that moves from a relationship of domination with regard to nature to one of care for both human and non-human beings (Curtin 1991). The radio acts as a space for personal transformation of participants, and for prefiguring social, cultural, economic and ecological relations that adhere to the notions of interdependence and ecodependence (Svampa 2015), and steer explicitly away from capitalist notions of profit and growth.

2.8 Conclusion

In a finite world, where it is accepted that resources are depleting rapidly, and a series of potentially catastrophic ecological transformations apparently looming, then a narrow focus on accelerating and expanding economic 'growth' can only be self-defeating—not least because presumptions around the kinds of stable futures and guaranteed resource-availabilities that will be sufficient to furnish the widely anticipated expansion of production, are beginning to look very dubious indeed. The creative economy is not exempted from the ecological crisis—and is indeed partly culpable for its amplification and extension. We suggest that however desirable a commitment to unlimited creative economy expansion might appear, such a goal cannot be sustained indefinitely, either as ideal or as practice.

By highlighting the cases of the radio El Brote and the *cartonera* publisher Eloísa Cartonera, we aim simply to draw attention to the suggestive and inspirational aspects of these emergent ‘post-growth’, ‘post-extractivist’ and ecologically oriented forms of cultural and creative economy production. Such initiatives are of course small-scale, fragile and localised. And while these and similar activities are growing in Argentina (and in Latin America, and regions beyond) we are not suggesting that they will easily supplant dominant forms of creative economy organising and production, nor come to fully replace existing socio-economic arrangements—at least not yet. Indeed, as we write, the resurgence of right wing and strongly growth-oriented (and anti-ecological) governments once again threatens to undermine the alternative cause. Rather we raise these initiatives as harbingers of something else—further evidence of the progressive raising of a more fulsome ecological consciousness amongst cultural producers and a hopeful sign of the kinds of new cultural praxes that might be occasioned in the face of expanding economic and ecological crises. What has happened in Argentina over two decades may be more likely to happen elsewhere as neoliberal regimes of growth further stall and the need to survive and sustain collective forms of life—in the creative economy and more generally—assumes a greater urgency and precedence. At the very least, this urgency might help put creative and cultural practitioners and producers more firmly at the forefront of necessary attempts to imagine more sustainable and just economic futures for all. For the future, we might even invoke the hope that the creative economy may come to matter less as an ‘engine of growth’ and rather more for its capacity to provide a valued context and resource for evaluating the current order of *life*—including the role played by growth in sustaining or suppressing it.

Acknowledgements This chapter draws on empirical research supported by a British Academy/ Leverhulme Trust Small Research Grant.

References

Acosta A (2008) El Buen Vivir, una oportunidad por construir. Ecuador Debate 75:33–47

Avogadro E (2016) Is Latin America ready for a creative economy? World Econ Forum. https://www.weforum.org/agenda/2016/06/is-latin-america-ready-for-a-creative-economy

Banks M (2017) Creative justice: cultural industries, work and inequality. Rowman and Littlefield International, London

Banks M (2018) Creative economies of tomorrow: limits to growth and the uncertain future. Cultural Trends 27(5):367–380

Bazalgette P (2017) The independent review of the creative industries. DDCMS. https://www.gov.uk/government/publications/independent-review-of-the-creative-industries

Bell L (2017) Recycling materials, recycling lives: cardboard publishers in Latin America. In: Johns-Putra A, Parham J, Squire L (eds) Literature and sustainability. Manchester University Press, Manchester, pp 76–96

Boyle D, Oakley K (2018) Cooperatives in the creative industries. Co-operatives UK, Manchester

British Council (2016) Scoping the creative economy in East Africa. British Council, London
Canada Heritage (2017) Creative Canada policy framework. Government of Canada. https://www.canada.ca/en/canadian-heritage/campaigns/creative-canada/framework.html
Caraway B (2017) Literal media ecology: crisis in the conditions of production. Telev New Media 19(5):486–503
Chan J, Pun N, Selden M (2016) Chinese labor protest and trade unions. In: Maxwell R (ed) The Routledge companion to labor and media. Routledge, New York, pp 290–302
de Peuter G, Cohen N (2015) Emerging labor politics in creative industries. In: Oakley K, O'Connor J (eds) The Routledge companion to the cultural industries. Routledge, London, pp 305–318
Cubitt S (2015) Integral waste. Theory Cult Soc 32(4):133–145
Curtin D (1991) Toward an ecological ethic of care. Ecol Femin 6(1):60–74
D'Alisa G, Demaria F, Kallis G (eds) (2015) Degrowth: a vocabulary for a new era. Routledge, London and New York
Daly H (2018) Ecologies of scale: interview by Benjamin Kunkel. New Left Rev 109:81–104
DDCMS (2018) Culture is digital. DDCMS, London
Delgado Ramos GC (ed) (2013) Ecología política del extractivismo en América Latina: casos de resistencia y justicia socio-ambiental. CLACSO, Buenos Aires
Demaria F, Scheider F, Sekulova F, Martinez-Alier J (2013) What is degrowth? From an activist slogan to a social movement. Environ Values 22:191–215
Devine K (2019) Decomposed: the political ecology of music. MIT Press, Cambridge, MA
Escobar A (2014) Sentipensar con la tierra. Nuevas lecturas sobre desarrollo, territorio y Diferencia. Ediciones UNAULA, Medellín
France Créative (2013) Création sous tension 2e Panorama de l'économie de la culture et de la creation en France. http://francecreative.org/
Gibson-Graham JK (2006) A post-capitalist politics. University of Minnesota Press, Minneapolis
Government of Australia (2013) Creative Australia: National Cultural Policy. http://apo.org.au/node/33126
Grodach C, O'Connor J, Gibson C (2017) Manufacturing and cultural production: towards a progressive policy agenda for the cultural economy. City Cult Soc 10:17–25
Gudynas E (2011) Más allá del nuevo extractivismo: Transiciones sostenibles y alternativas al desarrollo. In: Wanderley F (ed) El desarrollo en cuestión. Reflexiones desde América Latina. La Paz, Oxfam & CIDES UMSA, pp 379–410
HM Government (2018) Creative industries sector deal. HMRC, London. https://www.gov.uk/government/publications/creative-industries-sector-deal
Hruby A (2018, March 22) Tap creative industries to boost Africa's economic growth. Financ Times. https://www.ft.com/content/9807a468-2ddc-11e8-9b4b-bc4b9f08f381
Jackson T (2009) Prosperity without growth: economics for a finite planet. Earthscan, London
Jackson T (2018) The post-growth challenge: secular stagnation, inequality and the limits to growth. CUSP working paper no 12. https://www.cusp.ac.uk/publications/?_sft_publication_type=working-papers
Kagan S, Hahn J (2011) Creative cities and (un)sustainability: from creative class to sustainable creative cities. Cult Local Gov (Culture et gouvernance locale) 3:1–2
Kallis G (2018) Degrowth. Agenda Publishing, Newcastle
Kon A (2016) On the creative economy chain in Brazil: potentials and challenges. Brazil J Polit Econ 36(1). http://www.scielo.br/scielo.php?script=sci_arttext&pid=S0101-31572016000100168
Krugman P (2014) Four observations on secular stagnation. In: Teulings C, Baldwin R (eds) Secular stagnation: facts, causes and cures. CEPR Press, London. https://voxeu.org/content/secular-stagnation-facts-causes-and-cures
Lepawsky J (2018) Reassembling rubbish: Worlding electronic waste. MIT Press, Cambridge, MA
Martinez Alier J (2002) The environmentalism of the poor: a study of ecological conflicts and valuation. Edward Elgar, Cheltenham

Martinez Alier J (2009) Socially sustainable economic de-growth. Dev Chang 40(6):1099–1119
Maxwell R, Miller T (2017) Greening cultural policy. Int J Cult Policy 23(2):174–185
Murdock G (2018) Media Materialities: for a moral economy of machines. J Commun 68 (2):359–368
Novy J, Colomb C (2013) Struggling for the right to the (creative) City in Berlin and Hamburg. Int J Urban Reg Res 37(5):1816–1838
O'Connor J (2018) Tasmanian creative island report. http://find.creativeisland.com.au/creative-and-cultural-research-released/
Oakley K, O'Connor J (2015) Culture and the city. In: Oakley K, O'Connor J (eds) The Routledge companion to the cultural industries. Routledge, London, pp 201–211
Oakley K, Ward J (2018) The art of the good life: culture and sustainable prosperity. Cult Trends 27 (1):4–17
Piketty T (2014) Capital in the twenty-first century. Harvard University Press, Cambridge
Qiu JL (2016) Goodbye i-Slave: a manifesto for digital abolition. University of Illinois Press, Champaign
Roth S (2017) Marginal economy: growth strategies for post-growth societies. J Econ Issues 51 (4):1033–1046
Sandoval M (2017) From passionate labour to compassionate work: cultural co-ops, do what you love and social change. Eur J Cult Stud. Published online 11 Aug. http://journals.sagepub.com/doi/abs/10.1177/1367549417719011
Serafini P (2019) Community radio as a space of care: an Ecofeminist perspective on media production in environmental conflicts. Int J Commun 13:5444–5462
Sitrin M (ed) (2006) Horizontalism: voices of popular power in Argentina. AK Press, Oakland, CA
Sternberg R (2017) Creativity support policies as a means of development policy for the global south? A critical appraisal of the UNESCO creative economy report 2013. Reg Stud 51 (2):336–345
Summers L (2014) Reflections on the 'new secular stagnation hypothesis'. In: Teulings C, Baldwin R (eds) Secular stagnation: facts, causes and cures. CEPR Press, London. https://voxeu.org/content/secular-stagnation-facts-causes-and-cures
Svampa M (2011) Argentina, una década después: Del «que se vayan todos» a la exacerbación de lo nacional-popular. Nueva Sociedad 235:17–34
Svampa M (2015) Feminismos del Sur y ecofeminismo. Nueva Sociedad 256:127–131
Svampa M (2019) Las fronteras del neoextractivismo en América Latina. Conflictos socioambientales, giro ecoterritorial y nuevas dependencias. CALAS, Guadalajara
Svampa M, Viale E (2014) Maldesarrollo: La Argentina del Extractivismo y el Despojo. Katz, Buenos Aires
UNDP/UNESCO (2013) Creative economy report special edition: widening development pathways. United Nations, New York
WEF (2016) Factors for enabling the creative economy. World Economic Forum, Geneva
Wilkinson R, Pickett K (2013) The Spirit level: why equality is better for everyone. Penguin, London
Zimmer Z (2014) The unmanageable: exposing the literary commons in Buenos Aires. Chasqui 43 (2):94–109

Mark Banks is Professor of Cultural Economy at the Univeristy of Glasgow. For two decades he has researched working lives and policy-making in the cultural and creative industries and produced many articles and books, including the monographs *The Politics of Cultural Work* (2017) and *Creative Justice: Cultural Industries, Work and Inequality* (2017).

Paula Serafini is Research Associate at the CAMEo Research Institute for Cultural and Media Economies, University of Leicester. Her research is in the field of cultural politics, focusing on issues such as cultural labour, the politics of arts institutions, and the role of cultural production in the context of social and environmental justice movements. Paula is author of *Performance Action: The Politics of Art Activism* (Routledge 2018).

Chapter 3
Creative Workers in Permanent Crisis: Labor in the Croatia's Contemporary Arts and Culture

Jaka Primorac, Valerija Barada, and Edgar Buršić

Abstract Work in Croatia's independent cultural sector demands a specific type of individual. A typical worker is female, lives and works in the capital, Zagreb, and is mostly paid by honoraria. She is well educated and has well-educated parents that provide her with the safety net. She is burned out, but overall, she is satisfied with her position and life. She is also middle aged, single, and in most cases childless with only a few younger collaborators who are working with her. As an independent cultural worker, she is in a state of permanent crisis created by broader structural socioeconomic conditions in Croatia. These conditions do not encourage viable and sustainable cultural production, especially independent cultural production and especially in communities outside the capital. In order to work in such an unstable environment, independent cultural workers must be persistent, resourceful, multitalented, loyal to their profession, well embedded in the community, and privileged with a family that can function as a safety net. In short, to work precariously in this sector, one must belong to the elite, as only the elite can afford to work precariously.

Keywords Culture · Elite · Independent cultural sector · Inequalities · Precarious work

J. Primorac (✉)
Institute for Development and International Relations, Zagreb, Croatia
e-mail: jaka@irmo.hr

V. Barada
Department of Sociology, University of Zadar, Zadar, Croatia
e-mail: vbarada@unizd.hr

E. Buršić
Faculty of Interdisciplinary, Italian and Cultural Studies, Juraj Dobrila University of Pula, Pula, Croatia
e-mail: edgar.bursic@unipu.hr

I. Kiriya et al. (eds.), *The Industrialization of Creativity and Its Limits*, Science, Technology and Innovation Studies, https://doi.org/10.1007/978-3-030-53164-5_3

3.1 Introduction

Over the last decade, there has been a proliferation of research on the structural and individual conditions of work in arts and culture, with a specific emphasis on the precariousness of the work–life balance of cultural and creative workers (Banks 2007; Banks and Hesmondhalgh 2009; Banks et al. 2013; Barada 2012; Barada et al. 2016; Blair 2001; Blair et al. 2001; McRobbie 2002; Pratt 2004, 2008; Primorac 2008; Randle et al. 2015; Ross 2004, 2007, 2008; Standing (2011); Wing-Fai et al. 2015). These research endeavors, which are primarily centered in Europe and have a strong research influence in UK scholarship, have unraveled the complexity of the fragile social position experienced by cultural and creative workers, intersecting it with class, gender, and the ethnic inequalities of cultural and creative industries. This research has also shown that these sectors are far from rewarding for workers and that many policy actions are needed to achieve a creative justice (Banks 2017) that would enable more openness and equality for people with different social backgrounds.

Authors have also highlighted the importance of understanding the regional differences of working in this field (Avdikos and Kalogeresis 2018: 200). However, it is fair to say that not many voices from the European periphery and semi-periphery have been heard on these issues. Preliminary research from selected countries in Southeast Europe has shown both the similar and culturally specific trends of the precarious nature of creative work in the region and of the socioeconomic inequalities engrained within it (Cvetičanin and Krstić 2017). Furthermore, research on cultural and creative work has focused on conditions in cultural and creative industries in general, while conditions in other subsectors, such as the independent cultural scene, have been neglected. In this chapter, we aim to address these shortcomings by analyzing workers' positions in the independent cultural sector—that is, in civil society organizations involved in contemporary culture and the arts. In addition, with this analysis, we want to provide a voice on this issue from a European and semi-peripheral context—specifically, we want to provide a Croatian voice.

Croatia has a population of about 4.2 million and, in 2013, became the most recent country to join the European Union. After the Croatian War of Independence in the 1990s, the country's socioeconomic and political transitions were somewhat turbulent, reaching their climax during the global economic crisis of 2008, the echoes of which are still strongly felt. All of this has impacted the country's structural limitations, which has resulted in a decade-long socioeconomic crisis that is still palpable in high unemployment rates and emigration, especially among young people.[1] Unsurprisingly, the cultural and creative sectors have also been influenced by these events. In 2007, before the economic crisis, Croatia had an

[1]In October 2018, the general unemployment rate was 9.1%, while the youth unemployment rate was 23%. Since 2008, more than 200,000 people have emigrated from Croatia (www.dzs.hr, November 16, 2018).

emergent local market of cultural and creative products (Švob-Đokić et al. 2008), whereas over the last decade, a decline has occurred and has been exacerbated by continuous cuts to national subsidies (Primorac and Obuljen Koržinek 2017: 36). Additionally, the independent cultural sector has been heavily influenced by these cuts, with continuous underfunding at both the national and local levels (Primorac and Obuljen Koržinek 2017: 37) and additional cuts in specific subsectors, notably nonprofit media (Bilić et al. 2018: 8).

In this chapter, when speaking about the independent cultural sector, we define it as composed of nongovernmental civil society organizations in the field of contemporary arts and culture. This field has managed to establish itself as an important player in Croatia's overall culture mainly through its continuous advocacy, networking, and lobbying efforts in (local and national) cultural policy (Vidović 2012). These activities contributed to the 2011 establishment of the Kultura Nova Foundation, which is dedicated to the financing and development of contemporary arts and culture.[2] Although it has a modest budget relative to Croatia's other cultural institutions, the Kultura Nova has become the primary actor in the independent cultural sector's development. Nevertheless, the sector remains fragile, inviting the question of who works in the sector. More specifically, considering the burgeoning research on inequalities in the cultural sector, who in Croatia can afford to work in this sector?

To answer these questions, we conducted a type of census. Using a mixed methods approach (Creswell and Plano Clark 2007), we undertook an empirical study in 2014 and 2015 on the conditions of work in Croatian civil society organizations operating in the field of contemporary arts and culture (Barada et al. 2016).[3] Together with an analysis of Kultura Nova's database, the empirical work consisted of two online questionnaires, meaning that we had three sources of quantitative data. The database provided information about the finances, geographical data, and contact information of the cultural civil society organizations that applied for funding between 2011 and 2014. It must be noted that Croatia's cultural civil society organizations have substantial difficulties raising funds from personal donations, tickets, the European Union, etc. In such a situation, a foundation such as Kultura

[2]After the successful lobbying and policy advocacy activities of several civil society organizations, the Croatian government established the Kultura Nova Foundation in 2011 with the aim to financially support cultural civil society organizations in the fields of contemporary arts and culture. Kultura Nova does not finance institutionally funded organizations that enjoy national and/or local state subsidies. Rather, it is solely intended for noninstitutional arts and culture. While the Ministry of Culture oversees Kultura Nova, its calls for financing proposals are independent, although its budget comes from the State Treasury, namely from the National Lottery. This setup makes the Croatian model of financing independent culture and arts rather unique in the European context. According to the Kultura Nova's website, "[it] is an additional measure within the Croatian system of financing culture that contributes to the stabilization and development of civil society organizations in the fields of contemporary arts and culture." (http://kulturanova.hr/english, 20 November 2018).

[3]This study was funded by the Kultura Nova Foundation. However, this chapter reflects the views of the authors, and the Kultura Nova Foundation cannot be held responsible for any use of the information contained herein.

Nova, as previously explained, offers a unique means of funding cultural civil society organizations, which is why almost all Croatia's active cultural civil society organizations have applied to it at least once. Regardless of organizations' success in their applications, Kultura Nova recorded their data. Therefore, the database contains detailed information about the civil society organizations, including their projects, budgets, funding, and employees. The data of 380 organizations that applied in the 2011–2014 period was available. In the final research design, this number was reduced to 215 organizations whose activities fell strictly under the scope of contemporary arts and culture, i.e., the independent cultural sector.

More information about the cultural civil society organizations was gathered through an online questionnaire constructed with LimeSurvey[4] and emailed to the representatives of the 215 previously filtered organizations. The representatives of 93 organizations replied. The questionnaire asked for more detail about funding and budgets as well as the type of employees and number of long-term, limited contract workers who had contracts for six or more consecutive months. Representatives were also asked to provide the email addresses of the people they considered as employed in the field, including those not from their specific organizations. Considering that various and overlapping employment statuses can be found in the independent cultural sector, we asked respondents to define "employment."[5] Such consecutive sampling means that the second data set was based on information from the first (Kultura Nova's database) and that it was used to construct the third data set, which contained detailed information about the employees.[6] The third data set was collected with a second online questionnaire, which was also constructed with LimeSurvey, and more detailed personal questions were asked. We sent the questionnaire to 323 people and received 111 usable replies. This last data set was most relevant to the analysis presented here.

Additionally, 22 semi-structured interviews (with elements of in-depth interviewing) were conducted in nine cities in different regions of Croatia[7] with leaders of the longest running cultural civil society organizations, thus providing a comprehensive take on the field's labor conditions and processes. We addressed the reproduction of inequalities in the independent cultural sector on regional, gender-based, and sociodemographic levels, thus focusing on how sociocultural conditions create economic inequalities and vice versa. These somewhat historical social, cultural, and economic factors firmly structure the individual and institutional labor practices of Croatia's independent cultural sector. As this chapter continues, we will show how this structuring puts workers in particularly ambivalent social and labor positions. Structurally, they represent the elite of the Croatian labor market and

[4]LimeSurvey is an open-source survey tool available at: http://www.limesurvey.org

[5]It will later be shown that even ongoing and long-lasting volunteering is seen as work in this sector.

[6]The questionnaires were answered anonymously, and none of the personal identifiers of the respondents were saved.

[7]Zagreb, Split, Rijeka, Pula, Dubrovnik, Zadar, Karlovac, Vukovar, and Vinkovci.

society as a whole,[8] while on an individual level, their everyday personal and working lives are characterized by precarious practices (Morgan et al. 2013; Ross 2008). We argue that such an ambivalent social and labor position puts these workers in an iron cage of precarity, meaning they must work constantly in order to provide themselves with options and possibilities to continue working (compare with Graeber 2018). However, this chapter will also show the sector's unequal labor conditions. The data show that one must belong to the elite in order to manage the precarious nature of this sector, as only the elite can afford to work precariously.

3.2 A Reproduction of Inequalities? Regional, Gender-Based, and Sociodemographic Differences in the Independent Cultural Sector

Creative labor in Croatia's independent cultural sector is characterized as a permanent crisis. This crisis has both globally and nationally specific traits that exist on a societal-structural level, an organizational and professional level, and in the personal lives of the creatives in question. Croatia's independent cultural sector suffers from global developments that define creative labor in general. The risks and challenges of globally mediated creative work (Hesmondhalgh and Baker 2011; Huws 2014) manifest as precarious conditions and define the sector's specific national context. Independent cultural production is engulfed in the country's insecure economic flows as well as in a sociopolitical context that does not value cultural and creative work apart from the nominal claim of possible financial gain. This societal distance and suspicion toward the independent cultural sector define its organizational and professional plain. Although elements of a vibrant and productive sector have been noted (Buršić 2014; Vidović 2012), the stakeholders working in the independent cultural sector have opted to work within the legal scope of civil society organizations. This legal form has proven itself as more organizationally resilient to Croatia's social, economic, and political fluctuations than others (Barada et al. 2016). All these processes produce a complex intertwined network of regional, gender-based, and socioeconomic specificities in the everyday personal lives of independent cultural creatives. Our research shows that a nuanced and multilevel analysis is needed to explain and understand the perpetual crisis of inequalities in Croatia's independent cultural sector.

[8]We use a working and vernacular definition of "elite" in a reductive and normative way. In comparison to the general population, our research sample represents the elite in terms of their educational attainments and family backgrounds, meaning that their parents were mostly clerks and low- to mid-level managers, not manual workers. Also, our research sample, unlike most of the Croatian labor force, does not work in the low-paid service sector but in self-employed, self-managed positions. See the section on socioeconomic differences for more.

3.3 Regional and Gender-Based Differences

Regional differences related to working in this sector are rooted in the socioeconomic relationship Zagreb has with other parts of Croatia. Our data show that most organizations are concentrated in Zagreb (54.8%), followed by the Adriatic Coast cities of Rijeka (9.7%), Split (7.5%), and Pula (4.5%). When looking at the European Union's Nomenclature of Territorial Units for Statistics (level NUTS 2), if we isolate Zagreb from Continental Croatia, the dominance of the capital is confirmed, again followed by Adriatic Croatia, which is the second most developed region due to tourism. Furthermore, when we examined the location of the Zagreb civil society organizations in more detail, our data showed that most of them can be found on a few downtown streets. This somewhat extreme centralization in the capital is unsurprising, as Zagreb is the country's most developed region and where most of the economic, political, and cultural activities take place.[9]

This aligns with research from other countries that have explored the regional differences of creative labor, notably London versus noncapital-city regions (Coyle and Rosewell 2014). Such regional differences are also visible in other Southeastern European countries, including those of the former Yugoslavia and Greece (Avdikos and Kalogeresis 2018). To emphasize and reiterate regional differences and specificities, an analysis of our semi-structured interviews showed the important work civil society organizations do in smaller urban communities outside Zagreb, since our interviewees said they brought content to their communities that were not generally available regionally or locally. Most civil society organizations also develop cooperation mechanisms and inter-sectorial connectivity. For example, they form cooperation networks for exchange of cultural programs, capacity building, and knowledge transfer (e.g., Clubture network, see: Buršić 2014; Vidović 2012). This type of cooperation and connectivity is especially important for organizations in smaller cities where there are fewer opportunities for paid cultural work.

Gender differences among cultural workers mainly mirror typical work–family balance dynamics, but they are also connected to more specific gender-based creative labor imbalances (Barada 2012). In our research, we found that there is an overrepresentation of female employees in independent cultural civil society organizations; indeed, two-thirds of our sample were women. To be more precise, of respondents to our civil-society-organizations employee survey, 71.2% (79) were women and 28.8% (32) were men. The same results were found in the questionnaire for civil society organizations themselves: 63.24% (74) were women, and 36.75% (43) were men.[10] In addition, 51.1% of organizations said they do not employ a man.

[9]As Croatia's capital, Zagreb is home to more than a quarter of the country's population. It also accounts for more than a third of Croatia's gross domestic product and has an index of 174.8 of gross domestic product per capita compared to Croatia as a whole (data for 2016, Croatian Economic Chamber).

[10]The difference between the two results was not significant ($p < 0.01$: χ^2 [2, $N = 228$] $= 1.62$, $p = 0.20$). www.hgk.hr/documentswww.hgk.hr/documentswww.hgk.hr/documentswww.hgk.hr/documents

One-off contracts were issued equally to both men and women, but women were overrepresented in flexible employment (persons working on six or more consecutive contracts). According to questionnaire respondents, 213 women and 50 men received six or more consecutive honoraria. This is an important result of our research, as women's employment is traditionally—especially in creative jobs—characterized by informal and more flexible contracts, which is a reproduction of broader gender inequalities and puts women in disadvantaged positions primarily because of the associated long-term lower income and social insecurity (Barada 2012; Galić 2011). For women, employment in the independent cultural sector does not bring employment security and income stability.

3.4 Socioeconomic Differences Between Workers in the Independent Cultural Sector

Socioeconomic differences can be interpreted as class differences or differences in the social and cultural capital of cultural workers. In our research, we looked at the following elements to better understand these differences: a person's level of education, their parents' level of education, the self-evaluation of their social status, the self-evaluation of their living standard, their salary, and their motivation to work. In order to better understand the work trajectories and social backgrounds that can form worker resilience in such a fragile sector, we focused on workers who were either employed or who had been engaged in the sector over the long term. Regarding workers' employment status, their strong identification with civil society organizations and the entire sector was interesting to note, as even those who were not officially employed in an organization considered themselves employed (Barada et al. 2016: 55).

When we look at the education level of the workers in our sample, the data show that most had a higher education degree. Meanwhile, 29.7% had an undergraduate university education from before the Bologna reforms were introduced, 10.8% had a bachelor's, 19.8% a master's, and 10.8% have an arts academy diploma. We found a similar situation when we looked at the education level of participants' parents, as outlined in Table 3.1.

The workers' mothers and fathers both fell into the more educated strata of Croatian society, as most had some kind of university-level education, including a master's or doctorate (54% of mothers and 62.1% of fathers). Their education levels were significantly above the Croatian average, which was 24.3% for people aged 25–34 years in 2013 and 18.2% for those aged 25–65 years (File et al. 2013: 10). We can thus conclude that the workers in our sample came from the higher classes of Croatian society. The reproduction of social classes in Croatia's independent cultural sector has also been found in other recent research on higher education (Farnell et al. 2014; Potočnik 2014), and it was confirmed by five decades of research on higher education in Croatia (Doolan et al. 2017).

Table 3.1 Educational level of parents

	Mother		Father	
Highest level of education	Freq.	%	Freq.	%
Incomplete elementary school	1	0.9	1	0.9
Elementary school	3	2.7	0	0
Vocational secondary school (3 years)	6	5.4	5	4.5
Vocational secondary school (4 years)	24	21.6	25	22.5
Grammar school	14	12.6	5	4.5
Professional higher education	23	20.7	27	24.3
University diploma before Bologna reforms	24	21.6	30	27.0
Bachelor's after Bologna reforms	0	0	0	0
Master's after Bologna reforms	2	1.8	1	0.9
Arts academy	1	0.9	2	1.8
Master's before Bologna reforms	7	6.3	4	3.6
PhD	3	2.7	5	4.5
Unknown/no answer	3	2.7	6	5.4

The claim of the reproduction of social classes is strengthened by further examination of the occupations of the surveyed workers' parents. Most had white-collar jobs, which is typical in Croatia for people with academic degrees (Doolan et al. 2017). Over 50% of them were clerks, occupied administrative positions, or were doctors, entrepreneurs, or something similar (see Table 36 in Barada et al. 2016: 63). This must be put into perspective, since Croatia is primarily a service sector economy; therefore, workers' parents held elite jobs in Croatian society. This indicates that the workers in this sector have safety nets. For example, they can probably borrow money from their parents.

The respondents affirmed this conclusion by self-evaluating their and their parents' social status on a scale of 0–10 (0: extremely low; 10: extremely high). They assessed their own social status to be somewhere in the middle of the social stratification structure ($M = 5.68$, SD $= 1.51$), which is also how they assessed their parents ($M = 5.40$, SD $= 1.79$). The Pearson correlation between the respondents' social status self-evaluation and their evaluation of their parents' social status was significant at the 0.01 level (2-tailed) in which $r = 0.309$, $n = 111$, and $p = 0.001$ (Table 3.2).

In short, workers' class backgrounds did not differ from those of cultural workers in the European Union (European Commission 2011), as data show that people from higher classes have easier access to the cultural sector, thus proving that class disparities in the sector exist (Hesmondhalgh and Baker 2011; Randle 2015; Randle et al. 2015).

The socioeconomic position of creative workers becomes more complex when the data on salaries are analyzed (Table 3.3). The workers in the civil society

Table 3.2 Self-evaluation of social status

	Personal		Parents	
Social status	Freq.	%	Freq.	%
0 (extremely low)	1	0.9	1	0.9
1	1	0.9	2	1.8
2	1	0.9	2	1.8
3	2	1.8	8	7.2
4	10	9.0	20	18.0
5	43	38.7	30	27.0
6	18	16.2	14	12.6
7	24	21.6	20	18.0
8	8	7.2	12	10.8
9	3	2.7	1	0.9
10 (extremely high)	0	0	1	0.9
Total	111	100	111	100

Table 3.3 Salaries

	Req.	%
Up to 2500 HRK (approx. 326 EUR)	5	4.5
From 2501 HRK (approx. 326 EUR) to 5000 HRK (approx. 654 EUR)	25	22.5
From 5001 HRK (approx. 5654 EUR) to 7500 HRK (approx. 1000 EUR)	31	27.9
From 7501 HRK (approx. 1000 EUR) to 10,000 HRK (approx. 1300 EUR)	21	18.9
From 10,001 HRK (approx. 1300 EUR) to 12,500 HRK (approx. 1635 EUR)	12	10.8
From 12,501 HRK (approx. 1635 EUR) to 15,000 HRK (approx. 2000 EUR)	6	5.4
From 15,001 HRK (approx. 2000 EUR) to 20,000 HRK (approx. 2600 EUR)	6	5.4
From 20,001 HRK (approx. 2600 EUR) to 25,000 HRK (approx. 3270 EUR)	3	2.7
Unknown	2	1.8
Total	111	100

organizations earn average Croatian wages.[11] Therefore, it comes as no surprise that survey respondents stressed the importance of having opportunities for self-development and expression (Barada et al. 2016: 80), even though working in the independent cultural sector entails continuous work without free weekends or holidays (Barada et al. 2016: 81–82). Labor in the independent cultural sector is therefore more of a calling than ordinary paid work (compare: Dobrow 2012).

Creative labor is precarious almost by definition because the people involved in it usually work on several projects simultaneously and flexible hours and different types of contracts in order to make ends meet (Murray and Gollmitzer 2012). The interview excerpt below illustrates this instability and also raises questions about future poverty and the availability of basic health insurance. The consequences of occasional, insecure, and unstable income will come into play when our study's

[11]The average monthly net wage in Croatia at the time of the survey in July 2015 amounted to 5716 HRK (approx. 747 EUR) (brutto salary HRK 7953 amounts to approx. EUR 1039).

Table 3.4 CBI scores

		CBI-WB	CBI-CB
CBI-PB	Pearson correlation	**0.829**	**0.495**
	Sig. (2-tailed)	0.000	0.000
CBI-WB	Pearson correlation		**0.493**
	Sig. (2-tailed)		0.000

participants retire. 'I always work from project to project. Currently, I am unemployed, but then you get a project and work. I was employed for 2 years, and it was great to have pay, good pay, and not only honoraria' (female interviewee).

The insecurity that comes from precarity, together with other factors, can cause occupational burnout and influence workers' job satisfaction. We, therefore, measured burnout among our respondents by using the Copenhagen Burnout Inventory (CBI) (Kristensen et al. 2005),[12] measuring all three of its dimensions: personal burnout (CBI-PB), work-related burnout (CBI-WB), and client-related burnout (CBI-CB) (Kristensen et al. 2005: 197). For our respondents, CBI-PB was high on average ($M = 47.94$, SD = 17.39), with 53.5% of respondents scoring 50 or higher. CBI-WB was lower ($M = 35.23$, SD = 18.85), with 26.7% of respondents scoring 50 or higher. CBI-CB was the lowest ($M = 31.61$, SD = 18.61), with just 19.2% of respondents scoring 50 or higher. The correlations were highly significant at the 0.01 level (2-tailed) between all the subdimensions, as depicted in Table 3.4. The correlation between CBI-PB and CBI-WB was significantly high ($r = 0.829$, $n = 111$, $p = 0.000$). There was no difference between females and males in any subdimension.

In order to measure job satisfaction, we used the Brief Index of Affective Job Satisfaction (BIAJS) (Thompson and Phua 2012), which is among the most used instruments for measuring affective job satisfaction (Muñoz and Topa 2018). The instrument measures affective job satisfaction with four items using a five-point Likert-type scale, the score being the average of the answers. In our case, the results showed that the workers were generally quite satisfied with their work ($M = 3.84$, SD = 0.63). There were no differences between women ($M = 3.83$, SD = 0.65) and men ($M = 3.86$, SD = 0.59) in job satisfaction ($t[109] = -0.252$, $p = 0.80$), and there was a high negative correlation between job satisfaction and burnout in general, except regarding CBI-CB (Table 3.5).

[12]CBI is tested in different cultures and settings with balanced results (Fong et al. 2014; Milfont et al. 2008; Molinero Ruiz et al. 2013; Parr et al. 2016; Yeh et al. 2007). The instrument's scoring ranges from 0 to 100 on a five-degree Likert-type scale. In our research, Cronbach's alpha for CBI was high for all the individual sub-dimensions as well for all of them combined. For CBI-PB, Cronbach's alpha was 0.88; for CBI-WB, it was 0.89; for CBI-CB, it was 0.88; and for the entire inventory, it was 0.93. When the score of a subdimension is equal or above 50 ($M \geq 50$), burnout is high, and when it is lower than 50 ($M < 50$), burnout is low (Borritz et al. 2006: 101).

Table 3.5 Correlation of CBI and BIAJS

		BIAJS
CBI-PB	Pearson correlation	**−0.363**
	Sig. (2-tailed)	0.000
CBI-WB	Pearson correlation	**−0.477**
CBI-CB	Pearson correlation	−0.130
	Sig. (2-tailed)	0.173
BURNOUT	Pearson correlation	**−0.377**
	Sig. (2-tailed)	0.000

As one might expect, the more our respondents were burnt out, the more they were unsatisfied with their jobs. Usually, they were burnt out on a personal level, but this was highly correlated with job-related burnout. However, when compared to the general Croatian population, they claimed to be happier on average. On a scale from 0 ("I'm not happy at all") to 10 ("I'm extremely happy"), our population had a higher score ($M = 7.10$, SD = 1.81) than the general Croatian population in 2014 ($M = 6.6$, SD = 2.35) ($t[1100] = 2086$, $p = 0.037$; Pilarov barometar hrvatskoga društva 2014: 12). The same was true for the question "How satisfied are you with your life as a whole?" (Pilarov barometar hrvatskoga društva 2014: 11). Our sample ($M = 7.00$, SD = 1.93) fared better than the general Croatian population ($M = 6.00$, SD = 2.44) ($t[1101] = 4.031$, $p < 0.0001$). Affective job satisfaction is highly correlated with the feeling of happiness and life satisfaction. Regarding feelings of happiness and affective job satisfaction, our scores were: $r = 0.387$, $n = 102$, $p < 0.0001$; for life satisfaction and affective job satisfaction, they were: $r = 0.411$, $n = 103$, $p < 0.0001$. Pearson's correlations for happiness and life satisfaction were high and negative.

From these results, we can conclude that respondents worked in situations in which they felt somewhat burnt out but were more satisfied than not with their work and lives. The respondents said their three key motivators for working in the sector were: "the possibility of self-development," "my own ideals and beliefs," and "getting new skills and knowledge." The qualitative data from the semi-structured interviews supported these findings. The interviewees felt it was necessary to be a "special kind of person" to survive in the sector, which they did not even consider as an area of employment. To illustrate this further, we present two quotes from the interviews:

> Most people work out of satisfaction in this sector, or sometimes they have to because they need the pay, but few people in this really independent sector are paid adequately according to their knowledge (male interviewee).

> I do not know if I have adjusted the work in the sector to myself or myself to the work in the sector. I suppose I have, but I have never felt deprived in any way . . . In fact, my lifestyle is possible because I work in the sector. For example, I travel 10 months in a year. That would be hard if I worked somewhere else. And even more, I am working and doing something meaningful. That is the source of great satisfaction but also sometimes dissatisfaction because it can be a little strenuous (male interviewee).

3.5 Everyday Life as a Result of Regional, Gender-Based, and Socioeconomic Specificities

When summing up the data, an image of a worker in Croatia's independent cultural sector emerges: she lives and works in Zagreb, is mostly paid by honoraria, and is the well-educated child of well-educated parents, burned out but satisfied overall with her position and life. However, further analysis sheds more light on this typical creative. For example, we have found that the sector is aging—that is, we can speak about it as a greying sector. The youngest of our respondents was 23 and the oldest was 58, but the mean age was 35.77 (SD = 7.83). This means that creatives are approaching middle age. The Pearson correlation between the age of respondents and their years of work in civil society organizations shows a high correlation ($r = 0.522$, $n = 111$, $p = 0.000$). It is viable to say that creatives tend to stay longer in their independent cultural organization, which means that working in civil society organizations is more of a long-term career or calling than just a stage in life. Moreover, half of the respondents were married or cohabitating, while 39.6% were single, and an additional 4.5% were divorced. Therefore, more than 44% of respondents were not in a relationship but were strongly tied to their civil society organization. The following excerpt illustrates the effect of this intense work on an interviewee's personal life:

> Well, my personal life has suffered, especially family life, because there is no moment when you do not work. If you want to be successful and survive, you basically work seven days in a week, or eight days in a week for 26 hours. . . . But I am really happy with my life, although I could shoot myself sometimes. But that is also beautiful (male interviewee).

Furthermore, most of the respondents did not have children. When asked if they did, 38 (34.2%) said, "yes," 42 (37.8%) said, "No, but I plan to have them," and 31 (27.9%) said, "No, and I don't plan to have them." A t-test on the independent samples did not show significant differences in any kind of burnout or in affective job satisfaction between people who have children and people who do not. Family life and personal lifestyle choices were not a source of burnout. However, a never-ending labor process can be. Our respondents reported working most of the time, as 44.1% worked overtime without getting paid for it (Barada et al. 2016: 82). Their time was occupied with constant multitasking and applying for various funding schemes, followed by increasingly demanding administrative procedures. These procedures sometimes even made a project's financial management risky. However, this forced financial frivolity did not extend to workers' personal finances. Eighty respondents (72.1%) said they did not have loans or mortgages (Barada et al. 2016). It is possible that such a situation is the result of the previously discussed family safety nets on which they relied. However, they might not have been eligible for loans because they were in a type of employment that banks do not find suitable in the context of lending money. The data show that only 6.3% of respondents had a car loan, and 15.3% had a mortgage (Barada et al. 2016: 84).

Many of their familial and personal decisions were mediated by work in the independent cultural sector. Still, in comparison to the broader Croatian socioeconomic context, creatives find themselves to be privileged. This crisis-stricken elite is surrounded by workers who are even more disadvantaged. Working in contemporary culture and the arts is a self-made and self-proclaimed safety net:

> I absolutely think that there is precarization everywhere, not only in the independent and creative sectors. But some things are incomparable. No matter how uncertain our work is, it cannot be compared to the fact that people lose jobs, that they work for six months without pay, [and] that they are degraded as workers (female interviewee).

3.6 Conclusion

Creative labor in Croatian contemporary arts and culture is conducted in the context of an almost permanent crisis that is reproduced both structurally and individually. This finding has been substantiated by the regional, gender-based, and sociodemographic specificities of working in this sector that has been analyzed and interpreted using the mixed method research study presented in this chapter. First, this sector is burdened with the global risks of creative labor (Hesmondhalgh and Baker 2011; Huws 2014), and second, it is situated in a crisis-stricken local emergent market of cultural and creative products and, more importantly, in the political setting and structural limitations of Croatia's socioeconomic conditions. This leaves individuals who are professionally engaged in cultural civil society organizations in an ambivalent social and labor position.

On a structural level and from a sociodemographic stance, these individuals represented the elite of the Croatian labor market and overall society, while on an individual level, they were faced with precarity. The research results presented in this chapter show that these members of the cultural and creative class structurally represented a small part of Croatian society, as they had university degrees and were raised by university-educated parents who worked in the tertiary sector. Although the unemployment rate in Croatia is high, these creatives found a working arrangement that enabled them to have employment with a rather stable income. Despite the continuing economic crisis, they have created a labor market niche in publicly funded civil society.

Our data show an unequal regional distribution of creatives, with Zagreb dominating as the political, economic, and cultural capital of Croatia and overrepresentation in coastal cities that are hubs for recent economic growth fueled by tourism. Globally, this resonates with the higher attractiveness of larger cities (Davis and Dingel 2014), and locally, it means that workers in Croatia's cultural and creative sector flock to cities that are centers of economic, social, and cultural growth and wealth. These cities are structurally better off than the rest of Croatia, and subsequently, creatives are better off in them than the general Croatian population.

However, on an individual level, creatives' everyday personal and working lives are characterized by precarious practices (Morgan et al. 2013; Ross 2008). Their personal and working time is consumed by never-ending labor, and they are constantly involved in material and symbolic production and reproduction. Although they have a rather stable income, its level is lower than other employed persons of the same education, and their remuneration comes from several funding sources, demanding quite intensive administrative schemes. Because they work for civil society organizations, creatives are not eligible for mortgages or loans and are more prone to being single and childless. Gender differences show the feminization of this fragile sector, proving it to be an alluring professional ghetto for women, regardless of its precarious conditions. The gendered nature of this labor enhances social and economic differences and inequalities, putting women at long-term risk of poverty due to long-term low income and social insecurity.

Furthermore, creatives constantly multitask, with most of their time allocated to financial and bureaucratic tasks that overshadow their basic artistic and cultural interests. The data show that although they are satisfied with their profession, they are burned out as workers. They have found themselves in the iron cage of precarity, constantly working in order to provide themselves with options and possibilities to continue working. For them, falling out of production and the never-ending loop of project-funding applications is not an option. The structural background of cultural and creative workers gives them the opportunity to pursue ideas they find important and feel passionate about. Those entering this sector remain loyal to it, but only a certain type of individuals can afford this loyalty, since it comes at a high cost. Although their work-life balance is laden with crisis on the societal and—even more so—individual levels, only the elite preconditions of these workers enable them to reproduce satisfying but still precarious labor conditions. This raises questions about the reproduction of class inequalities in people's chances of entering and remaining in the cultural sector. In addition, it raises questions about the sustainability of creative work in the foreseeable future. The geographically centered, elderly, overworked, underpaid, but loyal female creative with the memory of an elite social position may still fall through the cracks of Croatia's contemporary arts and culture sector.

References

Avdikos V, Kalogeresis A (2018) The uneven regional geography of labour precariousness: the case of Greek design industry. Cult Trends 27(3):187–202. https://doi.org/10.1080/09548963.2018.1473981

Banks M (2007) The politics of cultural work. Palgrave Macmillan, Basingstoke

Banks M (2017) Creative justice. Cultural industries, work and inequality. Rowman & Littlefield International, London

Banks M, Hesmondhalgh D (2009) Looking for work in creative industries policy. Int J Cult Policy 15(4):415–430

Banks M, Gill R, Taylor S (eds) (2013) Theorizing cultural work. Labour, continuity and change in the cultural and creative industries. Routledge Taylor and Francis Group, London and New York

Barada V (2012) Žensko iskustvo rada u kreativnim industrijama—primjer dizajnerica vizualnih komunikacija u Hrvatskoj. Doktorska disertacija (Women's experience of labour in creative industries—Example of female visual communication designers in Croatia. PhD thesis), Filozofski fakultet Sveučilišta u Zagrebu, Zagreb

Barada V, Primorac J, Buršić E (2016) Osvajanje prostora rada. Uvjeti rada organizacija civilnog društva na području suvremene kulture i umjetnosti (Defining the area of work. Labour conditions in civil society organizations in contemporary culture and art). Zaklada 'Kultura nova', Zagreb

Bilić P, Petričušić A, Eterović R (2018) Monitoring media pluralism in Europe: application of the media pluralism monitor 2017 in the European Union, FYROM, Serbia and Turkey. Country Report, Croatia. http://cmpf.eui.eu/wp-content/uploads/2018/11/Croatia_MPM2017_country-report.pdf. Accessed 8 Jan 2019

Blair H (2001) 'You're only as good as your last job': the labour process and labour market in the British film industry. Work Employ Soc 15(1):149–169. https://doi.org/10.1017/S0950017001000071

Blair H, Culkin N, Randle K (2001) From Hollywood to Borehamwood—Exploring nepotism and networking in US and UK freelance film careers (Business School Working Papers, vol. UHBS 2001–6) (Film Industry Research Group Paper, vol. 7). University of Hertfordshire

Borritz M, Rugulies R, Christensen KB, Villadsen E, Kristensen TS (2006) Burnout as a predictor of self-reported sickness absence among human service workers: prospective findings from three year follow up of the PUMA study. Occup Environ Med 63(2):98–106. https://doi.org/10.1136/oem.2004.019364

Buršić E (2014) Mreža Clubture: mapiranje organizacija izvaninstitucionalne kulture. Istraživački izvještaj (The Clubture network: The mapping of the non-institutional culture organizations). Savez udruga Klubtura/Mreža Clubture, Zagreb. https://bib.irb.hr/datoteka/810264.clubture_kb.pdf Accessed 12 Dec 2018

Coyle D, Rosewell B (2014) Investing in city regions: how does London interact with the UK system of cities and what are the implications of this relationship? https://assets.publishing.service.gov.uk/government/uploads/system/uploads/attachment_data/file/429129/london-and-UK-system-of-cities.pdf. Accessed 12 Dec 2018

Creswell JW, Plano Clark VL (2007) Designing and conducting mixed methods research. Sage, London

Croatian Economic Chamber. https://www.hgk.hr/documents/bdp-po-zupanijama-u-2015-godini-final25ad8955342dfa.pdf. Accessed 15 Jan 2019

Cvetičanin P, Krstić N (2017) Culture of austerity, household survival strategies and revival of mechanical solidarity. In: Presentation on the 1st of September 2017 at the 13th Conference of the European Sociological Association. (Un)making Europe: Capitalism, solidarities, subjectivities. https://www.europeansociology.org/sites/default/files/ESA-2017-Athens_Abstract-Book_final.pdf. Accessed 8 Nov 2018

Davis DR, Dingel JI (2014) The comparative advantage of cities. Working Paper 20602, National Bureau of Economic Research, Cambridge. https://www.nber.org/papers/w20602.pdf. Accessed 25 Oct 2018

Dobrow SR (2012) Dynamics of calling: a longitudinal study of musicians. J Org Behav 4 (34):431–452. https://doi.org/10.1002/job.1808

Doolan K, Puzić S, Baranović B (2017) Social inequalities in access to higher education in Croatia: five decades of resilient findings. J Furth High Educ 42(4):467–481. https://doi.org/10.1080/0309877X.2017.1281891

European Commission (2011) Cultural statistics. Publications Office of the European Union, Luxembourg. http://ec.europa.eu/eurostat/documents/3930297/5967138/KS-32-10-374-EN.PDF/07591da7-d016-4065-9676-27386f900857?version=1.0. Accessed 12 Dec 2015

Farnell T, Matković T, Doolan K, Cvitan M (2014) Socijalna uključivost visokog obrazovanja u Hrvatskoj: analiza stanja. Institut za razvoj obrazovanja, Zagreb. http://www.iro.hr/userdocs/File/Publikacije/Socijalna_ukljucivost_visokog_obrazovanja.pdf. Accessed 28 Dec 2015

File J, Farnell Th, Doolan K, Lesjak D, Šćukanec N (2013) Financiranje visokog obrazovanja i socijalna dimenzija u Hrvatskoj: analiza i preporuke. Institut za razvoj obrazovanja, Zagreb.

http://www.finhed.org/media/files/04_ ACCESS_Analize-i-preporuke_web.pdf. Accessed 17 Dec 2015
Fong TCT, Rainbow THH, Ng SM (2014) Psychometric properties of the Copenhagen burnout inventory—Chinese version. J Psychol 148(3):255–266
Galić B (2011) Žene i rad u suvremenom društvu—značaj orodnjenog rada (women and work in modern society—the importance of "gendered" work). Sociologija i prostor 49(1: 189):25–48. https://doi.org/10.5673/sip.49.1.2
Graeber D (2018) Bullshit jobs. A theory. Simon & Schuster, New York
Hesmondhalgh D, Baker S (2011) Creative labour. Media work in three cultural industries. Routledge, London and New York
Huws U (2014) Labor in the global digital economy. The cybertariat comes of age. Monthly Review Press, New York
Kristensen TS, Borritz M, Villadsen E, Christensen KB (2005) The Copenhagen burnout inventory: a new tool for the assessment of burnout. Work Stress 19(3):192–207. https://doi.org/10.1080/02678370500297720
Kultura Nova Foundation. http://kulturanova.hr/english. Accessed 20 Nov 2018
McRobbie A (2002) From Holloway to Hollywood: happiness at work in the new cultural economy? In: Du Gay P, Pryke M (eds) Cultural economy. Cultural analysis and commercial life. Sage, London, pp 97–114
Milfont TL, Denny S, Ameratunga S, Robinson E, Merry S (2008) Burnout and wellbeing: testing the Copenhagen burnout inventory in New Zealand teachers. Soc Indic Res 89(1):169–177. https://doi.org/10.1007/s11205-007-9229-9
Molinero Ruiz E, Basart Gómez-Quintero H, Moncada Lluis S (2013) Fiabilidad y validez del Copenhagen Burnout Inventory para su uso en España. Rev Esp Salud Publica 87(2):165–179
Morgan G, Wood J, Nelligan P (2013) Beyond the vocational fragments: creative work, precarious labour and the idea of 'flexploitation'. Econ Labour Relat Rev 24(3):397–415. https://doi.org/10.1177/1035304613500601
Muñoz JJF, Topa G (2018) Older workers and affective job satisfaction: gender invariance in Spain. Front Psychol. https://www.frontiersin.org/articles/10.3389/fpsyg.2018.00930/full. Accessed 8 Nov 2018
Murray C, Gollmitzer M (2012) Escaping the precarity trap: a call for creative labour policy. Int J Cult Policy 18(4):419–438. https://doi.org/10.1080/10286632.2011.591490
National Bureau of Statistics. https://www.dzs.hr/. Accessed 16 Nov 2018
Parr JM, Pinto N, Hanson M, Meehan A, Moore PT (2016) Medical graduates, tertiary hospitals, and burnout: a longitudinal cohort study. Ochsner J 16(1):22–26
Pilarov barometar hrvatskoga društva (2014) Institut društvenih znanosti Ivo Pilar, Zagreb. http://barometar.pilar.hr (Croatian Barometer)
Potočnik D (2014) Social status of Croatian students. In: Ilišin V (ed) Sociological portrait of Croatian students. Institute for Social Research, Zagreb, pp 57–96
Pratt AC (2004) The cultural economy. A call for specialised 'production of culture' perspectives. Int J Cult Stud 7(1):117–128
Pratt AC (2008) Locating the cultural economy. In: Anheier H, Isar YR (eds) The cultural economy, the cultures and globalization, series 2. Sage, London, pp 42–51
Primorac J (2008) The position of cultural workers in creative industries. The south-east-European perspective. European Cultural Foundation, Amsterdam. www.eurocult.org/uploads/docs/902.pdf. Accessed 6 Feb 2008
Primorac J, Obuljen Koržinek N (2017) Compendium of cultural policies and trends in Europe. Country profile: Croatia, 18th edition 2017. Council of Europe/ERICarts. http://www.culturalpolicies.net. Accessed 16 Feb 2018
Randle K (2015) Class and exclusion at work: the case of UK film and television. In: Oakley K, O'Connor J (eds) The Routledge companion to the cultural industries. Routledge, New York, pp 330–343

Randle K, Forson C, Calveley M (2015) Towards a Bourdieusian analysis of the social composition of the UK film and television workforce. Work Employ Soc 29(4):590–606
Ross A (2004) No-collar: the humane workplace and its hidden costs. Basic Books, New York
Ross A (2007) Nice work if you can get it. The mercurial career of creative industries policy. In: Lovink G, Rossiter N (eds) My creativity reader. A critique of creative industries. Institute for Network Cultures, Amsterdam, pp 17–39
Ross A (2008) The new geography of work: power to the precarious? Theory Cult Soc 25 (7–8):31–49
Standing G (2011) The precariat: the new dangerous class. Bloomsbury Academic, London
Švob-Đokić N, Primorac J, Jurlin K (2008) Kultura zaborava. Industrijalizacija kulturnih djelatnosti (The Culture of Oblivion. The Industrialization of Culture). Naklada Jesenski i Turk, Zagreb
Thompson ER, Phua FTT (2012) A brief index of affective job satisfaction. Group Org Manag 37 (3):275–307. https://doi.org/10.1177/1059601111434201
Vidović D (2012) Razvoj novonastajućih kultura u gradu Zagrebu od 1990. do 2010. Doktorska disertacija (The emergence of new cultures in Zagreb from 1990 until 2010. PhD thesis). Filozofski fakultet Sveučilišta u Zagrebu, Zagreb
Wing-Fai L, Gill R, Randle K (2015) Getting in, getting on, getting out? Women as career scramblers in the UK film and television industries. Sociol Rev 63(1_suppl):50–65. https://doi.org/10.1111/1467-954X.12240
Yeh WY, Cheng Y, Chen CJ, Hu PY, Kristensen TS (2007) Psychometric properties of the Chinese version of Copenhagen burnout inventory among employees in two companies in Taiwan. Int J Behav Med 14(3):126–133. https://doi.org/10.1007/BF03000183

Jaka Primorac works as a Senior Research Associate at the Department for Culture and Communication, Institute for Development and International Relations (IRMO), Zagreb, Croatia. She holds a PhD (2010) in Sociology from the Faculty of Humanities and Social Sciences, University of Zagreb, Croatia. Her research interests include cultural and creative industries, cultural and creative labor, women's work, media and cultural policy, digital culture, and qualitative research methods. She is the co-author (with Valerija Barada and Edgar Buršić) of a book on labor conditions in civil society organizations in contemporary culture and arts in Croatia (published in 2016 by Foundation 'Kultura Nova', Zagreb) and is the co-editor (with Paško Bilić and Bjarki Valtysson) of the book *Technologies of Labour and the Politics of Contradiction* (Palgrave Macmillan 2018). Her work has been published in the *International Journal for Cultural Policy, Forum Qualitative Sozialforschung/Forum: Qualitative Social Research* (FQS), *Medijska istraživanja/Media Research*, etc.

Valerija Barada is a Head of the Department of Sociology and an Associate Professor, University of Zadar, Croatia. She holds PhD (2012) in Sociology from the University of Zagreb and has also completed the Centre for Women's Studies Programme in Zagreb. She teaches on interpretative approaches in sociological theory and qualitative methods. Her primary research interests include issues of gender, labor, and professions, but she has also worked on the topics of youth social and work inequalities. Barada has authored and co-authored several articles, books, and research reports on quality of life, labor conditions, and gender relations in local coastal communities of Croatia. With Jaka Primorac and Edgar Buršić, she has published a book on labor conditions in civil society organizations in contemporary culture and arts in Croatia, resulting from a 2-year research project (published in 2016 by Foundation "Kultura Nova," Zagreb). Recently she has been working on gendered work biographies transformed by recent socioeconomic changes in Croatia.

Edgar Buršić is a Senior Lecturer at the Faculty of Interdisciplinary, Italian and Cultural Studies, Juraj Dobrila University of Pula, Croatia. He holds a master's degree (2003) from the University of Trento, Italy ("Joint European Master of Local Development"), and a PhD (2013) in Sociology from the University of Trieste, Italy. He teaches courses in various sociological fields (general sociology,

sociology of education, sociology of literature, and sociology of culture, sociology of tourism, creative city, and methods of research in the humanities) to students of various profiles. Buršić has been volunteering and working for years in the not-for-profit sector (from independent culture to the free software community). He has conducted several surveys regarding the working conditions in the independent cultural sector, but also qualitative research in cultural organizations. His research interests include topics in urban sociology and urban studies, sociology of culture, social networks analysis, and research methodology in general.

Chapter 4
The Only Place Where One Can Feel Connected to an International Context and Still Speak Russian: Hybrid Creative Work in Post-Soviet Contemporary Art Institutions

Margarita I. Kuleva

Abstract This chapter focuses on the hybrid creative labor of managers in Moscow-based contemporary art institutions. The Russian context is of interest because its young contemporary art market is still transitioning from the Soviet cultural monopoly to an open-market economy, and it, therefore, lacks established standards of cultural production, especially in the case of institutional organizations. The research examines Moscow's new private centers and contemporary art museums, which were founded in the late 2000s. Conceived as Russian versions of the Tate or Guggenheim, these institutions offer workers and their visitors the unique experience of belonging to the international art world in the center of Moscow. In this context, creative work organization is filled with negotiations and experiments, forming an ideological battlefield where both neoliberal creative entrepreneurialism and the Soviet heroization of work, such as praise for the new Stakhanovites, can be encountered. This chapter is based on a 2016 ethnographic study composed of 25 in-depth interviews with full-time cultural workers and 20 observation visits by the researcher to the art centers' offices and exhibition areas.

Keywords Art centers · Art managers · Creative labor · Cultural workers · Hybrid · Moscow · Russia

4.1 Introduction

In recent decades, the global structural position of culture and creativity has changed dramatically. First, when transitioning to a postindustrial society, knowledge-based industries, such as culture and art, science and education, and information

---

M. I. Kuleva (✉)
National Research University Higher School of Economics, Centre for German and European Studies St Petersburg State University and Bielefeld University, St Petersburg, Russia

I. Kiriya et al. (eds.), *The Industrialization of Creativity and Its Limits*, Science, Technology and Innovation Studies, https://doi.org/10.1007/978-3-030-53164-5_4

technologies, come to the fore of global and local economies. Creativity has been recognized as a full-fledged industry at the national level (departments of creative industries were first opened in Britain, then in other countries) as well as the global, including in the latest edition of the *International Standard of Industrial Classification* (a list of existing industries provided by the United Nations). As a result of the sector's increased attention, investment, prestige, and economic growth, the sphere of culture and creativity has begun to face new challenges. These include the hardships of the neoliberal industrialization of culture, the commodification of creative outputs, and the application of market criteria in evaluating the success of art, its creators, and cultural organizations. This issue was explored by the research strand known as creative labor studies, which emerged in the second half of the 1990s and in the 2000s (e.g., McRobbie 2002, 2018; Gill 2002, 2010; Gill and Pratt 2008; Taylor and Littleton 2012; Oakley 2014; Hesmondhalgh and Baker 2010, 2015; Conor et al. 2015).

These studies critically cover the issues caused by the transformed and sped-up markets of creative labor and production. However, they also leave some gaps: they present the rather specific experiences of creative sectors in the large cities of Western Europe and North America (the so-called cultural capitals) as universal, and they focus on the individual experience of creative workers who are characterized as atomized free agents of the new economy. In this way, critical creative labor studies fail to contribute to the de-Westernization and decolonization of research on the production of culture and new forms of labor, but more importantly, they raise the following research question: how do the features of non-Western cultural production systems frame the conditions of creative work?

To answer this question, I offer Moscow's new privately funded art centers as extreme cases (Seawright and Gerring 2008).[1] In the second half of the 2000s, several private cultural institutions simultaneously appeared in Moscow, all supported by big businesses. In 2007, Roman Trotsenko, adviser to the president of PJSC Rosneft Oil Company and his wife, Sofia, opened the Winzavod Centre for Contemporary Art in a former brewery. In 2008, Dasha Zhukova and Roman Abramovich, eleventh on the Russian *Forbes* 2018 list of Russia's richest people, founded the Garage Museum of Contemporary Art, which was then a contemporary culture center and is located in the Bakhmetevsky Garage. In 2009, Alexander Mamut, fortieth on the *Russian Forbes* list, supported the launch of the Strelka Institute of Media and Design in the courtyard of the Red October factory. Meritocratic neoliberal principles formed the basis of their ideological opposition to the previous system of cultural production. Their ambitious attempts to express this opposition can be seen in the new Tate Moderns and MoMAs (Museums of Modern Art) they have created along the Moskva River.

[1]Some of the conclusions drawn is this chapter were presented in Kuleva (2018). Turning the Pushkin Museum into a "Russian Tate": Informal creative labour in a transitional cultural economy (the case of privately funded Moscow art centers). *International Journal of Cultural Studies.*

This chapter investigates the space and function occupied by informal hybrid creative labor in the shifting cultural economy. It is expected to contribute to the debate on creative labor in the following ways: I track how multiple international agents, not just cultural policy alone, frame the conditions and ethos of cultural production; as I consider these agents competing for cultural hegemony in this chapter's context, I define these regimes of work as "hybrid"; and I see privately funded institutions as especially prominent examples of this complexity, as state control is limited in this arena (although still present), which gives visibility to other stakeholders.

4.2 Methodology

The research is founded on a Moscow-focused ethnographic study. As mentioned above, specific cultural venues were selected as the objects of my study in order to better understand cultural labor in changing creative economies in general and in Russia in particular. The fact that they are privately funded sets them apart from most of Russia's cultural institutions. These organizations are not financed or operated according to grassroots principles, and they, therefore, possess enough capital to achieve ambitious goals. As a result, their labor organization is less rigid than that of public sector institutions, which are coached in conservative bureaucratic structures, or in self-sustained private institutions—so-called self-organization—because of a lack of resources. The selected institutions constitute an extreme case as defined in the field of quantitative studies:

> [A]n extreme value is understood here as an observation that lies far away from the mean of a given distribution; that is to say, it is unusual. If most cases are positive along a given dimension, then a negative case constitutes an extreme case' (Seawright and Gerring 2008: 301).

For the second stage, I selected 10 of Moscow's largest private cultural institutions working in visual arts. The research consisted of 20 in-depth interviews with private sector employees. Two main criteria were applied to the selection process: first, the employees were mainly employed full time; second, as I selected two interviewees per institution, they had to be from different departments and occupy different levels of authority (e.g., junior and senior). The research guide required interviewees to respond to questions about the quality of their on-the-job learning process, their career trajectory, day-to-day routines, and the organization of the workplace (for the latter, interviewees were required to sketch out the management structure of the art center they worked at). I also conducted 20 observational sessions in offices and at public events held at the art centers. Due to differing levels of access, the observations varied in terms of their content and level of observer participation.

Regarding the issue of accessibility in the field, half of the institutions (five) were accessed via my personal connections. I then used snowball sampling to approach the remaining half. In two instances, I had to interact with employees via official channels, and the quality of communication reflected this. Interviewees who had been accessed via personal connections felt more comfortable sharing thoughts and concerns, as they might with a colleague. Interviewees with whom I was newly acquainted naturally kept a more formal distance. In terms of observations, I was taken on a guided tour of the newly discovered institutions, while in a few of the better known, I was able to play an active part in the workspace during the observations, and this took the shape of working alongside interviewees in the office, staying in the center overnight, and helping with the installation of new displays.

The follow-up data collection continued through 2017–2018. It consisted of a series of less formal observations conducted during my visits to the aforementioned institutions. Additionally, I kept track of the institutions' media and press materials and all conversations with study participants.

4.3 New, Sexy, and International: Moscow's Private Cultural Centers in the 2000s

In Moscow, the new private sector art centers that emerged in the second half of the 2000s stood in contrast to the traditions set by state museums, choosing to emphasize foreign rather than domestic experiences. For example, on the Strelka Institute's website, it describes its work on the concept of change:

> In 2009, Strelka was founded with the aim of reshaping Russia's metropolitan landscape, both culturally and physically. Strelka's educational initiatives push for positive change and new sets of ideas and values. These fresh educational opportunities are run by the institute, while it continues to maintain the City at the heart of its overall research program (Institute for a Social City 2016).

Newly founded institutions present the concept of internationalization in their ideas and practices: classes and lectures are given in English and much of the teaching staff is made up of foreign experts, such as Rem Koolhaas, the first program director. Garage Museum of Contemporary Art (MoCA) promotes future-orientated work and global experiences: "Garage is a special place since it is managed by the post-Soviet generation, born in the 80s and 90s. In fact, as a whole, Garage captured the fresh mentality of that generation when it comes to culture, and managed to find new ways of putting the ideas of our time into effect in the society around us" said Kate Fowle, chief curator, in a video about their new building.[2] Her colleague, Snezhana Krastevam, added, "[the curator] Viktor Misiano described Garage in a fascinating way—he said it's the only place in Moscow where he feels one can exist and belong in an international context while still speaking Russian."

[2]Garage Museum of Contemporary Art Opens June 12th! https://www.youtube.com/watch?v=2l_Ma6J6b1o. Accessed 17 March 2020.

Moscow's art centers exist as portals, connecting their local urban setting to the art of the wider, international world. These centers exhibit both high culture as well as an array of cultural leisure pursuits, such as interactive classes and lectures, tours and walks, restaurants and shops, bicycling and roller-skating, and outdoor activities. The design and layout of the centers are crucial parts of these transitional zones, since they clearly separate the centers from other urban areas and the general public, reinforcing their high status as places to be visited. The art centers' well-designed environments also attract employees. A designer taking part in a Garage video presentation said: "I remember when I first visited Garage. I said to myself, 'Oh, this is somewhere I should be. This is somewhere I should live and die.'"[3] This approach to art centers, as more than workplaces—as living spaces hosting life (or even death!)—has knock-on effects for the other criteria used when workers decide on places of employment. Despite the many difficulties faced by the research participants, the interview and observation data showed that the makeup of the workspace and the esthetic quality of the work it produced were among the main reasons employees might continue working at a particular art center. Indeed, the interviewees said they enjoyed attending the exhibitions as visitors ("[This is] the coolest place in Moscow," a project administrator laughed. "That is why I'm here."). Therefore, it can be concluded that employees share a feeling of belonging and are proud of contributing to ambitious projects that amaze international guests, including important experts. As said one female deputy director, "Important people from all over the world come here . . . it's like a miracle, just wow! This is where my pride and loyalty come from."

Researchers who focus on creative work internationally have also remarked on the passion and interest that creative workers employ in their projects; however, these sentiments are typically less concerned with specific industry trends or projects than with a given workplace itself. The interviewees too also pointed out the global agenda of these institutions. First, these workplaces answer a demand for cosmopolitanism, striking a balance between the old system of cultural production, on which their educations focused, and international institutions found abroad, for which they do not feel sufficiently experienced to work. Second, the art centers offer their employees a sense of belonging to the wider, international art world. The belonging has been largely romanticized, and in certain cases, art and media stars serve as the embodiment of this engagement. As one of the study participants explained, the rushing of an intoxicated Woody Allen to a private viewing offered her an experience of internationalization.

[3]Garage Museum of Contemporary Art Opens June 12th! https://www.youtube.com/watch?v=2l_Ma6J6b1o. Accessed 17 March 2020.

4.4 Open Calls and the New *Blat*

This section is devoted to the hybrid recruitment practices of the new art centers. Since Moscow's MoCAs follow the principles of meritocracy, open calls are their main recruitment instrument. They include temporary fellowships, small grants, and full-time jobs. Here, meritocratic recruitment principles go hand in hand with inherited informal procedures. For instance, as Ledeneva (1998) wrote in her book on *blat*,[4] although institutional conditions have changed, the practices themselves are still in use: "informal contacts still remain primary where money is not accepted as a mean of exchange—that is, at the upper level, where there are much corruption and nepotism, or at the very bottom level, where informal networks are used to tackle scarcity" (Ledeneva 1998: 180). Surprisingly, old Soviet practices of service and goods exchange, such as *blat,* have found a place not only in general post-Soviet society but in this rather specific environment as well. One individual who works for a fund contended:

> Yes, we do open calls, but it doesn't make much sense: there is only a small number of specialists who can carry out higher quality research in Moscow. We are especially interested in projects on [historical] museology. [Tell me] where I [can] find any specialists of that kind, and I would be happy to support them. Unfortunately, there aren't any. This was also truth . . . when I did the Young Artists Awards [for the Moscow Art Center]. Of course, I was receiving loads of rubbish [applications] from all over. I had to do a fair amount of preparatory work to develop better applications. I knew a few interesting artists, but their initial applications weren't strong enough, or the concept was boring. We would collaborate to expand on the ideas and then they would apply (male artist and curator).

This demonstrates a more complicated mixture of recruitment techniques: a curator is willing to discard the principles of an open call, not in order to provide *blat* to his friends or relatives and snatch some profit for himself, but to make the project happen and improve the quality of the works presented. Nevertheless, the curator relies on a network of personal contacts, making allowances for people he knows while failing to do so for people he does not. Despite these methods clearly having their roots in the modus operandi of the previous generation of museums, they are far from incongruent with a neoliberal meritocratic approach.

It should also be noted that these open calls, while well-publicized and frequently posted on all the researched institutions' websites, are not required when advertising vacancies and openings and thus can always give way to their informal analogues:

> If you look at the top of our institution, you will see that there are actually a lot of people who were not particularly engaged in contemporary art but were close to certain circles (*tusovka*). [As for] how they are working [and] what their salaries are like, that is a completely different matter (female keeper).

As in the previous instance, it is possible to interpret this in two ways. One is that this is a reworking of *blat*—the founders of a cultural institution hire their friends for

[4] *Blat* can be defined as a form of corruption in the Soviet Union based on the informal exchange of services, connections, and goods.

a top position even though they do not have relevant work experience. Another interpretation is that, if one considers that professional competence in Russia's contemporary art world has not yet fully matured and educational institutions have not fully adapted, then the principle of trust is a definite factor of hiring. Research has explored this from a Western perspective as well (e.g., Wreyford 2015).

4.5 Mundane Work and (in)Visibility

The subjects of focus in this section are personal work timetables and working conditions, and these are examined within the framework of the aforementioned characteristics of a Muscovite cultural institution's work environment.

Employees are not only controlled by a formalized, hierarchical management structure but also by a stricter sense of self-regulation: they take individual responsibility for a product and equate their professional success with that of the art institution. This unformalized characteristic of their work is highly significant:

> We have additional criteria that act in tandem with professional qualities, which we call "the [art centre] match." "I'd just sat that we have a very good group of people here because the style and tempo of work does not easily facilitate efforts to advance your personal career (deputy director, female).

As such, a supposed good employee does not fight for working rights because those rights do not indicate the disparity between the written contract and the actual work. Rebelling against the shock-work principle may then come as a result. In this case, such employees would drop out:

> They quit and leave, not because I dismiss them but simply because they drop out. That is why I say this is a self-regulating system because you do not have [to fire someone], but when you have a nice team, you cannot, you would not want to refuse the workload (deputy director, female).

As such, it is more often unspoken rather than spoken rules that define the working environment. Peer recognition is invaluable and even defines whether someone works passionately, or merely fulfills the professional obligations of the job. "No one is forcing anybody" is the soft enforcement mantra that dictates the relationships between workers and their creative environments. To this regard, below is an illustrative excerpt from an interview I conducted (my questions in italics) with two creative professionals:

> I know I shouldn't like my work, but I just can't resist the charm of the place. It gives you a nice feeling (female librarian).
>
> What is a working day like for you?
>
> I'm here at the bar drinking coffee and chatting to people.
>
> It looks very nice.
>
> That's the thing! It all looks very nice! That's the secret [of the art center]—it all looks very nice. The only little add-on is that, on a daily basis, I work like this for 16 hours (female deputy director)

Interviewees were seduced by the esthetic layout, quality architecture, and self-recognition that they were part of a bold and exceptional project. However, in opposition to this, many employees mentioned a trendy lifestyle imposed on them regardless of whether they desired it (even though they might have been able to afford it). Bearing in mind the above exchange, working in an art center cafe is not always an esthetic choice but a scenario imposed by a lack of office space. Likewise, eating at these trendy venues was often not a lifestyle choice but necessitated by a lack of options.

The risks experienced by art center employees are akin to those of a typical creative industry worker. The disparity appears when these workers are not credited in the same way as artists, designers, and musicians. There is a lack of public recognition and therefore a lack of compensation for their poor working conditions. One clear example can be found in the texts on the walls of exhibitions; creative workers are rarely credited for writing these, whereas the artist and sometimes head curator are acknowledged for their work. These employees remain nameless and are conceived of as part of the organization rather than as individuals. "Our director does not even know that I was the one who suggested the idea for this project," said a female curator. Projects and exercises that are generally seen as creatively expressive and stimulating are reserved for only a select few.

Meanwhile, activities such as hanging out and having a chat are part of a curator's workday, while their juniors have to pick up the everyday tasks and therefore operate at a very different tempo in the same environment. Tasks that could be classed as creative are far from open to all. Because of this, many interviewees took on extra, voluntary work that was well beyond the scope of their contracts. As a result, despite receiving a regular salary, creative workers undertake significant additional work that is effectively free labor. To wit, a female art manager relayed a conversation with her curator boss: "Hey, how come you're being so serious? Come hang out in the studio," said [the curator]. I replied, "Hey, I've got work to get on with. You're my boss—you should know that."

4.6 The Pyramid Model: Visibility, Pay, and Creativity

The contemporary art world and creative industries, in general, are known for their high degree of social inequality: while a tiny minority of the artistic community shares most of the visibility and cultural and economic capital, the rest is excluded (Cattani and Ferriani 2008; Bull 2011). However, this observation is primarily based on studies of the art market's free agents, such as artists, and the role of the institution is rarely considered. In the following section, I use my data to develop a hierarchical model—a pyramid—that shows how resources of visibility, pay, and creativity are spread among art center employees. It should be noted, however, that a worker's responsibilities are not fixed; for example, additional work is sometimes required on top of existing duties. Some additional tasks are rewarded with supplementary payment, while others are not. Visible, recognized forms of work are intertwined

Table 4.1 The creativity pyramid

	Pay	Visibility	Creativity
Curator/director	+	+	+
An external (contractor)	–	+	+
An occasional creative	–/+	–	+
A technician	+	–	–
An intern	–	–	–

with forms that are effectively invisible, i.e., they were never mentioned in the contract. Another feature of this pyramid is its unsteadiness: while its foundation (the lower stratum) and peak (art center CEOs) are relatively stable, the levels in between are volatile. From this point of view, the pyramid is reminiscent of the sandpile metaphor put forward by Giuffre: "career ladders in the art world are not so much ladders as they are sandpiles. The movement of actors within the field changes the shape of the field" (Giuffre 1999: 829).

Thus, the pyramid's ranks are not only slippery and unstable but highly dependent on the moves of other actors. The classification of creative workers' positions presented below is, therefore, closer to a Weberian-ideal-type system (Weber 2011) than a strict typology. Before presenting the pyramid, I offer definitions of the positions within it (Table 4.1).

Curator/director: This peak position consists of formal work that is considered creative, and the name of the person holding the position is usually known. A curator is, for example, responsible for the conception of new exhibitions. This kind of work is a rarity—in each institution studied, not more than five to 10 people worked on such projects. These high-profile creative professionals often represent the institution in the media.

External: This position was added to balance the existing classification, although high-profile external collaborators are beyond the actual scope of this chapter. Indeed, while externals are not involved in financial exchange as institutional employees, they do impact the hierarchy of prestige and visibility. Additionally, they are potential human resources for curators/directors.

Occasional creative: The second-best opportunity is informal labor that is considered creative. This could take the form of a manager or coordinator who undertakes some research for a new exhibition. This work is usually performed in addition to the responsibilities that this person already formally has. This work is anonymous and unpaid.

Technician: Formal, and according to the interviewees, noncreative work has a lower status, as all full-time employees already perform this kind of work.

Intern: Informal noncreative work, usually described as "help," is left for interns and volunteers. Commonly, this position is the lowest level of the pyramid.

4.7 Conclusion

The main objective of this chapter was to explore the specificity of creative labor in the hybrid conditions of the new Moscow Guggenheims or Tates. I employed an extreme-case strategy by taking new nongovernmental art centers as empirical subjects because such institutions oppose the traditions of cultural production in Russia, especially methods such as informal recruitment or nepotism ("*semeistvennost*" in Russian). However, public and private assertions of this kind are undermined by this study's discovery of continued methods of informal recruitment, organization establishment, and workflow organization, with either striking or faint similarities to those of the Soviet and post-Soviet state museums. New institutions discursively counterpose themselves against the previous generation of cultural producers, even though their practices have roots in unreformed higher education bodies and institutions as well as methods passed on from older colleagues. However, the Soviet-style informality of working practices was not the only workplace system exposed at the studied art centers: there was also a tendency for many to be organized like start-ups despite their sizes. This disparity underlines the supposition that cultural institutions are still transitioning.

Funding The author hereby discloses receipt of the following financial support for the research, authorship, and/or publication of this chapter: this research was supported by the National Research University Higher School of Economics Academic Fund Program under grant No. 19–01-012: Creative Labor Revisited: A Toolkit for Fair Cultural Production in Distinct Institutional Environments.

References

Bull M (2011) The two economies of world art. In: Harris J (ed) Globalization and contemporary art. Wiley-Blackwell, Oxford, pp 179–190
Cattani G, Ferriani S (2008) A core/periphery perspective on individual creative performance: social networks and cinematic achievements in the Hollywood film industry. Organ Sci 19 (6):824–844
Conor B, Gill R, Taylor S (2015) Gender and creative labour. Sociol Rev 63:1–22
Gill R (2002) Cool, creative and egalitarian? Exploring gender in project-based new media work in Europe. Inf Commun Soc 5(1):70–89
Gill R (2010) 'Life is a pitch': managing the self in new media work. In: Deuze M (ed) Managing Media Work. Sage, Thousand-Oaks, CA, pp 249–262
Gill R, Pratt A (2008) In the social factory?: immaterial labour, precariousness and cultural work. Theory Cult Soc 25(7–8):1–30
Giuffre K (1999) Sandpiles of opportunity: success in the art world. Soc Forces 77(3):815–832
Hesmondhalgh D, Baker S (2010) 'A very complicated version of freedom': conditions and experiences of creative labour in three cultural industries. Poetics 38(1):4–20
Hesmondhalgh D, Baker S (2015) Sex, gender and work segregation in the cultural industries. Sociol Rev 63(1_suppl):23–36
Institute for a Social City (2016) http://www.strelka.com/en/idea. Accessed 15 Oct 2019

Garage Museum of Contemporary Art Opens June 12th (2015) https://www.youtube.com/watch?v=2l_Ma6J6b1o. Accessed 10 Nov 2019
Kuleva M (2018) Cultural administrators as creative workers: the case of public and non-governmental cultural institutions in St. Petersburg. J Cult Stud 32(5):727–746
Ledeneva AV (1998) Russia's economy of Favours: blat, networking and informal exchange. Cambridge University Press, Cambridge
McRobbie A (2002) Clubs to companies: notes on the decline of political culture in speeded up creative worlds. Cult Stud 16(4):516–531
McRobbie A (2018) Be creative: making a living in the new culture industries. Polity Press, Cambridge
Oakley K (2014) Good work? Rethinking cultural entrepreneurship. In: Bilton C, Cummings S (eds) Handbook of management and creativity. Edward Elgar Publishing, Cheltenham, pp 145–159
Seawright J, Gerring J (2008) Case selection techniques in case study research: a menu of qualitative and quantitative options. Polit Res Q 61(2):294–308
Taylor S, Littleton K (2012) Contemporary identities of creativity and creative work. Ashgate, Farnham
Weber M (2011) Methodology of social sciences. Transaction Publishers, Brunswick
Wreyford N (2015) Birds of a feather: informal recruitment practices and gendered outcomes for screenwriting work in the UK film industry. Sociol Rev 63(1_suppl):84–96

Dr. Margarita Kuleva (PhD in Sociology) is a senior lecturer in sociology at the National Research University Higher School of Economics, St. Petersburg. Since September 2018 she also works as chair of the Department of Design and Contemporary at the same university. She held a position of a research fellow of the Centre for German and European Studies, St. Petersburg State University, and Bielefeld University. Kuleva has collaborated as a researcher and curator with a number of Russian and international cultural institutions, including Manifesta Biennale, Goethe Institute, and New Holland St. Petersburg. One of her main research interests is creative labor. In 2012–2016, she studied post-Soviet creativity, looking at the example of the careers and professional identities of young cultural workers in the hybrid cultural economy in Russia. Some findings from these studies are presented in recent journal publications, for example, *Cultural Studies* (2018).

Chapter 5
Creative Writing Courses Are Useless: Creative Writing Programs and the Italian Literary System

Cecilia Ghidotti

Abstract Creative writing schools and programs are weird creatures. They have been around for decades and have become increasingly popular despite their relatively recent addition to the curricula of higher education. This chapter investigates the public discourse around creative writing programs: it looks at how creative writing degrees are received both in the English-speaking world (the United States and the United Kingdom) and in Italy, and it investigates the reasons behind this reception. In the Anglo-American case, creative writing is part of university education, but this is not the case in Italy, where universities do not offer degrees in creative writing. The teaching of creative writing thus is entirely entrusted to private enterprises such as schools, associations, charities, cooperatives, and bookshops. This chapter looks at how, in Italy's case, the reception of creative writing has been shaped by the country's historic understanding of high and popular culture and by the position of the Alessandro Baricco, best-selling author and founder of the Holden School, the most famous Italian creative writing school. These themes are relevant to the scholarship on creative and cultural industries because they offer insights into the role of creative writing programs as mechanisms for the inclusion and exclusion of cultural workers. They also reveal the programs' growing influence over literary production and cultural production more generally.

Keywords Creative writing · Cultural work · Higher education

5.1 Creative Writing Studies?

When we talk about creative writing and creative writing schools or programs, we are usually referring to a discipline created in the 1920s during the U.S. progressive education movement, a pedagogical approach that focused on fostering the creativity

---

C. Ghidotti (✉)
Institute for Media and Creative Industries, Loughborough University London, London, UK
e-mail: C.Ghidotti@lboro.ac.uk

I. Kiriya et al. (eds.), *The Industrialization of Creativity and Its Limits*, Science, Technology and Innovation Studies, https://doi.org/10.1007/978-3-030-53164-5_5

of young scholars in primary and secondary education (McGurl 2009). From that period on, creative writing changed, becoming especially popular within higher education.

Traditionally, the origin of creative writing programs traces back to 1936, when the Iowa Writers' Workshop was established. Since then, and especially in the last 30 years, creative writing programs in the United States have increased in number, from 79 in 1975 to 1269 in 2014 (Harbach 2014). In the United Kingdom, the figures are smaller, but there is nevertheless a considerable offering of creative writing degrees, and the same is true for Australia, as the national associations for creative writing confirm (Australian Association of Writing Programs and National Association of Writer in Education). Educations in creative writing differ considerably depending on the specificities of each country, ranging from full integration into the higher education system to less formalized arrangements, which is the case in Italy. In the Italian higher education system, creative writing is not recognized as a formal degree, thus representing a sort of vocational path that may be combined with, or act as an alternative to, a university education. For more than 15 years, the Holden School, which is not a university, has been the only institution offering full-time creative writing courses in Italy.

In terms of studies on this phenomenon, there is a lack of comprehensive approaches. Creative writing studies are a discipline that practitioners and professionals have established during the last 10–15 years because of the increase in programs. The scholars, who are usually involved in the teaching of creative writing, aim to differentiate creative writing from literary and composition studies, and they seek to build a space for it in contemporary academia (Harper and Kerridge 2004; Donnelly 2009; Mayers 2016). This literature addresses the techniques, pedagogy, and philosophy of creative writing; it focuses on how aspiring writers build skills as well as on practical issues, such as how they stimulate their imaginations and build stories and the pros and cons of workshops as teaching formats.

Creative writing degrees produce, or should produce, authors of literary texts. For this reason, one might expect them to be of interest to literary studies. However, literary studies tend to pay little attention to the products of workshops and to workshops as cultural phenomena. This is, at the very least, counterintuitive, considering the relevance that creative writing programs have assumed in the last 30 years.

The works of Myers (1996), Dawson (2005), and McGurl (2009) are exceptions to this trend. They presented the history of creative writing and its literary outcomes as a history of tensions between creative writing practices and literary studies and between writers, critics, and scholars. McGurl approached the development of creative degrees in the United States as a history of the changing processes that led to entrance into the literary field. Before the programs, a system of patronage in which established writers mentored emerging authors was in place. Programs did not completely replace this form of patronage,[1] but they represented a remarkable

[1]See Harbach (2014) for a detailed account of how the two systems of American fiction work: one depends on writing programs and the other is connected to the New York literary economy.

change in the mechanisms that allowed aspiring writers to attempt to fulfill their aspirations. I argue that the institutionalization of creative writing education and its impact on the processes of access to the literary field are a matter of relevance for scholars interested in cultural production and for those who develop critical approaches to the study of cultural and creative industries.

While it is true that the profession of the writer is not one that developed as a consequence of the post-2000s expansion of the cultural and creative economy, it is also true that "journalists, book authors, screenwriters, poets, bloggers, advertising copywriters, and the publishing industries" (Hesmondhalgh 2013: 6) are among the professionals working in the cultural industries, and they are therefore worthy of as much interest as other creative professionals that are more often at the center of these studies, such as new media workers, TV professionals, actors, designers, and people working in the music industry or visual arts.

Critical approaches to cultural and creative industries (McRobbie 2002; 2016; Oakley 2009; Hesmondhalgh and Baker 2011; Banks et al. 2013; Scharff 2017; Alacovska 2018) usually focus on a wide range of issues related to working in various creative sectors. With this chapter, I intend to draw attention to the stage that predates accessing a job in the creative industries, namely the stage of education. As argued by the editors of a collection exploring the intersections between the creative industries and higher education (Ashton et al. 2013), this stage has so far received limited attention. However, the phase of education is important because it is when values regarding creativity are taught, professional expectations are shaped, and, more generally, material, symbolic, and emotional investments are made in a process that is supposed to lead to a job in the cultural industries. For this reason, more attention should be given to the transitions between a creative education and the access to a job in the creative industries. This would allow taking into consideration not only those who managed—albeit partially—to acquire a creative job but also those who, after having devoted their education to this aspiration, eventually fail to secure an occupation in the cultural and creative industries.

I start this discussion from a perspective that might appear of secondary importance: the reception of creative writing degrees and the ways in which they are discussed. However, this perspective is crucial. As I will explain further below, pursuing a degree in creative writing is often framed as a waste of time because of the widespread belief, which may appear contrary to common sense, that one does not learn how to write. Writing is impossible to teach because being a writer is a quality that one either possesses or not.

The focus on Italy contributes to the scholarship on cultural and creative industries by showing how the aspiration to work in a creative profession and build a creative identity exist in a country that remains peripheral to the global production of literature (with some exceptions, such as evidenced by the success of Elena Ferrante's novels). Relative to the United Kingdom, Italy did not experience a growth of investments in and government policies on creative industries (Belfiore 2006; Bodo 2016).

5.2 A Peculiar Kind of Education

Paradoxically, creative writing programs exist and prosper because of the belief that it is impossible to teach whatever they promise to teach because writing cannot be taught and courses are therefore useless. This belief is common both in public discourse on programs and in the scholarly debate, but it is rarely investigated in its components. I will now discuss some examples of this belief as it surfaces for the US and UK cases, after which I will look at the Italian case, which presents some similarities but also some substantial differences.

Creative writing programs are not widely debated in public, but they usually reach the public debate when a teacher or former teacher (often a writer) decides to publicly claim how useless the degrees are and how talentless the students. Here are some examples: celebrated author Hanif Kureishi said that his students "just can't tell a story. They can write sentences but they don't know how to make a story go from there all the way through to the end without people dying of boredom in between. It's a difficult thing to do and it's a great skill to have. Can you teach that? I don't think you can" (Jones 2014). He completely rejected the idea of paying for such a degree. Instead, he suggested that the aspiring writer should find a good teacher and pay them for teaching instead of attending a program (Flood 2014), as if this would be a viable option for an aspiring writer with no connections. Lucy Ellmann, a novelist and former creative writing teacher, believes that creative writing programs are an example of how universities went from being "culture-preserving institutions" to "culture-destroying institutions." She suggested that, instead of taking a creative writing program, one should read "as much good literature as you can get your hands on, for years and years, rather than wasting half your university life writing stuff you're not ready to write" (Flood 2014). This assumes, once again, that young people who are trying to develop their skills can learn how to write through the simple act of reading. How does one choose what to read? Who decides what is good writing in the absence of the mediation provided by a school?

US writer and academic Elif Batuman declared that she is "not a fan of program fiction" (Harbach 2014: 243). She added that, for her, program fiction has an anthropological value similar to the literature produced in developing countries, but if she wanted to read literature from developing countries, she would read literature written by less privileged writers instead of the literature written in the programs attended by privileged writers. This argument implicitly reflects a bias against creative writing students that are considered spoiled kids not worth being read, while at the same time it does not address Batuman's own privilege as a US author at the center of the global literary system.

The case of Ryan Boudinot is another example of an author taking a controversial stance. A writer and former teacher of creative writing, Boudinot argued in a personal essay (*Things I can Say About MFA Writing Programs Now That I No Longer Teach in One*) that writers are born with talent, which is something one can even read on the Iowa Writers' workshop website,[2] but he also said that talent cannot be developed, which is the opposite of what Iowa and other programs promise. This is something that many writers seem to believe, though they seldom dare to state so openly. Boudinot also said that most MFA students do not have that talent (with the exception of so-called real-deal students), and that they use the program as a therapy: "Just because you were abused as a child does not make your inability to stick with the same verb tense for more than two sentences any more bearable" (Boudinot 2015).

The piece caused quite a controversy, and many responded, including C.J. Sevcik, who unveiled himself as the abused child Boudinot was referring to (Sevcik 2015). At the time, Boudinot was the chair of a committee that was working on the application for Seattle's UNESCO City of Literature Program. The episode led to his removal from the chair position and eventually resulted in the withdrawal of the application (Gwinn 2015; Seattlish 2015). Other writers, like Sevcik, wondered why Boudinot decided to go public with such a statement. Others (Electric Literature 2015) noted that while the article's most visible targets were aspiring writers and students, Boudinot was actually criticizing the over-proliferation of MFAs: a Ponzi-like scheme that does not produce writers but teachers of creative writing, and which keeps reproducing itself. These examples are relevant because they prove how controversial the reception of creative writing programs remains.

The emphasis on the endless nature of the debate also proves that there is an ongoing debate happening and that these are not just occasional occurrences. The discourse around the legitimacy of creative writing education might not be very visible because it usually does not reach the level of public debate. However, it is well known to professionals working in the industry, aspiring writers, and teacher-writers.

In the scholarly literature, a reference to this debate can be found already in Myers' *The Elephants Teach* (2006). As the blurb notes, the book "explores more than a century of debate over how writing should be taught, and whether it can or should be taught in a classroom at all." The complex issue of the uselessness of creative writing degrees is addressed by Childress-Gerber (2015) in *The MFA in Creative Writing: The Uses of a "Useless" Credential*. The authors move from the taken-for-granted belief that creative writing degrees are useless for teaching how to write and even for securing industry jobs to an investigation of former students' actual uses of their degrees. They interviewed about 120 teachers, students, and publishing professionals. "I don't know why we do it. I know why I do it, but we're tasked with teaching the unteachable," (8) said one of the teachers-participants, who seemed to share Boudinot's opinion on talent: if teachers are supposed to teach the unteachable, then students who succeed already had what it takes. Publishing

[2]"Though we partially agree with the popular insistence that writing cannot be taught, we exist and proceed on the assumption that talent can be developed, and we see our possibilities and limitations as a school in that light. If one can 'learn' to play the violin or to paint, one can 'learn' to write, though no processes of externally induced training can ensure that one will do it well." Iowa Writers' Workshop, Philosopy https://writersworkshop.uiowa.edu/about/about-workshop/philosophy

professionals are "highly dubious of the claim that one learns how to write well in MFA-CW programs." They believe "that the quality of writing can even be adversely affected by MFA-CW attendance" (9). Students claim that programs are useful for securing time to write, establishing networks, or learning informally good publishing practices than for actual learning.

This shared distrust over the fact that courses can help in developing writing skills is relevant and warrants further investigation. The idea that writing is part of a domain separated from everyday life and that it is an ontological attribute that one either possesses or not might sound surprising given that the idea of art as autonomous from society has been challenged in many disciplines over the last 30 years, from art sociology and cultural studies to contemporary art theory. However, these disciplinary fields are not part of the curricula of creative writing programs, and their knowledge is not a prerequisite. In the 1980s, David Foster Wallace noted this phenomenon when he said that few programs "require of applicants any significant preparation in history, literature, criticism, composition, foreign languages, art, or philosophy; fewer still make attempts to provide it in curricula or require it as a criterion for graduation" (2014: 79). Furthermore, a high number of creative writing teachers received their education from the same programs[3] they end up teaching in. It is therefore possible to think that, in general, practitioners involved in teaching creative writing are not necessarily familiar with or open to the idea that art production is more complex than the product of an innate genius or, to use Boudinot's words, the "real-deal student." Therefore, if a teacher says that writing cannot be taught, it is clear that they subscribe to an idea of art as an autonomous domain, which is an approach to making art that surfaced during the modern age. As Shiner recalled, the modern system of art or fine art is neither universal nor something that has existed unchanged through the times. Rather, it emerged in the West, particularly in Europe, around the eighteenth century as a consequence of a shift that modified the broader, more utilitarian conception of art that was previously in place (Shiner 2001).

From Ancient Greece until the eighteenth century, art was not a matter of spiritual elevation and contemplation but rather referred to a wider range of meanings and practices. Art was "any human activity performed with skill and grace" (Shiner 2001: 5). Both the Greek word "*techne*" and the Latin term "*art*" refer to a series of activities and practices that only loosely correspond to what has been considered the homogeneous system of the arts since the eighteenth century. Although this transformation varies in time and place, the eighteenth century marked the first moment when authors of treatises on rhetoric, painting, architecture, and music started to discuss various art forms on the basis of common principles, whereas before then, these disciplines were not considered as subgroups of the general domain of art. The eighteenth century was also a period when scholars began to elaborate on one of the most influential pieces of Kant's philosophy, namely his ideas on esthetics. For Kant, the esthetic experience—and hence the experience of beauty—is a pure,

[3]Myers (1996: 146), Harbach (2014) and Bennett (2014: 52).

disinterested pleasure produced in the domain of philosophical thought. This idea implies a separation between the spheres of art and practical utility, and between art and everyday life (Kant 2007). The notion of art as pure contemplation and as disinterested pleasure excluded from the field of fine arts all the creative manifestations that could be of practical use, leading to a separation between the artist and the artisan, the fine arts and the crafts.

A long historical distance runs between this turn and the idea that writing cannot be taught. However, I argue that the root of this belief and the distrust toward creative writing lie precisely in the modern idea of art as a separate domain from everyday life, which, despite having been challenged by many art sociologists, such as Becker (1982), Bourdieu (1984), and Wolff (1981), has somehow survived unscathed in the specific field of creative writing.

5.3 Italian-Style Creative Writing: The Controversial Reception of the Holden School

In the remainder of this chapter, I will explore how the criticism of creative writing initiatives operates in Italy. As discussed above, the main difference between the Italian and the US and UK cases is that in Italy, universities do not offer degrees in creative writing[4] and this kind of education is completely entrusted to private institutions. Charities, associations, private academies, and bookshops are examples of the venues that might offer creative writing classes. Among them, only a single institution offers a full-time program: the Holden School.

The Holden School was established in Turin in 1994. In Italy's Northwest, Turin was known until the early 1980s as the core of the national automobile industry. Over the last 30 years, the city went through a process of transformation because of the downsizing of FIAT's manufacturing operations. Eventually, after the 2006 Winter Olympic Games, the city slowly managed to shift its image from a former working class identity to a new, postindustrial identity, one that remains debated and controversial (Vanolo 2008, 2015).

The Holden School started as a small enterprise accommodating about 30 students a year, and it now offers a wide range of courses: weekly online and offline workshops, residential retreats, workshops for companies, and programs for children. However, it is especially famous for its two-year program in storytelling, which is similar in structure to a master's degree. This program is now organized into five colleges. The specialism of each college has something to do with the world of storytelling, with different emphases on social media, television, cinema, and

---

[4]In January 2019, the Holden School launched the Holden Academy, a three-year program that will award a qualification recognized as a bachelor's degree by the Ministry of Education, University and Research. The Holden Academy will not replace the Holden School's two-year program, which will award the same qualification as before.

fiction. There is a general scarcity of information available about the school, and indeed, part of its appeal is generated by the mystery surrounding its pedagogical offering. Since 2013, the school has offered approximately 100 places a year, and the fees are around 10,000 euros, almost five times the most expensive fees for an Italian MA at a public university.[5] At the end of the two-year program, there is neither an examination nor a dissertation to submit. The school's website defines the diploma as a "business card" that can be used to gain consideration from the "professionals of storytelling." The school claims that the Holden degree is valuable for positions in the creative industries at large (television, radio, movie, theater, and advertising industries), and it does not mention publishing and writing as occupational ends, while, in the alumni section, it lists a number of people who managed to publish at least one book of fiction.[6] The Holden School is an expensive institution that offers an informal entry point into the creative industries at the national level, while avoiding to claim this too explicitly, possibly as a means of not generating too much hope or controversy if this does not occur.

The founder of the school, Alessandro Baricco, was already a prominent writer when he started it. He has a playful, combinatory, fully postmodern approach to literature and arts (Nicewicz 2011), and he belongs to the second wave of Italian postmodernism, which came after Umberto Eco (Casadei 2007). In terms of reputation, the Holden School is often subject to criticism that is in part consistent with the general argument regarding the impossibility of teaching people how to write. However, this strand of criticism is also influenced by the specific features of Italian cultural history and by the peculiar position of Baricco in the Italian literary system.

Below, I will discuss how a certain notion of culture shaped the reception of creative writing schools in Italy. Then, I will discuss how Baricco's position in the Italian literary and cultural fields influenced both the school's reputation and the professional paths of Holden graduates.

In Italy, the teaching of creative writing began around 1985, when writer Giuseppe Pontiggia launched a series of writing workshops at Teatro Verdi in Milan (Lepri 1997). In the early 1990s, Brazilian writer Julio Monteiro Martins started the Sagarana School in Lucca. He described the reactions that the school generated as "open mockery" (Treves 2003). When he started the school, Monteiro Martins was familiar with both North and Latin American approaches to creative writing, and he was not likely ready to deal with the criticism that he encountered. In his opinion, this criticism was because Italy's writing society was outdated and writers lived in the past and believed in the old Romantic values of the writer as a pure genius. Francesco Piccolo, now a famous writer, claimed that in Italy back then

---

[5]According to the data from the Organisation for Economic Co-operation and Development (OECD 2017), the average fee for a master's degree in Italy in 2017 was about 1800 USD (1580 euros).

[6]"For over 20 years, this diploma has been acknowledged in all working storytelling environments, TV, the radio, cinema, theatre and advertising. It's always been a business card which allows whoever has it in their pocket to present themselves as a professional storyteller with the acknowledgment they deserve" (Holden School Website 2019).

"if anyone tries to discuss creative writing programs in public, they are immediately asked: are creative writing schools useful? It is impossible to decide whether they are or not, but those who think that they aren't, they don't ignore them, they claim loudly that creative writing schools are a disgrace, even dangerous"[7] (1997: 252).

While this negative reception bears some similarity to the aforementioned criticisms of creative writing programs, it also shows some specificities such as the ones I will illustrate below tied to the meaning of the word "culture" in the Italian context, and the discourse on creative writing is one of the places where these tensions openly manifest. In Italy, "culture" mostly refers to the highest manifestations of literary culture, and attempts to open the culture to diverse and not necessarily high cultural manifestations are met with strong resistance and opposition, especially from literary critics and academics. This is possibly due to the role played by literature in building a sense of belonging to the nation-state in the aftermath of the country's unification in 1861.

Literature and literary language represented one of the core values of the Italian identity in a country that was deeply divided and fragmented at the linguistic, economic, and political levels. The canon of national literature was thus shaped to build a shared sense of belonging to a new national identity, and that original inspiration shapes higher education curricula even nowadays (Ceserani 1997). Italy's national culture was built on the values conveyed by the literary tradition, and for this reason, since the very beginning of national history, the term "culture" has been mostly associated with the words "education," "literacy," and "print culture," and culture was "a value in itself, something which one either possess or should aspire to acquire" (Forgacs and Lumley 1996: 3). The term "culture" thus assumed a very narrow meaning and ended up referring mostly to literary culture or, at least, literary and philosophical culture (De Mauro 2004: 3). The identification of culture with education and literacy is also connected with the influence of neo-idealist philosophy on Italian culture during the nineteenth century, especially that of Benedetto Croce (1866–1952) (De Mauro 2004; Zinato 2010). Croce, who developed his philosophical system in opposition to positivism, believed that art is the realm of pure intuition. Craftsmanship, training, education, and social position do not play any role in the process of art creation.

However, considering the high status of literary culture in Italy and the role played by the teaching of national literary history in education curricula, the repudiation of creative writing programs might appear counterintuitive. After all, what is more deferential to the idea that culture equals literature than people who aspire to become writers? Within a context in which the meaning of culture embraces different manifestations—from popular to high forms—it is possible to consider the choice of teaching and learning writing techniques as acceptable and legitimate. However, this has not happened in Italy, where culture is mostly associated with the national literary past and where the concept is not open to new manifestations and meanings.

[7]Translations are mine.

The reception of creative writing programs in Italy is also shaped by Baricco's peculiar position in the Italian publishing industry. He was already a best-selling author when he established the Holden School. In the early 1990s, he published several successful novels and gained further popularity hosting shows on literature, opera, classical music, and theater on public television. While his popularity among readers and the general public steadily increased after the publication of his first novel, *Castelli di Rabbia* (1991), his critical appreciation decreased. Baricco is generally perceived as a *parvenu*, someone who betrayed the true value of literature and who—in his novels, critical essays, and television appearances—offers a poor and oversimplified version of literature (Ferroni et al. 2006). Interestingly, Baricco's intellectual biography is all but poor in cultural capital. He graduated in philosophy under the guidance of Gianni Vattimo, the postmodernist thinker and theoretician behind 'weak thought', and before becoming a full-time author, he wrote about theater and classical music for years.

While Baricco developed his profile as an acclaimed writer and public intellectual, Italian critics were in the middle of a debate about the death of the critic as a mediator between writers and readers' tastes. Critics belonging to the Marxist tradition rejected the postmodern literature of the period almost entirely. They warned that literature had lost its aura, social role, and prestige. They believed that literature no longer educated the elites, nor did it shape the middle class's taste (La Porta and Leonelli 2007). A variant of this position argued that intellectuals were secluded within universities and that literature was besieged by technology, media communication, advertising, and consumerism. Meanwhile, Italian was becoming polluted by American-style managerial jargon (Luperini 2002, 2005). Critics also complained that readers were unable to recognize postmodern literature's poor quality.

Baricco loudly made his way into this context, claiming on public television that when critics said a piece of art was good because it did not lower itself to the public's taste, they forgot that audiences pay to be entertained, not to be fed with difficult and enigmatic content (Baricco 1998). The relationship between Baricco and literary critics did not improve as the years went on. In a debate that reached the pages of the principal Italian newspapers, Baricco (2006) lamented that critics were not even giving him the dignity of a proper review, as they had just superficially dismissed his latest novel, *Questa Storia* (2005), as "sickening." (Ferroni 2006a : 22) One of them, Giulio Ferroni, reacted by pointing out how many times he had reviewed Baricco. According to Ferroni, Baricco did not write literature but rather entertainment. Ferroni said that literature was "passion, the emergence of the unexpected, the deep knowledge one cannot see," while Baricco wrote a "polished, advert-like literature" that was only "superficially captivating." For Ferroni, Baricco was an example of a "peculiar type of narcissistic and complacent nihilism." He was successful because he was "easy to read," "not threatening," and "light" (Ferroni 2006b).

Even today, Baricco's reputation has a huge influence on the way Holden School graduates are perceived. Here, I draw on 49 in-depth qualitative interviews I conducted with Holden graduates in 2018. While a full analysis of this material is beyond this chapter's scope, I provide an illustrative example of how Holden graduates are perceived by other professionals in the Italian literary field.

Several participants reported that the choice of attending the Holden School was seen in a positive light by people outside the literary field, such as parents and friends who did not have a strong interest in literature. However, people working in the publishing industry are often skeptical about this educational qualification. A participant who now works in a major publishing house reported: "I am always in doubt whether to disclose that I attended the Holden School. If I say that I attended it, I encounter two reactions: those who say, '[the] Holden School is shit; what a crappy place,' and those who say, 'Yes, you know, I went there too.' I always have to think about how much I want to disclose and how this is going to influence the way in which I am perceived."

Other participants reported similar experiences, all of which show that Italy's reception of creative writing programs is not only informed by the argument that writing cannot be taught, which is common in the United States and the United Kingdom, but also by features that are specific to the Italian literary field: the relevance of the national literary tradition and Baricco's fame. Holden graduates risk being associated with a superficial institution that, being commercially oriented, does not represent the values of the national literary canon. This perception is further exacerbated by the image of Baricco as an author who, according to critics, caters too explicitly to the masses.

5.4 Conclusion

This chapter aimed to show that a number of historical, social, and cultural factors shape the reception of creative writing programs in the United States and the United Kingdom and that these factors intersect with more national influences in Italy.

Overall, I demonstrated how criticism of creative writing programs is informed by a specific understanding of artistic creation that has its roots in the separation of the domain of art from the domain of craft. According to this view, literature belongs to the first domain, while creative writing programs have been steadily assigned to the second. This tension frames the public discourse about creative writing degrees and their negative reputation. Moreover, I showed that in Italy, the reception of creative writing programs is influenced both by the relevance of literary education in the building a national identity and by the conflicted relationship between Baricco, founder of the most popular creative writing program, and literary critics. I also showed that this conflict deeply influences the way in which Holden graduates are perceived once they attempt to enter the job market.

Through this exploration, I have argued that critical scholarship on the creative and cultural industries should pay more attention to creative writing programs, as they have become a key institution regulating the processes of inclusion in and exclusion from the literary field. These processes of selection are important because they regulate the production of literature (and culture more generally) and because they have an impact on the aspirations and biographies of students, which remain severely understudied.

References

Alacovska A (2018) Keep hoping, keep going': towards a hopeful sociology of creative work. Sociol Rev. https://doi.org/10.1177/0038026118779014

Ashton D, Noonan C (eds) (2013) Cultural work and higher education. Palgrave Macmillan, Basingstoke

Banks M, Gill R, Taylor S (eds) (2013) Theorizing cultural work: labour, continuity and change in the cultural and creative industries. Routledge, London

Baricco A (1998) Alessandro Baricco spiega il finale de 'Guglielmo Tell'. https://www.youtube.com/watch?v=QAcCMQxqJwU. Accessed 3 Nov 2019

Baricco A (2006, March 1) Cari critici ho diritto a una vera stroncatura. La Repubblica. http://www.repubblica.it/2006/c/sezioni/spettacoli_e_cultura/baricco/baricco/baricco.html. Accessed 3 Nov 2019

Becker HS (2008) [1982] Art worlds. University of California Press, Berkley–London

Belfiore E (2006) Ubi maior minor cessat: a comparative study of the relation between changing cultural policy rationales and globalization in post-1980s England and Italy. PhD thesis, University of Warwick

Bennett E (2014) The Pyramid Scheme. In: Harbach C (ed) MFA vs NYC: the two cultures of American fiction. New York, Faber and Faber, pp 51–72

Bodo C (2016) Italy/1. Historical perspective: cultural policies and instruments. In: Compendium of cultural policies and trends in Europe, 17th edn. Council of Europe/ERICart. http://www.culturalpolicies.net/web/italy.php. Accessed 3 Nov 2019

Boudinot R (2015) Things I can say about MFA writing programs now that I no longer teach in one. The Stranger. https://www.thestranger.com/books/features/2015/02/27/21792750/things-i-can-say-about-mfa-writing-programs-now-that-i-no-longer-teach-in-one. Accessed 3 Nov 2019

Bourdieu P (1984) Distinction: a social critique of the Judgement of taste. Harvard University Press, Cambridge

Casadei A (2007) Stile e tradizione nel romanzo italiano contemporaneo. Il Mulino, Bologna

Ceserani R (1997) Italianistica in crisi: l'insegnamento della letteratura. A proposito degli interventi di Gnisci, Merz e Fedi. Bollettino del '900, Gennaio-Giugno n 1. http://www3.unibo.it/boll900/numeri/1997-i/Ceserani.html. Accessed 3 Nov 2019

Dawson P (2005) Creative writing and the new humanities. Routledge, Oxon

De Mauro T (2004) La cultura degli Italiani. Laterza, Bari

Donnelly JD (2009) Establishing creative writing studies as an academic discipline. PhD thesis, University of South Florida

Electric Literature (2015) How the MFA glut is a disservice to students, teachers, and writers. https://electricliterature.com/how-the-mfa-glut-is-a-disservice-to-students-teachers-and-writers/. Accessed 3 Nov 2019

Ferroni G (2006a, February 26) Vassalli, un uomo contro il postumano. l'Unità, p 22

Ferroni G (2006b, March 2) Caro Baricco, io la recensisco ma lei non mi legge. La Repubblica. http://www.repubblica.it/2006/c/sezioni/spettacoli_e_cultura/baricco/critic/critic.html. Accessed 3 Nov 2019

Ferroni G et al (2006) Sul banco dei cattivi. A proposito di Baricco e di altri scrittori alla moda Donzelli editore, Roma

Flood A (2014, March 4) Creative writing professor Hanif Kureishi says such courses are 'a waste of time'. The Guardian. https://www.theguardian.com/books/2014/mar/04/creative-writing-courses-waste-of-time-hanif-kureishi. Accessed 3 Nov 2019

Forgacs D, Lumley R (eds) (1996) Italian cultural studies: an introduction. Oxford University Press, Oxford

Foster Wallace D (2014) [1987] Novelist as a critic. In: C. Harbach (Ed.) MFA vs NYC: the two cultures of American fiction (pp. 73–80). New York, Faber and Faber

Gwinn MA (2015) War of words sidelines Seattle's 'City of Literature' Bid. The Seattle Times. https://www.seattletimes.com/entertainment/books/war-of-words-sidelines-seattles-city-of-literature-bid/. Accessed 3 Nov 2019

Harbach C (2014) MFA vs NYC. In: MFA vs NYC: the two cultures of American fiction. Faber and Faber, New York, pp 9–28

Harper G, Kerridge R (2004) Editorial. New Writ 1(1):1–5

Hesmondhalgh D (2013) Introduction. In: The cultural industries, 3rd edn. Sage, London, pp 2–33

Hesmondhalgh D, Baker S (2011) Creative labour. Media work in three cultural industries. Routledge, Abingdon/New York

Holden School Website (2019) Original. https://scuolaholden.it/en/original/. Accessed 3 Nov 2019

Iowa Writing Worskshop. Philosophy. https://writersworkshop.uiowa.edu/about/about-workshop/philosophy. Accessed 3 Nov 2019

Jones A (2014, March 3) Bath literature festival: creative writing courses are a waste of time, says Hanif Kureishi (who teaches one). The Independent. http://www.independent.co.uk/arts-entertainment/books/news/the-independent-bath-literature-festival-creative-writing-courses-are-a-waste-of-time-says-hanif-9166697.html. Accessed 3 Nov 2019

Kant I (2007) [1952] The critique of Judgement (trans. James Creed Meredith). Oxford University Press, Oxford

La Porta F, Leonelli G (2007) Dizionario della critica militante. Letteratura e mondo contemporaneo. Bompiani, Milano

Lepri L (ed) (1997) Quaderni di Panta: la scrittura creativa raccontata dagli scrittori che la insegnano. Bompiani, Milano

Luperini R (2002) Breviario di Critica. Alfredo Guida Editore, Napoli

Luperini R (2005) La Fine del Postmoderno. Alfredo Guida Editore, Napoli

Mayers T (2016) Creative writing studies: the past decade (and the next). J Creat Writ Stud 1(1): Art 4. https://scholarworks.rit.edu/jcws/vol1/iss1/4. Accessed 3 Nov 2019

McGurl M (2009) The program era. Postwar fiction and the rise of creative writing. Harvard University Press, Cambridge—London

McRobbie A (2002) Clubs to companies: notes on the decline of political culture in speeded up creative worlds. Cult Stud 16(4):516–531. https://doi.org/10.1080/09502380210139098

McRobbie A (2016) Be creative: making a living in the new culture industries. Polity, Cambridge

Myers DG (1996) The elephants teach. Creative writing since 1880. The University of Chicago Press, Chicago

NAWE (National Education of Writers in Education). Writing Courses. https://www.nawe.co.uk/writing-in-education/writing-at-university/writing-courses.html. Accessed 3 Nov 2019

Nicewicz EM (2011) Il caso Baricco: nella trappola del postmoderno. PhD thesis, Università degli Studi di Padova

Oakley K (2009) From Bohemia to Britart—art students over 50 years. Cult Trends 18(4):281–294. https://doi.org/10.1080/09548960903268105

OECD (2017) Education at a glance 2017: OECD indicators (summary in Italian). OECD, Paris. https://doi.org/10.1787/cf1223b6-it. Accessed 3 Nov 2019

Piccolo F (1997) Non è vero che 'dopo aver scritto non posso più toccare nemmeno una riga perché quello era ciò che avevo dentro'. In: Lepri L (ed) Quaderni di Panta: la scrittura creativa raccontata dagli scrittori che la insegnano. Bompiani, Milano, pp 252–262

Scharff C (2017) Gender subjectivity and cultural work: the classical music profession. Taylor and Francis, London

Seattlish (2015) Ryan Boudinot killed Seattle City of lit and the stranger helped him to bury the body. https://seattlish.com/post/113982681386/ryan-boudinot-killed-seattle-city-of-lit-and-the. Accessed 3 Nov 2019

Sevcik JC (2015) I was the MFA student who made Ryan Boudinot cry. The Stranger. https://www.thestranger.com/books/features/2015/03/11/21856969/i-was-the-mfa-student-who-made-ryan-boudinot-cry. Accessed 3 Nov 2019

Shiner LE (2001) The invention of art: a cultural history. University of Chicago Press, Chicago

Treves S (2003) Lo spirito della Sagarana. Un'intervista a Julio Monteiro Martins. Libri Nuovi 24. https://www.el-ghibli.org/intervista-54-silvia-treves/. Accessed 3 Nov 2019

Vanolo A (2008) The image of the creative city: some reflections on urban branding in Turin. Cities 25:370–382. https://doi.org/10.1016/j.cities.2008.08.001

Vanolo A (2015) The Fordist city and the creative city: evolution and resilience in Turin. City Cult Soc. doi: https://doi.org/10.1016/j.ccs.2015.01.003

Wolff J (1993) [1981] The social production of art. London, Macmillan

Zinato E (2010) Le idee e le forme. In: La critica letteraria in Italia dal 1900 ai giorni nostri. Carocci, Roma

Cecilia Ghidotti is a doctoral candidate at the Institute for Media and Creative Industries, Loughborough University London. Her project focuses on processes of inclusion and exclusion from cultural work looking at the case of the Italian publishing industry.

Part II
Ideology: Creative Self-Expression and Aesthetics

Chapter 6
The Art Biennial's Dilemma: Political Activism as Spectacle in Aesthetic Capitalism

Panos Kompatsiaris and Nada Endrissat

Abstract In recent decades, the biennial has become the most widespread mode of showcasing contemporary art. Rather than acting as mere aesthetic containers, these shows aspire to be socially relevant by raising questions about capitalism, colonialism, inequality, environmental devastation, and gender imbalances. In this chapter, we draw from ethnographic observation of the 7th Berlin Biennale (2012) that took place in the context of a rising anti-capitalist discourse reflected in the Occupy movement and the movement of the squares. We explore the outcome of curators' attempts to disrupt existing practices by introducing the logic of activism. Drawing from empirical vignettes, we identify three institutional rationales that coexisted, clashed, and mutually displaced this logic, reaffirming rather than disrupting the idea that art has to preserve some distance from social reality, that neo-anarchist activism should prefigure social reality in the here and now, and that the configuration of the above through the organization's politics of visibility that promotes the spectacle of the Berlin Biennale and itself as a brand. These three rationales concomitantly and decisively structured the event's public performance and turned the idea of linking art to activism into the spectacle of a human zoo. We discuss our findings and link the micro-institutional logics to broader macro-level logics of aesthetic capitalism and spectacle.

Keywords Activism · Aesthetic capitalism · Art biennials · Institutional legitimacy · Occupy

---

P. Kompatsiaris (✉)
National Research University Higher School of Economics, Moscow, Russia
e-mail: pkompatsiaris@hse.ru

N. Endrissat
Bern University of Applied Sciences, Bern, Switzerland
e-mail: nada.endrissat@bfh.ch

I. Kiriya et al. (eds.), *The Industrialization of Creativity and Its Limits*, Science, Technology and Innovation Studies, https://doi.org/10.1007/978-3-030-53164-5_6

6.1 Introduction

> This publication is a report on the process of arriving at real action within culture . . . we have been witnessing a process of incapacitation whereby artistic radicalism is transformed into velvet critique. . . . Art needs to be *reinvented*, but not as some crafty option to aestheticize human problems in a novel way by turning them into a formal spectacle . . . The most important thing at stake . . . is art that *brings change*, art that is not critical in an empty fashion; art that does not produce pseudo-critique, but is genuinely *transformative* and *formative*.
>
> Curator's foreword to the 7th Berlin Biennale, Forget Fear, Zmijewksi 2012: 10 (emphasis added).

In the framework of neoliberal cultural policy, contemporary art is an area of economic productivity and is therefore both a subject of and servant to market logics. Apart from its association with the processes of gentrification, symbolic consumption, money laundering, and artwashing for corporations, the field is defined by immense inequalities that lead to exploitative and underpaid work. On the one hand, there is a small cadre of superstar artists, and on the other, there is the creative dark matter of all the shadowed, amateur, informal, and self-organized practitioners who remain invisible to the institutionalized art world, usually with little or no pay (Sholette 2011; Dimitrakaki 2012). To participate as a global actor in this field means to see and be seen within the transnational, cosmopolitan, and class-marked networks of art fairs, museums, biennials, and mega-exhibitions (Kompatsiaris 2014).

In addition, biennials and similar mega-events are economic boosters that contribute to a city's image and provide cool or Instagrammable experience scapes to middle-class audiences. These events are therefore infused with the logics of marketing, public relations, social media promotion, networking, and career promises, all of which are features of contemporary aesthetic capitalism (Böhme 2003, 2016; Murphy and de la Fuente 2014; Roberts 2003) or, more broadly and in a transhistorical manner, with the aesthetics of capital (Holm and Duncan 2018). Aesthetic capitalism is a further development of capitalism and its inherent imperative to grow and reinvent itself by co-opting its critics (Boltanski and Chiapello 2005). It signifies a turn from artistic criticism of capitalism to the "artistic spirit" of capitalism (Roberts 2014: 16), thereby turning business into art and art into business. The distinction between "culture and commerce once wide has shrunk" (Murphy and de la Fuente 2014: 3; duGay and Pryke 2002); art is increasingly commodified and used as a means for capitalism to grow and to sell and stage experiences and products (Böhme 2003, 2016), thus linking it to the new consumption patterns of the aspirational class (Currid-Halkett 2017).

At the same time, and somewhat counter intuitively, these contemporary art mega-shows present themselves as deviations from dominant culture and relations, hoping to disrupt, explore, and question processes of economic globalization, exclusion, migration, and social inequality. The curators and artists participating in perennial mega-exhibitions, or biennials, are typically socially and theoretically aware, left leaning, and interventionist (Hlavajova 2010). Generally, the idea of criticizing the system to which one contributes is particularly stark among critical contemporary art milieus and their public outlets, including journal publications, socially engaged artist and curatorial statements, or politically loaded exhibitions. Despite their different statuses, contemporary mega-exhibitions, such as biennials, triennials, and documenta, which recur at regular intervals in different locations, are sites where experimentation coincides with the logic of the spectacle, critical theory with gentrification, and flexible labor with branding techniques (Boltanski and Thevenot 2006; Green and Gardner 2016; Kompatsiaris 2017).

In this chapter, we explore how the world of aesthetic capitalism (macro level) provides a context that defines how artistic and curatorial resistance (micro level) is played out in the context of a biennial and its politics. This framework helps explain how institutional change does or does not take place on these sites. Through the description of several ethnographic moments, our empirical study addresses and investigates one radical attempt to disrupt the 7th Berlin Biennale (BB7) that took place in 2012 in Berlin, Germany. As this chapter's opening quote suggests, the curatorial idea was to uproot conventional ways of making biennials, escaping the institutional iron cage, and unleashing the potential for radical transformation that would enable social effects in the City of Berlin (Zmijewski 2012: 10). By inviting Occupy movement activists to take over the space, the main goal was to transform the BB7's premises from a space of spectatorship into a space of action with real consequences.

In the first section of this chapter, which is titled "Art Biennials and Aesthetic Capitalism," we discuss the biennial as a form of the mega-exhibition and position it within our historical present. This serves to outline the existing rationales that rule the macro level and to identify the crisis of legitimacy associated with contemporary biennials.

Subsequently, in the section entitled "Art Biennials and Institutional Dynamics," we introduce the concept of institutional logic to conceptualize how institutional change might take place through institutional work on the micro level, focusing our attention on the curator's role and decisions to initiate change.

Following that, in the section "The BB7" we present three ethnographic vignettes from the BB7 that highlight the institutional logics that coexisted, overlapped, clashed, and mutually displaced each other during the show: first, the rationale that art has to preserve some distance from social reality; second, the rationale that activism should prefigure social reality in the here and now (i.e., Occupy's neo-anarchism); and third, the configuration of the above through the organization's politics of visibility that promotes the spectacle and Berlin Biennale brand. We argue that these three rationales concomitantly and decisively structured the event's public performance and, despite the curators' radical intentions, turned (partly) counter-hegemonic politics into an aesthetic experience. In aesthetic capitalism, everything assumes commodity value, and because of this, even attempts to criticize art institutions through activism and radical gestures are commodified. This does not mean that art exhibitions have no social impacts, but that these impacts are filtered through an assemblage of market discourse, promotional culture, public relations, and the idea of art as an exclusive activity aloof from society. In this context, these shows often promote the neoliberal ethos of social responsibility and controlled transgression that is currently the norm. Furthermore, as a result of its temporary nature, the BB7 failed to develop a transformative (or formative) force and, as a one-off event, contributed to the tendency of art to aestheticize human problems in a novel way by turning them into a spectacle, a critique that Zmijewksi, the BB7 curator, had sought to overcome (see this chapter's opening quotation). In other words, the BB7 achieved the opposite of what its curatorial team had intended.

In conclusion, we assert that this paradox is part of the new spirit of aesthetic capitalism in which criticism, disruption, and the attempt to break from existing norms in many ways normalize existing structures insofar as they are incorporated into the aesthetic industry, a dynamic known to be at the heart of artistic critique since the early avant-garde (e.g., Leger 2012; Roberts 2015). We also conclude that anti-capitalist ways of being can be more effectively developed through political groups that question capital accumulation in its contemporary forms, including the valorization of experience and marketization of deviance.

6.2 Art Biennials and Aesthetic Capitalism

The established history of the art biennial begins with the 1895 Venice Biennale, which was the first exhibition of visual arts to adopt that name. Venice Biennale took its form from the world fairs of the nineteenth century that expressed the desire to establish their host cities as cultural and touristic centers (West 1995). Since Venice, the name "biennial," which literally means every 2 years, has evolved into a recognizable brand in the art world, carrying with it symbolic capital that provides the necessary legitimacy and promises to attract sponsors, artists, volunteers, and the public.

In the last 20 years, the number of contemporary biennials around the world has grown rapidly. Despite their positioning in the field of art, biennials are sites of dialogic encounters rather than aesthetic formalism, and they perform what the philosopher Peter Osborne, drawing on both Francois Lytorad and Fredric Jameson, called the "postconceptual condition"—that is, the "cultural logic of high capitalism today" (2018: 3). As postconceptual entities, biennials privilege ideas rather than the forms of works and their political statements rather than their colors, shapes, and appearance; biennials are expected to be within the action of events, to grasp the moment, intervene, and make statements rather than refer exclusively to artistic matters. In 1983, Hal Foster named artists' tendency to repudiate questions of form in favor of those of concept as the "anti-aesthetic" (xv). Debates around the anti-aesthetic contributed to the post-2000s dominance of relational aesthetics (Bourriaud 2002) in which art is not supposed to be found in the object and its materiality but in the relations, it institutes with audiences. Ideas such as resistance and criticality, very popular in the vocabulary of critical contemporary art, are part of this postconceptual condition (Elkins and Montgomery 2013). The birth of a series of new biennials in the 1990s, along with the rise of specialized curatorial magazines and master's programs, contributed to the institutionalization of conceptual art as the new artistic paradigm.

This institutionalization of conceptual practices relates to notions of aesthetic capitalism and the aesthetics of capital. The two refer to different yet overlapping and equally useful ideas for speaking about the relations between contemporary biennials and capitalist logic. As a term, "aesthetic capitalism" signifies a period in capitalist history, while the idea of the aesthetics of capital is a trans-historical concept that can be applied to any cultural artifact that prioritizes capitalist values on an ideological level. In the context of contemporary art mega-shows, both these concepts are applicable and coincide; historically speaking, these shows have been flourishing around the world since the 1990s because of the advent and domination of global capitalism, and as such, their overall aesthetics have to do with the promotion of their brand status.

Therefore, in these heavily marketized environments, postconceptualism, as a mode of both displaying and criticizing the status quo, becomes a form without content, and the aesthetics of capital override whatever political messages are present. As Böhme put it, in the aesthetic economy the principal distinction "between art and kitsch is quite consciously abandoned," and thus, the high aesthetics—in the exclusive sense of the term—that are usually antagonistic to market relations interweave with the low aesthetics of social media, marketing, and everyday culture so as to provide the experience of a mega-event (2003: 72). In other words, biennials are vehicles of leftist liberal politics that potentially empower local art scenes by bringing them into contact with international audiences while diffusing the logic of the spectacle, providing sites for public relations, networking, and city branding at the same time, thus creating manifold tensions on the ground (Kompatsiaris 2017).

In the context of the BB7, the curator wanted to change this positioning by resisting neoliberal market logic and changing the biennial into a political actor with real consequences. Our research interest for this chapter lays in mapping the contours of this attempted change. Theoretically, we draw from the concept of institutionalism that helps to explain the persistence of institutions despite attempts to change them (e.g., Meyer and Rowan 1977; Lawrence et al. 2009).

6.3 Art Biennials and Institutional Dynamics

Contemporary art biennials are institutions with symbolic power that authorize artistic practices, a power they regularly strive to maintain, legitimize, and expand (Born 1995). In traditional sociological accounts, institutions are thought to be created in order to serve certain social functions, helping, for example, to align "individual and collective interests" (Holm 1995: 399). For the purpose of this chapter, we are mostly interested in the institution of the biennial in terms of its moving, conflicting, and shifting positions rather than its determinate role in a social order. For this reason, we think of institutions as porous entities that strive to maintain and prove their usefulness in relation to often-changing social circumstances (e.g., Lawrence et al. 2009).

Scholars in the field of organization studies have looked at the ways in which institutional logics induce certain normative behavioral patterns in institutional and organizational actors (Meyer and Rowan 1977; Lawrence et al. 2009). According to this line of thought, as far as institutional preservation and survival are at stake and even though institutions may be inhabited by conflicting forces, actors will most often act in accordance with institutional interests. However, recent scholarship in the field stresses how actors within institutional settings may also attempt to use their positions of power to make the institutions work for causes not directly related to preordered institutional aims (e.g., Hirsch and Bermiss 2009; Lawrence and Suddaby 2006; Spicer 2010). In order to restore agency and explore the dynamics of organizational settings, Lawrence and Suddaby (2006) offered the term "institutional work" to refer to a kind of "purposive action of individuals and organizations aimed at creating, maintaining and disrupting institutions" (215). In this sense, practices of disrupting or escaping institutions may contribute to new institutional forms with differing rationales, scopes, and approaches. While the more traditional approaches may see strategies of repurposing institutional aims as attempts to maintain or reinforce the institution's original structure, the institutional work perspective focuses on the ways practices themselves affect institutions and their larger environments (Hirsch and Bermiss 2009).

In the context of biennials, the curator plays a central role, deciding on the higher meanings and providing the necessary framing for the biennial. The curator emerges as the figure who can "make sense of things," a connoisseur who has the capacity to orchestrate, organize, and give meaning to an otherwise chaotic universe (Balzer 2014: 40). In our narration of our empirical findings, we focus our attention on the curator and his institutional work, which aimed at disrupting and rearranging the power relations of the setting to address the legitimacy crisis and processes of deinstitutionalization (Hirsch and Bermiss 2009). To make a strong statement and distance himself from typical institutional practices, the BB7's curator framed it as a non-biennial. His focus was on employing "disruptive" practices and producing "real consequences," as this chapter's opening quote suggests. This included inviting the Occupy movement to take over the biennial space, the practice of symbolically resigning and implementing a more horizontal organization while the biennial was still running, the practice of inviting activists' transgressive behavior, and providing a stage for contested actors.

6.4 The BB7

Our case study is based on an ethnographic investigation of the BB7. Data were collected from a variety of sources, including 2.5 months of daily participant observations on the main site, informal chats with visitors and participants, our attendance of assemblies and most BB7 events, and 12 recorded interviews with participants of the Occupy movement, the Biennale organizers, and the curatorial group. We followed the BB7's social media sites before, during, and after the event, observing their posts and interactions and analyzing the reviews written about the show, especially those in the international press (for more information, see Kompatsiaris 2017).

The curatorial team of this show collaborated with several social movements and activist groups, including the Russian group Voina, which has achieved notoriety in Russia and the global art world for its scandalous performances that involve violence and the vandalism of state institutions; activists and members of the Occupy Berlin; and members of the Brazilian group Pixadores, a subsection of the graffiti movement in Sao Paulo whose main practice is the tagging of high-rises as a means of making themselves visible. Through these collaborations, the BB7 tried to incorporate political activism and render the biennale transformative in the fight against economic globalization, exclusion, and inequality.

We present three vignettes from our empirical data to highlight how the curator's above-described practices and the established institutional logics of art biennials in the context of aesthetic capitalism (see above) interacted and clashed. The following three logics are central to our analysis:

- Art must preserve some distance from social reality (R1).
- Activism should prefigure social reality in the here and now (R2).
- The above are configurated through aesthetic capitalism's modalities of the spectacle, brand, and visibility (R3).

The ethnographic vignettes recount how these logics were adopted, contested, and reconfigured by participants, providing the empirical base to argue how the curator's vision of critical, anti-capitalist political art was brought together and clashed with the commodified space of the spectacle in the same conceptual and spatial organizational arrangement.

6.5 Ethnographic Vignette 1: Activism Meets Spectators

The curator decided to invite activists from Occupy Berlin and give them the opportunity to invite and network with their international peers. The curator's intent was to turn the gallery from a space of representation to one of action. After debating whether to accept the invitation, Occupy Berlin decided to take over the BB7's most central site: the KW venue. By occupying this central space, the activists became the hosts of the exhibition. Rather than perceiving visitors as mere participants, the activists sought to mobilize them for the cause of social change.

Nevertheless, these two contradictory logics—the logic of the art gallery and that of the activist space—were not easy to navigate. One Occupy participant confessed that although the group was planning to subvert their prescribed roles as entertainers, before the opening, she and the other Occupy participants were distressed, wondering what they were going to show to the crowds that were arriving by the hundreds.

Despite the stress, there was little to show on opening night apart from a real-time assembly in which the activists continually invited guests and audience members through a megaphone to participate. However, most audience members, whose clothes and manners were those of bourgeois art visitors and not street activists, were baffled by the invitation. Our observations suggest that several audience members were bemused by the entertaining occupiers, while others hesitated to take part in the assemblies.

It seemed that the two worlds—that of gallery-based art and that of street activism—clashed, as visitors were indifferent, if not hostile, to the occupation. In many ways, visitors perceived the social movement as a participatory work of art itself, contextualizing it within recent art-world trends, the City of Berlin, or the contemporary political condition involving austerity and social movements. The dominant rationale that an art space is not exactly real but metaphorical, allegorical, and different from reality (R1) was forced into an encounter with the activist logic of direct action, which is literal and unambiguous (R2). In other words, the idea of turning spectators into activists was fraught with tension from the outset because spectators typically understand gallery visits as predetermined routines (e.g., the visit usually lasts a couple of hours and involves seeing rather than doing). In this case, the audience was neither prepared nor willing to get active.

Responding to the danger of the public viewing them as a type of living artwork, activists encouraged visitors to participate as they went about their activism and coordination. They had placed an imposing banner above their tents announcing that "This is not our museum. This is your action space" (see Fig. 6.1). This statement was performative in that it embodied the rationale of the movement to convert the art space into a real space (R2) rather than one that is distanced from reality (R1). The Occupy ethos insisted that this was not an art show in which people simply came to contemplate art. However, the statement alone was not enough to mobilize the audience to abandon their passivity.

This first vignette illustrates how the BB7's main project, which was to invite social activists involved in the Occupy movement to camp on its premises, was a project that involved different and incompatible logics. The activists were supposed to use the infrastructure, equipment, and brands of the Biennale and KW for international networking and resistant actions against austerity, nationalism, and neoliberal politics (R3). For the curator, this invitation was intended to reverse the role of the Biennale from an aesthetic container to a space that enabled pragmatic social impacts. Yet, this unorthodox invitation, bringing together three distinct logics—those of art, activism, and the spectacle-brand—inevitably foregrounded the predicament of their interweaving.

Fig. 6.1. "This is not our museum. This is your action space." The Occupy activists as hosts intended to transform the function of the gallery space

6.6 Ethnographic Vignette 2: Moving Toward Horizontality

This predicament produced discomfort among the Occupy activists and curatorial team, who came to terms with the fact that social change at the biennial was insufficiently real. This enabled the horizontalization of the exhibition so that equality would be achieved in practice. A landmark in this process was a statement issued in May 2012, 1 month after the opening of the biennial. In it, the curatorial team resigned its position and publicly spoke of itself as former curators. According to the official statement uploaded to the BB7's webpage,

> The invited global movements have challenged the hierarchical structure of the Biennale, initiating a move toward horizontality [that] means de-centering power . . . from leadership hierarchies and making decisions through group consensus. (See the full text here: http://blog.berlinbiennale.de/en/comments/7th-berlin-biennale-is-moving-towards-horizontality-30631.html)

This experiment was intended to then consist of "changing the positions of the curators relative to the Occupy Biennale and calling a series of assemblies with activists and KW staff" so as to "rethink the terms and conditions of labor."[1] The aim was to reconcile statements and practice, be truthful towards the activist ethos the BB7 set out to embrace, and be in "line with the stated claims to present art that

[1]Ibid.

actually works, makes its mark on reality, and opens a space where politics can be performed."[2]

This was not just the curators' initiative but part of the activists' reflexive practice in response to the way the public had cast them as a "living artwork". They had submitted a proposal called You Can't Curate a Movement, urging the curatorial team to practice what they were preaching—that is, to adopt a "horizontal, non-hierarchical organizational structure."[3] To the curators, this proposal was a response to "a disempowering situation that became … known as the 'human zoo." The term "human zoo" was a negative label that the press and audience gave to the Occupy members and the BB7 more generally in order to highlight that the whole setting reminded them of a colonial zoo in which the activists were seen by the audience as wild animals (e.g., Kimball 2012). The now-former curators accepted the credo "don't curate, supervise, or assess" for the remainder of the show, thereby following the activists' desire to de-exoticize themselves.

At the same time, the quest for horizontality led to a series of talks and assemblies concerning questions about the budget and labor rights context in which KW workers participated. However, these issues were only brought forward through this temporary rift in typical biennial politics rather than leading to permanent changes in the Berlin Biennale's hierarchies and lines of command. In this sense, the BB7's logic of the spectacle (R3)—specifically the idea that it should be seen as an art institution in order to find sponsors, maintain its visibility, and reproduce the status of its participants—cut short the change brought inside the institution by the activists. This logic would then act as a shield against efforts to radicalize the institution in a socially meaningful way.

6.7 Ethnographic Vignette 3: Transgressing Designated Areas—Unwelcomed Disruption

This step toward participatory inclusion in the institutional structure proved to be illusory both because of institutional limitations and the fact that it did not take into account power relations in which the curators themselves were entangled. This oversight caused issues in late-May 2012 event at the Elisabeth Church, one of the BB7's venues. For this event, the curators invited Brazilian group of *pixadores* for a workshop. These practitioners were involved in the urban tagging and protest practice known as *pixação*, a widespread graffiti-like movement mostly centered in Sao Paolo involving the tagging or marking of inaccessible areas, such as tall buildings, with letters and messages with meanings clear largely to a circle of insiders (Gupta 2015). Its practitioners come from disadvantaged backgrounds,

[2]Ibid.

[3]See the full text here: http://occupymuseums.org/index.php/actions/43-occupy-museums-and-the-7th-berlin-biennale

and the movement's political agenda strongly relates to working class visibility, transgression, and anti-institutionalism. The workshop was called Politics of the Poor and was expected to offer an insight into *pixação* and its practices as a form of protest against the class and race dynamics of Brazilian society. The church was prepared as venue by equipping its walls with white panels all around.

However, during the workshop, the *pixadores* transgressed their presumed role, namely that of poor Brazilians who would perform before a middle-class audience in Berlin. They moved beyond their specially designated area covered with white panels and started spraying the actual walls of the church. In so doing, they violated the terms of the agreement they had with the curator. The curator, furious over the breaching of the agreement, threw a bucket of water on one of the pixadores, saying, "This is also a transgression."[4] This action backfired, as a member of the group perceived it as an assault and doused the curator with yellow paint. The exchange of insults and staining liquids ended when the curator decided to call the police, who arrived to arrest and charge the *pixadores*.

A similar incident occurred some days later when newly arriving Occupy activists from Spain mistook a piece of work by Zmijewski in KW's central yard for a corporate advertisement. Expressing their anti-capitalist feelings, they climbed on top of a five-meter wall and painted over the assumed capitalistic banner with the words "Rise Up!" (Fig. Fig. 6.2). In the language of conceptual art that biennial crowds use, the banner was intended to mimic and parody corporate imagery (R1). The activists, however, who were unfamiliar with the language codes of the art world, perceived the banner literally, unfiltered, and without the mediating distance of conceptual art; rather, they perceived it for what it appeared to be: a corporate advertisement (R2). As the artwork and gallery's external wall were vandalized, the institution decided to fine the activists several thousand euros for the damages.

In a manner the curators had not expected, the transgressions of the *pixadores* and Spanish activists were indeed a politics of the poor as enactment of negativity and resistance rather than consensus with the aesthetic condition of the BB7. In this case, the curators opted to eradicate the distance between art (R1) and the streets (R2), bringing the streets into the gallery as a form of grassroots pedagogical practice. Yet, in the last instance, the dividing line was drawn by the persisting institutional mandate according to which the BB7 was decisively an art show, not an activist incubator, and it was organized as an economic and legal entity, not one that was self-run or self-organized, and it was one that was meant to secure and advance its own interests and those of its stakeholders (R3).

The curator had hoped to bring in proletarian artists to disrupt the bourgeois workings of the institution. However, when these proletarian artists refused to play by the rules, they encountered the same power arrangements that the curator had initially hoped to disrupt (e.g., the police and the insistence that the BB7 was an art show).

---

[4]This is shown in the film *Pixadores* (2014) directed by Amir Escandari (min 54–55).

Fig. 6.2 Former artwork painted over by Occupy activists

6.8 Discussion

The question of legitimacy and how to preserve or restore it has been a central question in ethnographic studies of Western art institutions. Similar to what we have tried to demonstrate in the vignettes above, those studies have focused on the multidimensional ways that institutional legitimacy is preserved. Examples of such research include Sharon McDonald's 2020 study of the Science Museum, London, which looks at how the British government's implementation of neoliberal policies in the 1980s forced museums to reorganize their activities and explore new realms of financing while simultaneously maintaining their social relevance. In a similar fashion, Penelope Harvey's *Hybrids of Modernity* (1996) framed the Universal Expos as colonial institutions that strive to adapt to the changing reality of a postcolonial world. In *Rationalizing Culture* (1995), a study of the avant-garde center of musical research and electronic production funded by the French state, Georgina Born attempted to show how the contradictions in which modernist musical discourse found itself relative to the rise of postmodernism during the 1980s were negotiated and expressed within prestigious, state-funded musical institutions, such as IRCAM (Institut de Recherche et Coordination Acoustique/Musique), which is linked with the Centre Georges Pompidou and was then directed by the renowned avant-garde composer Pierre Boulez. Born demonstrated how IRCAM, through its public statements, productions, collaborations, and the influential command of its director, constantly strived to maintain its legitimacy as an institution supporting and enabling the circulation of serious music. Much as high art Western institutions have, according to Born (1995), the tendency to "absorb and conceal contradiction" (7), ethnography can "uncover gaps between the external claims and internal realities, public rhetoric and private thought, ideology and practice" (7). In this sense, ethnographic accounts can shed light on how certain patterns or scripts are involved in institutional power, untangling the ways through which institutional authority is preserved or expanded. This chapter has drawn on the above-mentioned studies to advance a critical ethnographic questioning of a major contemporary art institution: the biennial. In what follows, we will discuss the effect of the curator's attempt to disrupt established practices and restore the biennial's legitimacy as a transformative social force in aesthetic capitalism.

6.9 Extitution and the Quest for Legitimacy

Our case study highlights the curator's attempt to incorporate political activism into the sphere of art not just to make his institution more relevant and legitimate but also to preserve his position as a critical figure in the artistic marketplace. In our case study, we explored the consequences of inviting political activist groups to participate in the BB7. This practice has been described as "extitution" (Spicer 2010: 25). Accordingly, institutions, whether artistic, scientific, political, or otherwise, constantly proclaim and manufacture problems in order to find a role for themselves and expand their legitimacy (Spicer 2010). After defining the problems, the institutions then announce themselves as experts in resolving these problems. For example, it is in the strategic interest of medical institutions to extend the category of medical problems to a wide range of states and activities, from alopecia to madness, so as to continue proving—justifying and legitimizing—their social relevance.

In other words, extitution refers to all these areas of formless quality in social life that institutions seek to domesticate and colonize in order to maintain legitimacy, expand their scope, and/or overcome crises of deinstitutionalization. Following Deleuze, Spicer (2010) described this institutional opening to new areas of life as a process perennially fraught with tension. Attempts to expand the institutional scope "open up new areas for institutionalization," while the failure of the institution to honor its promises "creates many cracks and fissures in which noninstitutionalized life grows" (26). From this perspective, the emergence of activism and social engagement in contemporary art biennials is the rationalization and circumscription of a problematic area, and it justifies curatorial intervention and expansion into the areas in which curatorial practice can be regarded as useful.

Seen in this light, the activist qualities mobilized by biennials are efforts to rearrange the institution's legitimacy crisis by extituting artistic form to external processes related to resistant cultures and social movements. Therefore, the institution as a set of values, norms, roles, infrastructures, agents, and logics operating within various temporal and spatial frameworks can transform or adjust itself as a result of some larger social change. However, our findings suggest that the curator's institutional work (Lawrence and Suddaby 2006), especially his attempt to disrupt institutionalized routines, ultimately led to a reaffirmation of existing practices and a return to organizing art-oriented shows rather than disrupting them. That is, while legitimacy was maintained, the idea of radical transformation by occupying the institution failed. At the same time, we acknowledge that the process of incorporating the other side of institutions (Spicer 2010) in order to stretch and extend their public reach and social relevance might not occur in a straightforward manner but is likely to involve a more complex process that is open to transformation in both directions. As such, the case might represent a liminal point in the political turn of art biennials.

6.10 Aesthetic Capitalism and the Art Spectacle

> Spectacular capitalism is like a Möbius strip, where even the other side is a part of it.
> Gilman-Opalsky (2011: 29)

Our empirical material suggests that the attempt to make the BB7 more political and mobilize for real action was unsuccessful. To help explain this failure on the institutional level, we have drawn on the concept of logics and extitution. In this concluding section, we link our findings to the larger macro context that we have defined above as aesthetic capitalism.

From a critical perspective, we can conclude that the failed attempt to change the BB7 highlights the way aesthetic capitalism works. It puts a strong emphasis on stage value, inducing consumption practices while inhibiting political action. As such, the consequences of trying to associate itself with the Occupy movement might best be described as leading to a spectacle (Debord 1967/1998). Some critics of the BB7 have argued that the whole initiative to politicize the BB7 advanced neither the Occupy movement nor the BB7. In his analysis of why the experiment failed, Loewe (2015) concluded that taking part in the biennial turned the Occupy movement into a piece of art. It was perceived as kitsch and turned the BB7 and the clashes with the activists into a human zoo stripped of any political momentum. In other words, while the art world devoured the political aims of the Occupy movement by aestheticizing it (turning it into a conceptual piece of art), the Occupy movement had few politicizing effects on the BB7. Despite the Occupy activists' reflexive practices (see Vignette 2), they were caught in the rationales of the art world. The banner set up by the Occupy activists (see Vignette 1) reminds us of Margritte's famous surrealist painting *Ceci n'est pas une pipe*. As Debord (1967/1998) has pointed out: representation is always surreal. The attempted inclusion of activism was turned into a piece of art and became a symbolic representation (as opposed to the real thing) and was therefore unable to produce the intended real actions that would lead to real consequences. Rupture, surprise, and shock all contribute to drawing attention and entertaining the public. In 1967, Debord identified the "general acceptance of what is" (27) and the depoliticized passive attitude of spectator-consumers as the "greatest achievement of the society of the spectacle" as it "signals the subversion of both democratization and other, more radical aspirations" (Gilman-Opalsky 2011: 73). This conclusion might be as timely as ever.

In aesthetic capitalism, the staging of spectacular events to attract attention and visibility is part of the new spirit, as is the quest for disruption and reinvention. However, it is a trap: what is intended as critique is recuperated, incorporated, and fed into the dominant ideology. In Boltanski and Chiapello's (2005) historical and critical analysis of the new spirit of capitalism, the authors show how capitalism evolves by responding to its criticisms. At the heart of the so-called humanist or artistic critique "is a requirement for critical distance from the system and from its effects (power, comfort, and privilege). It is this type of critical distance that critical theory attempted to advance in theory and in practice. And it is precisely this type of critique that we now see at the heart of the spirit of the new capitalism" (Fisher 2010: 106). In other words, what was once the artistic critique has become the artistic spirit of contemporary capitalism (Roberts 2014).

This reveals the great tension that any form of disobedient practice faces today: to what extent should it engage in processes of instituting in order to transform existing patterns and structures, and when does this instituting turn into a Möbius strip, foreclosing any chance of escape? Rather than prioritizing fleeting encounters, we should think of building solid institutional arrangements that question capitalism, gender, and racial inequality. In other words, rather than enabling disruptions of the system by means of temporary counter-hegemonies, the task should be one of finding ways to organize imaginaries of radical equality in everyday life worlds, including workplaces, schools, and the streets.

References

Balzer D (2014) Curationism: how curating took over the art world and everything else. Coach House Books, Toronto

Böhme G (2003) Contribution to the critique of the aesthetic economy. Thesis Eleven 73(1):71–82

Böhme G (2016) Ästhetischer Kapitalismus. Suhrkamp Verlag, Berlin

Boltanski L, Chiapello E (2005) The new spirit of capitalism. Verso, London

Boltanski L, Thevenot L (2006) On justification. Economies of worth. Princeton University Press, Princeton

Born G (1995) Rationalizing culture: IRCAM, Boulez, and the institutionalization of the musical Avant-Garde. University of California Press, Los Angeles & London

Bourriaud N (2002) Relational aesthetics. Les presses du reel, Dijon

Currid-Halkett E (2017) The sum of small things: a tsheory of the aspirational class. Princeton University Press, Princeton

Debord G (1967/1998) Comments on the the Society of the Spectacle. Verso, London

Dimitrakaki A (2012) Art, globalisation and the exhibition form: what is the case, what is the challenge? Third Text 26(3):305–319

Du Gay P, Pryke M (eds) (2002) Cultural economy: cultural analysis and commercial life. Sage, California

Elkins J, Montgomery H (eds) (2013) Beyond the aesthetic and the anti-aesthetic, vol 4. Penn State Press, University Park

Fisher E (2010) Media and new capitalism in the digital age: the spirit of networks. Palgrave Macmillan, Basingstoke
Foster H (1983) The anti-aesthetic: essays on postmodern culture. Bay Press, Port Townsend, Wash
Gilman-Opalsky R (2011) Spectacular capitalism: guy Debord and the practice of radical philosophy. Minor Compositions, London
Green C, Gardner A (2016) Biennials, triennials, and Documenta: the exhibitions that created contemporary art. Wiley, New York
Gupta S (2015) Pixação and Tourist Appraisal. Wasafiri 30(2):40–46
Hirsch P, Bermiss S (2009) Institutional "dirty" work: preserving institutions through strategic decoupling. In: Thomas L, Suddaby R, Leca B (eds) Institutional work: actors and agency in institutional studies of organizations. Cambridge University Press, Cambridge, pp 262–283
Hlavajova M (2010) How to biennial: a consideration of the biennial in relation to the art institution. In: Filipovic E, van Hal M, Øvstebø S (eds) The biennial reader. Hatje Cantz, Bergen, pp 292–305
Holm P (1995) The dynamics of institutionalization: transformation processes in Norwegian fisheries. Adm Sci Q 40:398–422
Holm N, Duncan P (2018) Introduction: cultural studies, Marxism and the exile of aesthetics. Open Cult Stud. doi:https://doi.org/10.1515/culture-2018-0067. Published Online 31 Dec 2018
Kimball W (2012, June 18) Berlin Biennale may adopt OWS's horizontal power structure. Art F City. http://artfcity.com/2012/06/18/the-berlin-biennale-adopts-owss-horizontal-power-structure/. Last Accessed 24 Feb 2019
Kolb L, Flückiger G (2013/December) (New)Institution(alsim). OnCurating.org, (21)/December 2013. http://www.on-curating.org/files/oc/dateiverwaltung/issue-21/PDF_to_Download/ONCURATING_Issue21_A4.pdf. Last Accessed 3 Mar 2019
Kompatsiaris P (2014) 'To see and be seen': ethnographic notes on cultural work in contemporary art in Greece. Eur J Cult Stud 17(5):507–524
Kompatsiaris P (2017) The politics of contemporary art biennials. Spectacles of critique, theory and art. Routledge, New York
Lawrence T, Suddaby R (2006) Institutions and institutional work. In: Clegg SR, Hardy C, Lawrence T, Nord WR (eds) Handbook of organization studies. Sage, London, pp 215–254
Lawrence T, Suddaby R, Leca B (2009) Introduction: theorizing and studying institutional work. In: Thomas L, Suddaby R, Leca B (eds) Institutional work: actors and Agency in Institutional Studies of organizations. Cambridge University Press, Cambridge, pp 1–27
Léger MJ (2012) Brave new Avant Garde: essays on contemporary art and politics. Zero Books, Winchester and Washington
Loewe S (2015) When protest becomes art: the contradictory transformations of the occupy movement at Documenta 13 and Berlin biennale 7. FIELD: A Journal of Socially-Engaged Art Criticism 1:185–203
Macdonald S (2020) Behind the scenes at the science museum. Routledge, New York
Meyer JW, Rowan B (1977) Institutionalized organizations: formal structure as myth and ceremony. Am J Sociol 83(2):340–363
Murphy P, De la Fuente E (2014) Introduction: aesthetic capitalism. In: Murphy P, de la Fuente E (eds) Aesthetic capitalism. Brill, Leiden, pp 1–9
Osborne P (2018) The Postconceptual condition: critical essays. Verso, London
Roberts D (2003) Illusion only is sacred: from the culture industry to the aesthetic economy. Thesis Eleven 73(1):83–95
Roberts D (2014) From the cultural contradictions of capitalism to the creative economy: reflections on the new Spirit of art and capitalism. In: Murphy P, de la Fuente E (eds) Aesthetic capitalism. Brill, Leiden, pp 10–26
Roberts J (2015) Revolutionary time and the Avant Garde. Verso, London and New York
Sholette G (2011) Dark matter: art and politics in the age of Enterprise culture. Pluto Press, London
Spicer A (2010) Extitutions: the other side of institutions. Ephemera: Theory and Politics in Organization 10(1):25–39

West S (1995) National Desires and regional realities in the Venice biennale, 1895–1914. Art History 18(3):404–434

Zmijewski A (2012) Foreword. In: Zmijewski A, Warsza J (eds) Forget fear. KW Institution of Contemporary Art, Berlin

Weblinks

http://blog.berlinbiennale.de/en/comments/forget-fear-a-foreword-by-artur-zmijewski-19528.html. Last Accessed 9 Mar 2019

http://occupymuseums.org/index.php/actions/43-occupy-museums-and-the-7th-berlin-biennale. Last Accessed 9 Mar 2019

Panos Kompatsiaris is an Assistant Professor of Art and Media at the National Research University Higher School of Economics in Moscow. He holds a PhD in art theory from the University of Edinburgh (2015). He has published on art, culture, and politics in journals including the *European Journal of Cultural Studies, Communication, Culture & Critique, Journal of Visual Art Practice and Social Identities*. His monograph *The Politics of Contemporary Art Biennials: Spectacles of Critique, Art and Theory* (Routledge, 2017) looks at the politics of art biennials in the context of neoliberalism and its crisis. He is currently co-editing a special journal issue on art and value (*Journal of Cultural Economy*).

Nada Endrissat is a Research Professor at the New Work Institute, Bern University of Applied Sciences, Switzerland. She studied Psychology at Free University Berlin and holds a PhD in Management from Basel University. Her current research interests include the intersection of digital technologies and embodied encounters and the link between affect theory and value production in contemporary capitalism. Her research has been published in academic journals including *Human Relations, Organization Studies, Journal of Business Research, Leadership* and *M@n@gement*.

Chapter 7
Creativity in the Service of Economic Recovery and "National Salvation": Dispatches from the Greek Crisis Social Factory

Yiannis Mylonas

Abstract This chapter focuses on discursive constructions of creativity in the Greek public sphere in connection to the Greek government debt crisis. Instrumentalized by policy makers and pundits pursuing neoliberal reforms in Greece, creativity is understood to serve a mode of biopolitical governmentality. This is connected to the production of a national consensus over the necessity for neoliberal reforms and to the individualization of the risks and insecurity that such reforms entail. This chapter looks at specific public discursive constructions of creativity in Greece from 2010 onward. Specifically, the creativity discourse is approached in both its progressive and conservative articulations as articulated by the social democrat Giorgos A. Papandreou, Greece's prime minister during the first years of the crisis (2009–2011), and the conservative Kyriakos K. Mitsotakis, Greece's prime minister in 2019 and at the time of writing. Simultaneously, this chapter foregrounds the examples of success stories of creative ventures that received publicity in Greece so as to unfold other examples of a hegemonic discourse meant to motivate society on a post-political, entrepreneurial, and nationalistic basis. Such success stories develop through the didactic narratives that proliferate in Greece's mainstream news and lifestyle media, which are meant to establish a creative paradigm as a way out of unemployment and recession. Here, creativity forms a public repertoire that fabricates the crisis into a so-called opportunity for development that is borne through entrepreneurship.

Keywords Austerity · Entrepreneurialism · Meritocracy · Post-politics · Success stories

---

Y. Mylonas (✉)
National Research University Higher School of Economics, Moscow, Russia

I. Kiriya et al. (eds.), *The Industrialization of Creativity and Its Limits*, Science, Technology and Innovation Studies, https://doi.org/10.1007/978-3-030-53164-5_7

7.1 Introduction: Creativity, Crisis, and Reform

On a broad, popular level, creativity is loosely connected to productivity, entrepreneurialism, innovation, novelty, development, modernization, and sustainability, as well as to concepts such as merit, skill, talent, and hip lifestyles. On a structural level, it is associated with changes in the mode of production that "replace the steadily declining role of manufacturing in national economies" (Hesmondhalgh and Baker 2010, 4), and it is further associated with the advent of what is generally known as neoliberalism (Mould 2018, 12). To be more precise, according to Boltanski and Chiapello (2007), creativity developed as a paradigm of capitalist restructuring in response to the economic crisis of the early 1970s, capturing workers' demands for autonomy and meaningful work, and assimilating them so as to restructure the social relations of production into a more flexible mode of capitalist accumulation.

In the context of the 2008 global economic crisis and the subsequent intensification of neoliberal reforms that followed it, including austerity cuts and the privatization of public property, creativity has been integral to a hegemonic discursive framework that pursues a creative–destructive policy agenda in which welfare institutions, civic and labor rights, and established norms, social relations, and meanings are confronted by market-orientated transformations. As an inherent individual trait or potential charisma, the notion of creativity is instrumentalized by policy makers and pundits to serve a mode of biopolitical governmentality crucial to neoliberal economic restructuring. Here, creativity assumes an austere, mobile, proactive, and entrepreneurial mode of living that corresponds to the individualization of the risks and insecurities that neoliberal reforms entail.

Publicly displayed through a variety of discursive constructions and practices—what McRobbie (2016) called "the creative dispositive" (11)—creativity carries a highly affective dimension. It is meant to interpellate individuals into viewing neoliberal reforms, such as welfare cuts and labor deregulation, as "tasks" that may lead them to distinction, recognition, self-accomplishment, and material reward. Among other things, this also means the privatization of both risks and care, as well as the development of the "individuals' own market-conforming self-formation in the service of economic valorization" (Lorey 2015, 86). In societies where welfare institutions are shrinking and social solidarity networks are weakening, and in a globalized labor market characterized by increasingly reduced prospects of upward social mobility (Sennett 2008), people are constantly expected to independently reinvent themselves, update their skills, and even create, or "creatify" (Mould 2018, 108), their own work. Thus, by forcing citizens to be more creative, "austerity programs have imprinted the neoliberal ideology further into the social fabric" (Mould 2018, 105). The kind of creativity that policy makers encourage is connected to the mobilization and potential commodification of resources, institutions, and energies that have remained outside the capitalist market realm (Mould 2018, 100). In short, creativity in such a context of economic restructuring is meant to produce public consensus over neoliberal reforms, marginalize systemic criticism, and mobilize citizens to pursue their own individual way out of economic crisis.

In what follows, such critical theoretical approaches to creativity and creative work are deployed to deconstruct hegemonic discursive articulations of creativity in the Greek public sphere. This chapter looks at specific discursive constructions of creativity from the beginning of the Greek crisis in 2010 until February 2019, the time of writing. Creativity is approached in its both progressive and conservative dimensions, as articulated by the social democrat Giorgos A. Papandreou, Greece's prime minister during the first years of the crisis (2009–2011), and the conservative Kyriakos K. Mitsotakis, Greece's prime minister at the time of writing in late 2019. Simultaneously, this chapter scrutinizes specific "success stories" of creative ventures that received publicity in Greece in order to unfold examples of a hegemonic discourse to motivate society on a post-political, entrepreneurial, and also, nationalistic basis. Such success stories are developed through didactic narratives that proliferate in Greece's mainstream news and lifestyle media and are meant to establish a creative paradigm as an inspirational way out of unemployment and recession. Here, creativity forms a public repertoire that fabricates the crisis into a so-called opportunity for development that is borne through entrepreneurship. The empirical material selected is meant to present, through indicative examples or vignettes, the ways that creativity manifests in an economic crisis. This chapter reflexively draws on Ernesto Laclau's (1996) analysis of hegemony, which allows us to understand the ideas according to which creativity is manifested, the political visions it is meant to serve, and its affiliations to classist and nationalist pursuits.

7.2 Creativity and Conjunctures of "Race" and Class in the Greek Crisis

Critical research has stressed the culturalist and moralist construction of the Greek crisis, revealing the racist and classist underpinnings of such repertoires (e.g., Ervedosa 2017). Greece has been presented as an exception in the European Union and in the West; its oriental leanings were emphasized in order to dissociate it from the West. Austerity reforms and privatizations were presented as a realistic and urgent policy doctrine that would correct Greece's alleged irregularities. Thus, the neoliberal reforms took the form of a modernization and Europeanization project. The strategy of capitalist restructuring was publicly uttered in the depoliticized and "wooden language" of neoliberalism (Badiou 2018, 26), disregarding the destructive effects that neoliberal reforms have had on Greek society (Fig. 7.1). In this way, mainstream accounts of the crisis focused on its symptoms rather than its roots in the global capitalist crisis and Greece's vulnerability to it, which relates to its semi-peripheral position in the global economy.

As Balibar and Wallerstein (1991) noted, race and class are interrelated concepts. They signify the ideological tensions of capitalism in its efforts to create a universal ideology and a smooth global space for free market activity. According to critics (Berardi 2019), the endless accumulation of capital is only possible through the

Fig. 7.1 The crisis creates ruin and destruction without creation. A row of small-scale businesses, the backbone of the Greek economy (Lapavitsas et al. 2012, 224), closed after the emergence of the debt crisis and the launch of neoliberal reforms (downtown Thessaloniki, September 2018; photo by author)

commodification of potentially everything. This requires the free flow of commodities, finance, and labor. Particularisms of any kind that may block such a flow are incompatible.

Wallerstein, however, noticed that a seemingly contradictory movement exists in the process of capitalist accumulation, as it simultaneously encourages both universality and racism, allowing them to effectively coexist. On the one hand, a universal ideology is central to the spread and stability of the capitalist market system and the relations of production underlining it. To produce further growth, inclusion of difference is thus important for the assimilation of various populations and their effective proletarianization. On the other hand, competition and the division of labor produce social hierarchies that often lead to racism. Racism in this context emerges as a useful tool to minimize production costs and suppress dissent (Balibar and Wallerstein 1991, 33). In this sense, Wallerstein discussed the existence of a pattern of workforce ethnicization. This can be exemplified by the normalization of the social unevenness that exists between different social groups (e.g., migrants and "natives") with regards to entitlements, such as politico-economic rights, welfare benefits, and access to commodities. This ethnicization-of-work pattern is susceptible to changes because the boundaries of racism have always been flexible and contingent upon the demands of capitalist accumulation. Based on context, this ethnicization process can exclude different populations and social groups that can be declared unworthy of rights at a given historical conjuncture.

Wallerstein's analysis is appropriate to the Greek crisis. The culturalization of the crisis and the culturalist–moralist exceptionalization of Greeks from the realm of normality and the confines of Europeanness (however defined by Western bourgeois states) can be easily interpreted through the pattern of ethnicization outlined above. Imposing austerity on the non- or quasi-European other was justified by neo-orientalist technocratic assessments that deemed Greeks as corrupt, lazy, and unproductive. Simultaneously, the Western and Northern European communities justified themselves as entitled to privileges for incarnating the values of neoliberal capitalism related to entrepreneurialism, austere life, and hard work. Within Greece, the upper and aspiring middle-class groups reproduced the hegemonic, culturalist Greek crisis discourse in order to blame the poor and working classes for the country's state of insolvency, attributing to them the brutish traits (e.g., lazy, profligate, non-innovative, inflexible) that bankrupted the country and blocked its competitive and innovative potentials.

From a broader perspective, the creative-class narrative is based on the distinction between creatives and non-creatives: "the creative class is measured against the non-creative working class and the service class" (Mould 2018, 22). Valued for their economic potential for capitalist growth, those understood as creative in Richard Florida's (2005) sense—notably the educated, mobile, and multiethnic bobos (bourgeois-bohemian)—are preferred to those deemed as non-creative. Creativity and the creative class framework in capitalist globalization become benchmarks to assess different populations, social groups, and individuals based on their potential to produce value. Therefore, creativity surfaces as a biopolitical dispositif that governs inequalities (Lorey 2015, 65), normalizing the precarity and insecurity that austerity reforms produce and legitimizing classist and racist explanations of structural problems (such as an economic crisis) while triggering an individualized process of mobility and competition among the workforce. The collective crisis-stigma attributed to the Greek people here serves as a vehicle to boost individualist solutions to the crisis, while the fantasy of entrepreneurial creativity forms the horizon that orientates such individualized pursuits.

7.3 The Crisis and Austerity as Opportunities: The "Creative Greece" and Entrepreneurial Nationalism

Papandreou, a Third Way social democrat from the socialist PASOK party, was elected as the prime minister of Greece in late 2009 emphsizing the need for Greece's modernization through calls "to the country's creative forces"[1]to develop innovative practices. A few months after his election, his government signed the first

[1]Παπανδρέου: Προσκλητήριο στις Δημιουργικές Δυνάμεις [Papandreou: A Call to the Creative Forces]. https://www.capital.gr/epikairotita/806878/papandreou-prosklitirio-stis-dimiourgikes-dunameis; Accessed Feb 10, 2019.

memorandum of understanding with the European troika, an institutional body consisting of the European Central Bank, the European Commission, and the International Monetary Fund, that initiated vast neoliberal reforms entailing austerity and privatization in exchange for a large loan to support Greece's public debt repayment to different European and American banks and to avoid its defaulting on its debt (Roos 2019, 37). Up to then, Papandreou had campaigned for a modernized reform-policy framework that was to transform Greece into "Southern Europe's Denmark"[2] with Denmark being a country that scored high on Florida's creative class rankings (Florida et al. 2015, 22).

Shortly after Papandreou's electoral victory in fall 2009, Greece officially entered the crisis. Papandreou's modernizing, third-way reforms agenda then embraced austerity as another path of modernization for Greece. In his notorious speech of April 2010, delivered from the island of Kastelorizo, where Papandreou announced the activation of the troika's "rescue mechanism" in Greece, he closed his remarks with the following:

> Our ultimate goal, our ultimate destination, is to . . . liberate the powers of Hellenism and to free every Greek from perceptions, practices, and systems that have blocked his/her abilities for decades. Let's give oxygen where there is suffocation, justice and rules where there is injustice, transparency where there is darkness, certainty where there is insecurity, and development for all. The inspiration, our faith, is here, from Kastelorizo to Corfu, from Crete to Evros, these wonderful people, and our youth with their potential and visions. I am absolutely sure that we will succeed. What we Greeks need is to believe in our capacities, our values, and ourselves.[3]

Likewise, the plan to develop Greece and overcome the crisis was narrated in equivalent terms associated with neoliberal creativity. To refer to Papandreou's words from one of his later speeches, in 2018:

> How much would it cost to change structures in education to capitalize on and to invest in people, research, technology, knowledge, and in a high level of public education while opening it to the international market? [How much would it cost] to develop our education system into a product that could be exported, either through public or through non-state institutions? . . . How much would it cost to make better use of [European] Community funds in the agricultural sector so as to guarantee the production of high-quality and value Greek products, [to promote] the Cretan or the Mediterranean diet that form a brand name around the world, to develop competitive products with young farmers instead of selling our oil in bulk to the Italians? How can a worker feel creative if the state cannot secure a welfare system that guarantees a minimum standard of living and security? . . . How much would it cost for Greece to make use of its natural resources, [its] solar, wind, and green energy . . . [and to] help start-up businesses across Greece?[4]

---

[2]Πώς θα είναι η... "Δανία του Νότου" [How will the Denmark of the South be] http://www.enet.gr/?i=news.el.article&id=82857 Accessed 10 Mar 2020

[3]Απρίλιος 2010: Το Διάγγελμα Παπανδρέου από το Καστελόριζο [April 2010: Papandreou's Call from Kastelorizo]. http://www.thetoc.gr/politiki/article/aprilios-2010-to-diaggelma-papandreou-apo-to-kastelorizo Accessed Feb 15, 2019.

[4]Γιώργος Παπανδρέου: Υπάρχει Ελπίδα, Αρκεί να Πιστέψουμε στις Δυνατότητες του Λαού και της Χώρας Μας [George Papandreou: There is Hope if We Believe in the Potentials of the People and Our Country]. https://thecaller.gr/politiki/giorgos-papandreou-iparxei-elpida/ Accessed Feb 10, 2019.

In some ways, Papandreou's vision was similar to Tony Blair's for Britain in the 1990s; Blair sought to combine "a technological revolution, social liberalism, and the rise of a creative Britain" (Littler 2017, 86). In Britain, Blair strived to commodify the arts and attempted to "responsibilize" citizens by stressing personal vision, hard work, and self-confidence (Hewison 2014, 3) while criticizing state "paternalism" (Hesmondhalgh et al. 2015, 19). Such arguments have been articulated by (third way/neoliberal) social democrats against a background of deindustrialization and welfare cuts. To be sure, Britain is a highly industrialized former colonial empire with well-developed creative fields, while Greece is a semi-peripheral country with limited capacity to compete in the global market. In this respect, Streeck (2016) demonstrated that the European Union's integration policies liberated cross-market activity at the expense of the European periphery, thereby tightening the periphery's dependency on the core (Amin 2014, 90). At the same time, the literature notes that the most economically advanced countries have the greatest concentration of cultural production and cultural fields, thus offering more opportunities for creative employment (Primorac 2008, 16). During the first years of the Greek recession, 30.5% of Greece's creative workplaces were lost (Avdikos and Kalogeresis 2018, 190).

Papandreou's vision was connected to the creatification of already productive sectors, such as agriculture, which was in line with the demands of the global market and purported to boost productivity and gain a competitive advantage for established Greek products. Greece's educational, cultural, and other creative sectors were to advance as well, supposedly through the troika's structural adjustment reforms, which would transform these sectors into more open, marketable, and competitive entities. Papandreou offered a vision for a supposedly smart and creative rebranding of the country, one that would see Greek products gain market traction and attract creatives to the country's innovative ventures, students to its schools, and tourists interested in new services and experiences (e.g., more "sustainable" forms of tourism, such as outdoor activities) instead of those associated with its rather banal tourism image related to leisure and antiquity. In addition to this rebranding effort, the foregrounding of a healthy and balanced Mediterranean diet and overall lifestyle were meant to restructure the agricultural and culinary sectors by triggering entrepreneurialism related to green business, such as eco-farming, organic cafes, and new restaurants (also known as neo-tavernas) that are rebranding traditional esthetics.

Businesses that weathered the crisis are in the tourism and leisure sector and have tailored their offerings to the global upper-middle class. Following this strategy, many new bars, cafes, restaurants, nightclubs, and booming Airbnb properties have opened across the country. Since 2010, these have been key sites of entrepreneurship and market-based creativity, transforming public spaces and the social fabric in a spectacular and exclusionary way, as most Greeks struggle to make ends meet (Dalakoglou and Poulimenakos 2018).

Papandreou's vision for Greece, as retold in the 2018 speech quoted above, exemplifies the nature of creativity under neoliberal capitalism. Such creativity is about "seeing the world around you as a resource . . . because it feeds the notion that the world and everything in it can be monetized" (Mould 2018, 12). Competition, an export-driven economy, and smart and sustainable entrepreneurialism are supposed to create win–win situations for everyone, provided that they are flexibly directed and couched in a modernized state. The crisis and its resolution fall on the shoulders of average people and the Greek state. The social responsibilizing dimension of Papandreou's rhetoric should be emphasized, as it diluted responsibility for Greece's bankruptcy by stressing that everyone was immersed in a nepotistic and dysfunctional system (Littler 2017, 91), meaning it was everyone's—and most notably the working class's—duty to aid in the country's recovery according to the dictates of the free market.

It should also be noted though that Papandreou's government passed the Fast Track Law to attract rapid investment under a pretext of doing away with bureaucracy. Among other things, this compromised environmental, welfare, and labor protectionist laws. The launch of extractivist mining activities by the Canadian multinational corporation El Dorado Gold in the pristine forests of Chalkidiki, with similar plans to develop elsewhere in the country, has jeopardized local economies, culture, the natural environment, and public health (Velegrakis 2018, 128).

Papandreou represents Greece's progressive branch of neoliberalism, which practices a middle-class tolerance of diversity (Fraser 2017) while advancing a sustainable discourse that capitalism's progressive apologists often use as an excuse for inaction regarding the environmental and social crises that capitalism produces (Jacobsson 2019). Since the beginning of 2016, when Kyriakos Mitsotakis assumed leadership of the Nea Dimokratia (ND) party, a conservative strain of neoliberalism surfaced, framing creativity, and the creative sector with concepts that are part of a conservative repertoire, such as meritocracy (Littler 2017). Syriza's (the Coalition of the Radical Left that headed a collation government between 2015 and 2019) capitulation to the European Union's demands for austerity during the late summer of 2015 provided a strategic opportunity for ND to rebrand itself as a novel force of reform, innovation and development, even though the party represents Greece's most established conservative political force. During Syriza's administration (2015–2019), the creative aspirations of progressive neoliberalism (like those of Papandreou) were generally toned down. Although the general neoliberal reforms policy framework remained largely intact, on a public level, Syriza sustained a compromised public agenda that stressed social inequality as a major structural problem, without overstressing individualist solutions to the economic crisis (Stavrakakis and Katsampekis 2019).

7.4 The Creativity Cult: Entrepreneurial Success Stories

An entrepreneurial cult has been growing in Greece since the beginning of the crisis and is related to the construction of a "creative Greece" image, which is that of a nation emerging from the debris of a financial crisis. Throughout the crisis, the mainstream media presented successful businesspeople as role models and moral authorities. For instance, the conservative daily *Kathimerini* published a profile of

Greek entrepreneurs who had received an award for investing in innovation. There, one entrepreneur emphatically argued that "the country will exit the crisis when we all begin to pursue riches, for there is nothing shameful in being rich, because poverty is what one should be ashamed of."[5] Mass media are never short of success stories about self-made, confident, hardworking, and visionary entrepreneurs. As branding strategies that attract creatives, tourists, and investors, success stories are "based on selective storytelling, on the employment of a limited number of hegemonic, optimistic, and boosterish representations ... excluding dissident voices and negative representations ... therefore creating disparities between the promoted image of a place and reality" (Katsinas 2019, 3).

In the following example of an entrepreneurial success story, we see these characteristics in an individual's idea to appropriate free and still abundant seaweed from Greece's seashores in order to produce products such as mobile- phone cases. As with the aforementioned booming of new cafes and restaurants during the crisis years, examples of market-based, applied creativity show that capitalist innovation is not so much about novelty as it is producing more of the same (Mould 2018, 15). Indeed, the market is already overflowing with products such as mobile phone cases. Drawn from the Aegean Airlines' bimonthly magazine, Blue, one reads the following:

> Stavros Tsompanidis [is] a natural born Greek innovator. The 24-year-old founder of PHEE, who featured in this year's Forbes 30-under-30 list as one of Europe's most promising young industrial entrepreneurs, is a fine example of a new generation of Greeks who are setting themselves goals for themselves, working diligently, and ultimately succeeding.
>
> [After being] asked if he had a message for his peers in the brain-drain generation poised to seek opportunity beyond the recession-struck Greece, the young entrepreneur said that effort is always rewarded: "whoever tries hard—regardless of his or her educational background—and has a burning desire to create, will succeed. It is as simple as that. Anybody who is spoiled and expects solutions from others will never make a leap forward towards a better life.[6]

The narrative reproduces the foundational bourgeois myths of the successful, hardworking, gifted entrepreneur that can transform anything into riches, stressing the commonplace (bourgeois) morality tale that one can only thrive if one believes in oneself, works relentlessly, and is adequately determined and motivated. In this context, the failure to reach a better life is solely attributed to the individual. Therefore, the system causing failure and the degradation of life is abstracted and naturalized.

---

[5] Οι Πρωτοπόροι που Επένδυσαν στην Καινοτομία εν Μέσω Κρίσης [The Pioneers who Invested in Innovation in the Midst of the Crisis]. http://www.kathimerini.gr/956281/article/oikonomia/epixeirhseis/oi-prwtoporoi-poy-ependysan-sthn-kainotomia-en-mesw-krishs Accessed April 07, 2018.

[6] Συνέντευξη: Τσομπανίδης [Interview: Tsompanidis]. https://el.aegeanair.com/taksidepste/en-ptisei/periodiko-blue/blue-70/ Accessed Feb 05, 2019.

In a January 1, 2018, piece posted on the popular lifestyle website *Lifo* under the headline "The gastronomic revolution is coming from Thessaloniki," one reads the following:

> During the crisis, Thessaloniki went through its own darkness . . . that was followed by its "Renaissance." It all started in 2012 with Serbico: a restaurant cooperative set up by 12 (!) young guys who all had their roots in the anti-authoritative scene of the city and who were previously running the canteen of the Technical Schools [TEI] for seven years. [They created] a cuisine, brought in new techniques, made a grocery store, [created] a magical, posh hall with aesthetics that are not reminiscent to those of the old freaks of our Exarchia [an Athenian district where many anarchist/anti-authoritarian groups are situated] . . . [Not only] did they change the menu but also the way that a restaurant works: self-management, equality, and teamwork in the kitchen. The new generation of high-tech cooks finds shelter and courage in the view that you can set up your own business without being dependent upon any irrelevant businessman and turn your job into a partisan affair outside the known contours of a capitalism that they all detest.
>
> So when the Sebrico team broke up, Dimitris Tasioulas opened Thria . . . from the beginning, Thria had something different to say. Something more gastronomic, more creative, more gourmet, if I may say so. If Michelin would come to the city looking for [restaurants to give] awards [to], they would definitely have to come by here and try a crisp puff pastry with black sesame seeds . . . The decoration, the open kitchen that works like a TV—behind the glass, you envisage a show of young, stylish kids working through a ballet-style coordination in a choreography of the latest kitchen techniques, all civilized and clean cut. Without screaming and without hitting each other, they create a feeling that makes you think "Thessaloniki, just like New York," European and cinematographic.[7]

The long quotes above demonstrate a variety of creative trends in crisis-struck Greece. One may notice the expression of a "dialectic of the same" to unfold, with the restaurant business still at the forefront of Greece's entrepreneurialism, given that this is one of the main things that the market demands from Greece. Of further interest is the punk esthetics and mode of organization often found in such emerging businesses. As Angela McRobbie (2016) has shown, the pressures of austerity and uneployment often force people to mobilize countercultural practices for self-generated economic activity. From survival tactics (as the article mentions, the former anarchist activists used to run a self-organized school canteen, an illegal and highly precarious kind of work), specific practices become systematized into concrete and highly competitive and innovative schemes that refresh (or "revolutionize," to use the author's term) a specific market. Simultaneously, the author displays her Western-centric and middle-class fascinations. The restaurant appears as an experiencescape in which the cooks— besides preparing delicious, creative, and chic dishes—also perform elegant and sanitized choreographic spectacles of craftsmanship and civility. Here, the periphery's fascination with Europe appears. The making of a European Greece is a recurrent theme in Greek liberal narratives. Hence, entrepreneurial activity and, with it, austerity reforms emerge as crucial to the Europeanization of Greece.

---

[7] Η Γαστρονομική Επανάσταση Έρχεται από τη Θεσσαλονίκη [The Gastronomy Revolution Comes from Thessaloniki]. https://www.lifo.gr/articles/taste_articles/177201/h-epanastasi-erxetai-apo-ti-thessaloniki Accessed Feb 17, 2019.

Successful entrepreneurial stories are generally narrated by a variety of mainstream media, reproducing tropes that constitute a social logic meant to be post-ideological, technocratic, novel, and meritocratic. This logic is intended to interpellate citizens in the entrepreneurial ethos of neoliberal austerity, promising to suture, through hard work, mobility, and determination, Greece's allegedly sui generis ills. In a final example, a quasi-political site entitled Thousands of Voices (www.xiliadesfwnes.gr) posted the following to its Facebook group:

> Kostas Tzoumas sold his start-up company for 90 m euros to Alibaba. It is a company that offers processing services for vast data quantities, fraud detection, and direct communication with customers ... His company has developed partnerships with giant companies such as Netflix, ING, and others. Young people like Kostas show us the way to a Greece of the future. It is worth congratulating him for his huge achievement![8]

According to the theory developed above, such social media posts are meant to inspire individuals and breed in the general public a sense of hope and desire for the reaching of the exceptional. A standard bourgeois myth is reproduced here as well, and it sustains the illusion of a potentially rapid social elevation available to everyone, while creating a public admiration for the rich, who emerge as heroic and self-made figures. Reproduced by a page that proclaims its open support to Mitsotakis and the ND, the post is meant to associate such entrepreneurial ventures with ND's return to government and its agenda of building "the Greece of the future." What we can see here is a political dialectic of the same, as the old ruling conservative party of ND and its leader, the descendent of a well-established political family in Greece, are framed as the heirs of the new. The post reads as follows:

> We call to leave behind nihilism and intolerance. It is time to revive the values that are the symbols of Hellenism, such as bravery, inventiveness, solidarity, unselfishness, and pride. For us, these define [the essence of] contemporary patriotism. The politician who who today expresses 12 reasons for us to support him [a link is provided here in the original that explains these 12 reasons] is Kyriakos Mitsotakis. He is the only one who understands us and consistently fights for our vision. He is the only one who is not afraid to collide with what holds us back and has proven so. Kyriakos is the only one who can really change the terms of the game and take us out of today's quagmire. Are you part of the silent majority? Today, you are no more! We are no longer silent. We have a voice. Thousands of voices! We are the majority that will change Greece.[9]

The reference to Mitsotakis in quasi-messianic terms, as a figure who can "really change the terms of the game" offers an undemocratic understanding of politics as something that can be managed by supposedly charismatic individuals alone. Most importantly, such texts are meant to produce a personality cult and boost popular support for the politics, ideas, and practices represented by the leader. The politico-

---

[8]Ο Κώστας Τζούμας Πούλησε την Start Up Εταιρεία του για 90 Εκατομμύρια Ευρώ στην Alibaba! [Kostas Tzoumas Sells His Start Up Company for 90 Million Euros at Alibaba!] https://www.facebook.com/pg/xiliadesfwnes/posts/?ref=page_internal Accessed Oct 28, 2019.

[9]Είμαστε Χιλιάδες Φωνές [We Are a Thousand Voices]. https://www.xiliadesfwnes.gr/poioi-eimaste Accessed Oct 28, 2019.

ideological dimension of creativity can also be seen because the expressed creative fantasy is supposed to arrive with the coming of Mitsotakis to power and the reforms that he is meant to introduce. An entrepreneurial nationalism is also present in the essentialist features of "Greekness," are to naturalize a popular support for ND. For the authors of this text, ND's coming to power would mean the opening of the path toward Greece's resolute future (Laclau 1996, 28). The text posits potential in the essentialist features of the Greek identity, potential that remains untapped due to the reign of the leftist Syriza, which is charged with "nihilism and intolerance." This way, Syriza is blamed for the ills of the economic crisis and austerity.

7.5 Creativity and Meritocracy: Reinforcing the Status Quo

Though a nuanced idea that one can associate with different sociopolitical contexts, meritocracy is today a concept co-opted by neoliberals and conservatives to attack social welfare institutions and socialist politics (Littler 2017). Mitsotakis is a vocal advocate of meritocracy. However, his calls for meritocracy are controversial due to his own status. Despite his personal branding strategy, which was developed by his party and by Greece's mainstream media, and notwithstanding his efforts to publicly dissociate himself from his privileged background, Mitsotakis remains the beneficiary of a former prime minister, his father, Konstantinos Mitsotakis, who also headed the party of ND. Therefore, his meritocracy call represents the elites' reaction to the lower classes, the so-called plebes, which went so far as to elect a leftist party (Syriza) to power in Greece.

Mitsotakis's meritocracy vision is often blended with nationalist and racist tropes, as evidenced in the following:

> Greece has always been, in terms of its institutional tradition, a European country in the Balkans. Mr. Tsipras, Mr. Kammenos,[10] and their company turned us into a Balkan country in the European Union.[11]

A process of self-orientalization emerges here, along with the iteration of occidentalist and classist stereotypes with regards to the Balkans, presenting them as Europe's negative other.

Among other things, Mitsotakis took to Twitter to congratulate successful director Yorgos Lanthimos (member of the Greek weird wave cinema movement) after he was nominated for several Oscars for his 2019 film *The Favourite*:

---

[10]Here, Mitsotakis referred to the two main political partners (Alexis Tsirpas from Syriza and Panos Kammenos from the Independent Greeks) of the Syriza-led coalition that governed Greece between 2015 and 2019.

[11]Κυρ. Μητσοτάκης: Πλειοψηφία της Γκαζόζας, Εκβιαζόμενος Πρωθυπουργός ο Τσίπρας [K. Mitsotakis: A Soda Majority Government, Tsipras is a Blackmailed PM] https://www.liberal.gr/arthro/238852/politiki/2019/kur-mitsotakis-i-pleiopsifia-tis-gkazozas-katantia-gia-ti-chora-ekbiazomenos-prothupourgos-o-tsipras.html Accessed Feb 04, 2019.

> "Congratulations Yorgos Lanthimos for the great success of The Favorite at the #Bafta 2019. Very proud of your accomplishments! This is truly #Greece_at_its_best."[12]

However, in his Tweet, Mitsotakis misspelled the film's title (as one can see in the quoted tweet above, Mitsotakis wrote "The Favorite" instead of "The Favourite") while incorporating Lanthimos into his meritocratic vision for Greek excellence, closing with the hashtag "Greece_at_its_best." The idea of success certified by credible, market-driven institutions and media publicity seems to be a defining marker of meritocracy. Concerns about cinema and the arts are secondary to the accomplishment of "national success." Indeed, as Hesmondhalgh et al. (2015, 30) have noted, neoliberal cultural policy marks a shift "away from culture, and towards economic and social goals: 'competitiveness and regeneration.'"

The word "creativity" appeared in 53 posts to the party's online press center (https://nd.gr/grafeio-tupou/) from February 2016, shortly after Kyriakos Mitsotakis was elected as ND leader, until February 2019, when this study was conducted. These posts are composed of various speeches and comments provided by Mitsotakis and other leading party members. In them, creativity is articulated in a programmatic political discourse that includes signifiers such as "meritocracy," "competition," "mobility," "opportunity," "flexibility," "investing," "education," "low taxation," "business incentives," "work," "growth," "entrepreneurship," "Greece," and "Europe." The following excerpts are indicative:

> We do not want people to be trapped in poverty, forever dependent upon state benefits. We want to give them the opportunity to rebuild their life and to feel joy of creation (Nea Dimokratia 2018, 34).
>
> The well-studied ND program can really, I believe deeply, lead to a new "Greek miracle." At last, we may activate the so-called "growth accelerator," which today does not work, and mobilize the creativity of the Greek, to bring a self-sustaining spiral of positive expectations for another image at all levels.[13]
>
> I am now coming to the national insurance issue. The law of Katrougalos [Mitsotakis here refers to the unified national insurance law that Giorgos Katrougalos, Syriza's minister of Labor and Social Insurance passed in 2016] is a bad one. You all know this. Not only because it reduces pensions, but because it ultimately punishes creativity and work. Why should one work more if he knows that he will get the same pension as everyone else? How are businesses to recruit when labor costs rise unnecessarily due to high employer contributions? And why should a freelancer declare his actual earnings when the amount of his contributions is to be unsustainable? And who is nowadays motivated to join the insurance system—please observe this, because it is very important and I come across it whenever I talk to young people—if he believes that he will never get a pension? "I prefer to receive half of my earnings black, as I do not care about [paying for my insurance] stamps," a young man who works in a café told me.[14]

---

[12] https://twitter.com/kmitsotakis/status/1094935344754147329?lang=en, accessed Dec 17, 2019.

[13] Ομιλία του Προέδρου της Νέας Δημοκρατίας κ. Κυριάκου Μητσοτάκη στο Thessaloniki Summit 2018 [Speech Given by the President of ND at the Thessaloniki Summit 2018]. https://nd.gr/omilia-toy-proedroy-tis-neas-dimokratias-k-kyriakoy-mitsotaki-sto-thessaloniki-summit-2018 Accessed Feb 15, 2019.

[14] Ομιλία του Προέδρου της Νέας Δημοκρατίας κ. Κυριάκου Μητσοτάκη στην 83η Δ.Ε.Θ. [Speech Given by the President of ND at the 83th International Trade Exposition of Thessaloniki].

> And above all, we will unleash the dynamism of the Cretans, this great untapped resource of wealth that we have. We will liberate the creativity of the entrepreneurs of this place so as to allow them to invest. We will facilitate investment, simplify bureaucracy, and provide tax incentives, in order for Crete to become a true protagonist; as it deserves, as we deserve.[15]

For the Greek Conservatives, creativity is something that emerges through the further liberalization of the market and the state's support of the private economy. Pro-private economic regulation that combines low taxation and minimal state protectionism is supposed to "unleash" Greek creativity. At the same time, creativity also appears as something inherent to Greek identity. Work precarity is presented as desirable to and even demanded by the working class, which, through random but carefully instrumentalized examples picked by ND's public communication strategists, appears discontented with welfare and labor protection laws. The working class is forced to participate in the "joy of creativity," which, in Mitsotakis' articulations above, formulates the quintessence of human existence. Individualized workers are to self-govern in a precarious and uncertain market-orientated society in which they are urged to live according to an ethos of personal sovereignty related to individual decision-making and freedom; this "normalizing self-governance is based on an imagination of coherence, identity, and wholeness that goes back to the construction of a male, white, bourgeois subject" (Lorey 2015, 30).

Simultaneously, welfare dependency is targeted as anti-creative and anti-work, since it purportedly creates a flat and equal society that has detrimental effects on merit. In Mitsotakis's vision, welfare "traps people in poverty." In reality, Greeks have never enjoyed an extended welfare state of the kind that the core European Union states offer their citizens. Nevertheless, even minimal welfare is demonized as anti-productive and corrosive to character. Welfare and labor regulation are supposed to block investments and suppress the market's meritocratic potential, which, in the neoliberal imagination, emerges in a "pure" form, through an "unmediated" negotiation between the worker and the capitalist that is to take place in a labor market that is "undistorted" by pro-labor regulation. A pure form of liberalism is thus propagated by Mitsotakis and his followers, with the state to safeguard the free market competition framework from democratic demands and interventions.

Historian Quinn Slobodian (2018, 10) demonstrated that the free market is actually sustained by global institutions that impose and safeguard its norms and structure. Furthermore, "the neoliberal mantra that the socialized provisions of the welfare state should be gradually sold off to the private sector, piece by piece, has resulted in widespread 'asset stripping'" (Littler 2017, 118). Privatization has resulted in the skyrocketing of inequality and unprecedented levels of poverty and exclusion faced by societies around the world. Mitsotakis anti-welfarism is

---

https://nd.gr/nea/omilia-toy-proedroy-tis-neas-dimokratias-k-kyriakoy-mitsotaki-stin-83i-deth Accessed Feb 15, 2019.

[15]Συμμετοχή του Προέδρου της Ν.Δ. Κ. Μητσοτάκη σε σύσκεψη στην Ιεράπετρα για τη λειψυδρία στην Κρήτη [Participation of the President of ND K. Mitsotakis at a meeting in Ierapetra on water scarcity in Crete]. https://nd.gr/nea/symmetohi-toy-proedroy-tis-nd-k-mitsotaki-se-syskepsi-stin-ierapetra-gia-ti-leipsydria-stin Accessed Feb 15, 2019.

connected to a sweeping privatization agenda that his party is committed to developing during its reign. As Minister for Development and Investment Adonis Georgiadis bluntly stated in December 2019 at the 21st annual Invest in Greece forum held in New York, "Why don't we sell more? Why don't we privatize everything? ... our appetite [for privatization] is so huge that it increases by month."[16]

7.6 Conclusion: More of the Same

In this chapter, I provided an overview of the ideological configuration of creativity in the context of the Greek crisis. I traced this ideology in its public form as articulated by the neoliberal left and neoliberal right as well as through the mainstream media. I focused on the local context of semi-peripheral Greece during its prolonged economic crisis. Here, creativity has been a public repertoire that fabricates the crisis into an opportunity for development promised by entrepreneurship. Neoliberal creativity has a strong affective dimension, as it is intertwined with consumerist, middle-class, and occidentalist ideas, fascinations, and identities. This ideological assemblage interpellates subjects to hegemonic endeavors related to the economic and political restructuring processes, which are continuous in the neoliberal era. The process described by McRobbie through the notion of the creative dispositif is a catalyst in the production of competitive, mobile, anti-political, and austere subjects. In times of permanent crisis, austerity, and downward social mobility, the ideology of capitalism is also sustained by a regular propagation of its own foundational myths that reproduce promises of prosperity, growth, and achievement.

As David Harvey (2014) stressed, neoliberalism is a political project aimed at the reconstitution of upper-class hegemony. It is no wonder that between 2010 and 2016, Greece's richest 10% augmented their share of wealth from 38.8% to 54% (Hadjimichalis, 2019). The repertoire of meritocracy is an ideological expression of such politics (Littler 2017, 115). Here, creativity is intended to provide a positive public spin on the neoliberal reforms agenda, in line with the blaming of the poor for Greece's crisis. While racism makes a negative interpellation of the peripheral subject, creativity and entrepreneurial nationalism make a positive one. Together, both such interpellating moments are to orientate the peripheral subjects' mode of self-governance in a time of perpetual crisis and austerity.

During the crisis's early days, Papandreou launched what appeared to be a progressive entrepreneurial nationalism that combined essentialist notions of Greekness, and he further issued a call for what can be understood as biopolitical economic regeneration. Besides calling for the state's modernization, Papandreou—

[16]Γεωργιάδης Διαλαλεί "Καλώς Ήλθε το Δολάριο" [Georgiadis Declares "Dollar, Welcome"]. https://tvxs.gr/news/ellada/o-georgiadis-dialalei-kalos-ilthe-dolario Accessed 12 Dec 2019.

in line with the hegemonic Greek crisis narrative—attributed to the middle and lower classes the responsibility for the crisis of Greece's peripheral capitalism to their alleged consumerist lethargy, dependence on European Union funds, and lack of civic culture and entrepreneurialism.

Several years later, at the supposed end of the Greek crisis, Mitsotakis further stressed these tropes under an anti-leftist agenda that was tantamount to a deeper assault on worker and civic rights, this by defending the private sector and issuing his call for transnational capital investments in the country that he aspires to reform as business friendly. Like with Papandreou's aforementioned Fast Track Law, it should be further noted that Mitsotakis has also been a defender of particular extractivist investments (such as the extraction of oil and gas from deep-sea waters, among others) that jeopardize the natural environment and public health, while claiming that they supposedly bring jobs, growth, and "development". Neoliberal creativity on the periphery thus emerges from a pretext of proletarianization, land and assets grabbing, and extractionism, all protected by a powerful, pro-business state. Together, such features constitute the archetypical practices of capitalist accumulation.

References

Amin S (2014) The implosion of capitalism. Pluto Press, London

Avdikos V, Kalogeresis A (2018) The uneven regional geography of labour precariousness: the case of Greek design industry. Cultural Trends 27(3):187–202

Badiou A (2018) Greece and the reinvention of politics. Verso, London

Balibar E, Wallerstein I (1991) Race, nation, class: ambiguous identities. Verso, London

Berardi F (2019) Futurability: the age of impotence and the horizon of possibility. Verso, London

Boltanski L, Chiapello E (2007) The new spirit of capitalism. Verso, London

Dalakoglou D, Poulimenakos G (2018) Airbnbizing Europe: mobility, property and platform capitalism. https://www.opendemocracy.net/can-europe-make-it/dimitris-dalakoglou-giorgos-poulimenakos/airbnbizing-europe-mobility-property-and Accessed 4 Feb 2019

Ervedosa C (2017) The Calibanisation of the South in the German Public 'Euro crisis' Discourse. Postcolonial Studies 20(2):137–172

Florida R (2005) Cities and the creative class. Routledge, New York

Florida R, Mellander C, King K (2015) The global creativity index 2015. http://martinprosperity.org/media/Global-Creativity-Index-2015.pdf. Accessed 4 Feb 2019

Fraser N (2017) Progressive neoliberalism versus reactionary populism: a choice that feminists should refuse. NORA – Nordic J Feminist Gender Rese 24(4):281–284

Hadjimichalis K (2019) Z from Filoti, K from the Cafe of Kanaris street, and the Issue of the "Strategic Development for the Future". https://chronos.fairead.net/hadjimichalis-stratigiki-mellon?fbclid=IwAR1N2ExzucI89SXOr7RAlCQMrF1BlxJhgwNxPDXSbySQRpH2WLjFzu1v32g Accessed 18 Feb 2019

Harvey D (2014) Seventeen contradictions and the end of capitalism. Oxford University Press, Oxford

Hesmondhalgh D, Baker S (2010) Creative labour: media work in three cultural industries. Routledge, London

Hesmondhalgh D, Oakley K, Lee D, Nisbett M (2015) Culture, economy and politics: the case of new labour. Palgrave Macmillan, Houndmills, Basingstoke
Hewison R (2014) Cultural capital: the rise and the fall of creative Britain. Verso, London
Jacobsson D (2019) In the name of (un)sustainability: a critical analysis of how neoliberal ideology operates through discourses about sustainable progress and equality. tripleC 17(1):19–37
Katsinas P (2019) The international face of Thessaloniki: the "Greek Crisis", the entrepreneurial Mayor, and Mainstream Media Discourses. Area https://doi.org/10.1111/area.12545
Laclau E (1996) Emancipation(s). Verso, London
Lapavitsas C et al (2012) Crisis in the Eurozone. Verso, London
Littler J (2017) Against meritocracy: culture, power and myths of mobility. Routledge, London
Lorey I (2015) State of insecurity: government of the precarious. Verso, London
McRobbie A (2016) Be creative: making a living in the new culture industries. Polity, Cambridge
Mould O (2018) Against creativity. Verso, London
Nea Dimokratia (2018) Για Μια Καλύτερη □ωή: 12° Συνέδριο [For a Better Life; 12th conference]. https://nd.gr/sites/ndmain/files/u48/pds/gia_mia_kaluterh_zwh.pdf Accessed 15 Feb 2019
Primorac J (2008) The position of cultural workers in creative industries. The South-East-European Perspective. Amsterdam: European Cultural Foundation. https://www.researchgate.net/publication/299517882_The_Position_of_Cultural_Workers_in_Creative_Industries_The_south-eastern_European_Perspective Accessed 4 April 2019
Roos J (2019) Why not default? The political economy of sovereign debt. Princeton University Press, New Jersey
Sennett R (2008) The craftsman. Yale University Press, New Haven
Slobodian Q (2018) Globalists: the end of empire and the birth of neoliberalism. Harvard University Press, Cambridge
Stavrakakis Y, Katsampekis G (2019) The populism/anti-populism frontier and its mediation in crisis-ridden Greece: from discursive divide to emerging cleavage? Eur Polit Sci 18(1):37–52
Streeck W (2016) How will capitalism end? Verso, London
Velegrakis (2018) Εξορυκτικές Δραστηριότητες και Κοινωνικό-Οικολογικά Κινήματα σε Περίοδο Κρίσης: Το Παράδειγμα της Εξόρυξης Χρυσού στη ΒΑ Χαλκιδική [Extractivism and Socio-Ecological Movements in Times of Crisis: The Case of Gold Mining in Halkidiki, Greece]. Γεωγραφίες, 32, 124–128

Yiannis Mylonas is an Assistant Professor in Media Sociology and Cultural Studies in the School of Media, National Research University, Higher School of Economics in Moscow. He is the author of the monograph "The 'Greek Crisis" in Europe: Race, Class and Politics" (Brill 2019), and has previously published articles in journals such as *Critical Discourse Studies, tripleC, The Journal of Language and Politics, Continuum: Journal of Media & Cultural Studies, Subjectivity, Race and Class, The Journal of Political Ideologies, Javnost/the Public*, among others.

Hesmondhalgh D, Oakley K, Lee D, Nisbett M (2015) [illegible]
[illegible]

Chapter 8
Production of Cultural Policy in Russia: Authority and Intellectual Leadership

Tatiana Romashko

Abstract The chapter discusses different frameworks of knowledge production within the discourses and practices of Russian cultural policy. Russian cultural policy as an administrative sector has been developed in line with two distinctive governmental regimes, more precisely during the period of liberal decentralisation of the 1990s and the conservative centralisation from 2011 up until today. The study focuses on the main changes that have occurred in the framework of policy design and participation in policymaking.

An attempt is made to combine Foucauldian analytical frameworks of power and discourse with a Gramscian hegemonic approach to political studies that was mainly advocated by the Essex scholars—Ernesto Laclau, Chantal Mouffe, and David Howarth. Such a perspective opens up a possibility of considering the institutional rearrangements of intellectual leadership through which the post-2012 establishment has endeavoured to advance its sovereignty and planning capacities in both the symbolic and the normative dimensions of culture. Thus examined, Russian state cultural policy turns out to be intrinsically subordinated to the sovereignty of the presidential apparatus that privileges the conservative stance of the 'Russian World' project and neglects human rights and cultural diversity.

The research is based on a wide selection of national strategies and drafts of federal law on culture.

Keywords Russia · Cultural policy discourses · Hegemonic approach · Intellectual leadership · Sovereign power · Laclau and Mouffe · Foucault

T. Romashko (✉)
University of Jyväskylä, Jyväskylä, Finland
e-mail: tatiana.t.romashko@jyu.fi

I. Kiriya et al. (eds.), *The Industrialization of Creativity and Its Limits*, Science, Technology and Innovation Studies, https://doi.org/10.1007/978-3-030-53164-5_8

8.1 Introduction

Back in 2004, the Orange Revolution in Ukraine[1] became a kick-off for the first steps made by the Russian establishment towards consolidation of power within the Administration of the President of the Russian Federation (AP) and mobilisation of anti-Western rhetoric through a set of Kremlin-affiliated think-tanks. The antagonistic features of Putin's political project demonstrate its hegemonic character. Various researches have described the corresponding discursive practices of the Kremlin in many ways, e.g. as 'Putin's vertical of power' or 'federalism and electoral authoritarianism' (Ross 2015); 'supranationalism' or 'cultural and economic regionalism' (Kazharski 2019); and the 'Russian World project' (Suslov 2018). Nonetheless, a noticeable political and cultural turn towards conservatism occurred in the Russian Federation after the crisis of Putin's legitimacy in 2011–2013 (Ross 2015; Robinson 2017). Initially, thousands of metropolitan citizens took to the streets to protest against the unfair 2011 State Duma elections, and, later, massive peaceful anti-Putin protests shook the whole country in 2012–2015.

A literature overview (Gel'man 2015; Gudkov 2015; Bogush 2017) shows that the Russian establishment did not expect a chain reaction in the non-systemic opposition and, thus, took urgent measures. Primarily, the ideological shift in the post-2012 Kremlin's thinking sparked numerous changes in Russian legislation, which, in general, might be characterized as a 'state against civil society' confrontation (Ross 2015). Various restrictive federal and local laws led to a narrowing of the political space available for the non-systemic opposition, along with an institutional transformation of state governance as such. Additionally, such a squeeze on constitutional freedoms was accompanied by empowerment of both the repressive apparatus and the Kremlin-affiliated think-tanks (including the Russian Orthodox Church) in the promotion and preservation of traditional values, spiritual bonds, social stability and state sovereignty (Kalinin 2015; Grishaeva 2015; Yatsyk 2019). Within this context, Russian cultural policy became part of the national security strategy protecting 'traditional values and norms, traditions, and customs and patterns of behaviour of the Russian civilisation' (President of the Russian Federation 2014). According to the Presidential Decree № 808 (2004), 'culture' has been defined as 'a set of formal and informal institutions, phenomena and factors influencing the conservation, production, transmission and dissemination of spiritual values'. And ultimately, 'culture' has been turned into 'the guarantor of the preservation of the common cultural space and territorial integrity' of the country (Russian Government 2016).

Nevertheless, the post-2012 Russian state is neither totalitarian nor democratic. It is a 'hybrid regime', which simulates democratic institutions such as the Parliament but relies on 'repressive legislation inspired by the Presidential Administration'

---

[1]See 'Strategy of National Security of the Russian Federation' for an interpretation of the Ukrainian case as an 'anti-constitutional coup' supported by the United States and the EU (Russian President 2015).

(Noble and Schulmann 2018, 50). Following this course of thought, the chapter addresses a pivotal moment in Russian cultural policy development by examining the institutional background behind the conservative turn. A few critical studies show that today's Russian cultural policy tends to have features that differ from what the cultural policy supposedly was before. These are mainly associated with an 'instrumentalisation of culture' in an attempt to (1) legitimise the federal government (Turoma et al. 2018, 651), (2) establish 'cultural borders between Russia and the EU countries' and (3) reduce 'Russian society to a single national identity' (Romashko 2018, 90). In contrast, the mainstream national cultural policy discourse encourages conservative statements about the 'Russian distinctive path', 'Russian World civilisation' and 'Orthodox values' (Ministry of Culture 2015). In this vein, top Russian academics insist on the appropriateness of the new 'model of state cultural policy' (Vostryakov and Turgaev 2018), where the 'political will' comes from the president and his administrative apparatuses (see Gudima 2014; Turgaev et al. 2017).

Taking into account these existing contradictions, the chapter endeavours to explain the paradox of the novel framework of Russian *state* cultural policy and its post-2012 transformation. It is done through an analysis of the current political and legislative context, which is understood as an ensemble of power relations. The main research question is how the institutional conditions of the hegemonic conservative project affected the cultural policy framework in post-2012 Russia. In answering it, I pay special attention to the complexity of the relations between governmental rationalities and administrative techniques, as well as legislative proposals and institutions, which altogether constitute a specific governmental logic of cultural policymaking. In particular, I examine to what extent the sovereign power of the presidential apparatus[2] has embodied intellectual leadership and replaced network forms of governance in cultural policy.

Drawing on ideas from post-foundational political science and cultural theory (Gramsci 2000; Foucault 1969; Laclau and Mouffe 2001; Howarth and Stavrakakis 2000), I explore Russian cultural policy frameworks in terms of different governmental logics, ways of production and forms of intellectual leadership. In doing so, I scrutinise the recent legislative amendments on culture and the political discourses around them. The aim is to show the actual power relations and political decisions behind the empowerment of the Presidential Council for Culture and Art, PCCA (1996–2018), and the abrupt dissolution of the Russian Institute for Cultural Research, RICR (1986–2014), which for many years had played a leading role in cultural policy development. Thus, the research focuses on the dynamics of parliamentary lawmaking activity in the cultural sector and the political debates around it over the period from 2007 to 2018. Special attention is devoted to the analysis of

[2]It consists of the (1) Administration of the President of the Russian Federation (AP) and its profile departments; (2) members of the 'United Russia' party who hold (2.1.) leading positions in Kremlin-affiliated foundations and think-tanks; (2.2) the position of the Chairman of the Committee on Culture of the State Duma (since 2018) and those of other committees in the Parliament; and (3) the highest positions in the Russian Government, which are appointed by the President of the Russian Federation.

routine procedures of the RICR and PCCA and executive-legislative activities of the lower (the State Duma) and higher (the Federal Council) chambers of the Russian Parliament.

The chapter starts with a discussion on the post-Soviet cultural policy framework, addressing its legal system and political struggle for intellectual leadership. After that, I will explain the post-2012 mode of Russian state cultural policy and reveal its institutional background. Before doing so, I outline the methodological background of the study.

8.2 Hegemony, Intellectual Leadership, and Power in Russian Cultural Policy

Originally, Gramsci (2000, 249) defined 'hegemony' as an ensemble of 'domination' and 'intellectual and moral leadership', which is a precondition for the political authority of a supreme social group. Proposing a non-essentialist notion of 'hegemonic subjects', which Gramsci saw as the 'fundamental classes', Laclau and Mouffe (2001, 138) developed a post-Marxist theory of hegemony. They used the term to designate 'a political type of relations' that is incompatible with 'relations of subordination or power' because 'a hegemonic articulation' requires the 'presence of antagonistic forces and the instability of the frontiers which separate them' (Laclau and Mouffe 2001, 138). Their discourse theory emphasises 'a logic of equivalence' that explains how a specific constellation of 'nodal points' becomes a privileged signifier through converting 'elements' of heterogeneous discursive practices into 'moments' of a discursive formation (Laclau and Mouffe 2001, 114). As a result, Laclau and Mouffe tend to focus more on the symbolic dimension of hegemony and do not take into account the mutual interplay of power and discourse, which is a matter of importance in political studies.

For the purposes of political analysis, Howarth and Stavrakakis (2000, 5) state that they 'take discourse or discourses to refer to systems of meaningful practices that form the identities of subjects and objects'. Further, they deduce that 'moments' of discourse are the 'differential positions' (Howarth and Stavrakakis 2000, 5) that are visible at the political level due to their incorporation by the hegemonic forces, e.g. moral, intellectual, political and economic forces. Meanwhile, elements are those differences that exist in the complex discursive field, but their 'articulatory practices' and 'subject positions' lack a political will, and as a result, they do not obtain a higher degree of mediation, reproduction and dissemination within the 'hegemonic formation' (Laclau and Mouffe 2001, 136). In this respect, the Gramscian notion of *moral and intellectual leadership* might be interpreted as an ensemble of subject positions located within the *dominant* or *politically recognised discursive formation*, which is involved in policy formulation. Since intellectual leadership assumes both *authority* and *expert knowledge*, it articulates meaningful systems, identities and values that in a modern state support legal reasoning and political goals. Yet, neither Gramsci nor Laclau and Mouffe have much to say about the institutionalisation of a particular intellectual leadership and what kind of power pillars its subject positions. Moving beyond the most abstract comprehension of hegemony, this chapter seeks to extend the scope of the problem to different forms of power that might be mapped into a political logic of difference and a logic of equivalence. This is done in line with Laclau and Mouffe's observation 'that the logic of equivalence is a logic of the simplification of political space, while the logic of difference is a logic of its expansion and increasing complexity' (2001, 130).

A Foucauldian perspective on power and discourse can help to overcome this methodological challenge. Referring to Foucault's writings (1969, 1975), one may say that power operates not only from outside the discourse, investing a political will in the institutionalisation of a specific alliance of intellectual forces and constituting their discursive formations. But power is also exercised through the articulatory practices or discursive regularities of intellectual leadership. It follows that intellectual leadership might be endowed with authority either (1) by political forms of domination compatible with a democratic regime, which allows for the existence of political differences in collaborative governance; or (2) by the sovereign power of a particular institute or a supreme leader, which is typical for hybrid or authoritarian regimes with a centralised government. Apart from this, institutions of intellectual leadership themselves accumulate political features. This is due to the fact that they enunciate 'rules for the formation of objects, modalities of statements, concepts and theoretical choices' (Foucault 1969, 72). Therefore, those institutional entities that perform leading roles are capable of orchestrating a group of statements, norms of verification, critique and coherence, which a priori excludes certain possibilities, constructing lines of inclusion and exclusion within its sphere of competence. This kind of thinking is particularly relevant when considering the Russian case, because, on the one hand, as an *analytical category, intellectual leadership* carries political recognition or authority. On the other hand, as *a political category,* it reveals the struggle for domination among intellectual forces.

In this respect, a set of 'differential positions' (i.e. experts, opinion leaders and top officials of the cultural sector) located within the Presidential Council for Culture and Art[3] can be regarded as a coalition of Kremlin-elitist intellectual forces, which in exchange for privileges and economic rent authorise the 'power bloc' to speak out on behalf of the nation. An important fact is that, before 2012, this body was in charge of a limited number of functions, which were mainly related to the management of the national and presidential 'award in the field of literature and art'. Meanwhile, the political will and driving forces of cultural policy development resided dispersed within a network of different institutions of cultural policy, i.e. profile committees in regional governments and the Parliament, cultural and research agencies, independent think-tanks, and professional and academic units.

[3]Allegedly, this 'consultative body, established to inform the president of the situation in culture and the arts, coordinates his contacts with cultural and artistic organisations and members of culture and arts communities, as well as prepares draft proposals on topical issues concerning state policy in culture and the arts' (Kremlin 2001).

However, on the threshold of the 2014 National Year of Culture, Putin suggested that the honourable members of the Presidential Council for Culture and Art should 'formulate the central, basic objectives of the state cultural policy' (Kremlin 2013). Ironically, this initiative resulted in a public scandal. In April 2014, a ministerial document on the 'principles of state cultural policy',[4] which mainly consisted of Putin's quotations and instructions, caused public discontent. Quite a few academics[5] and research centres (e.g. the Institute of Philosophy of the Russian Academy of Science, https://iphras.ru/cult_polit.htm) were against radical statements proposed in the document, such as 'Russia is not Europe' (for more, see Gudima 2014, 44; Moroz 2016). This was a pivotal moment since, in order to resolve the situation, President Putin authorised his Council for Culture and Art to take intellectual leadership in cultural policy formulation. Later on in 2014–2016, proceeding in the same way, the president expanded the privileges of his 'consultative body' to legislative activity, bypassing parliamentary discussions and political representation. One may say that the redistribution of intellectual leadership has occurred through institutional alterations caused by the reinforcement of the sovereign power coming from the Presidential Administration. Thus, I argue that after 2012 the presidential apparatus has gradually established a monopoly on political and legislative initiatives in cultural policy through rearrangements of institutional apparatuses and consolidation of intellectual and moral leadership[6] within the Presidential Council for Culture and Art. In particular, it is important to stress that the shift from the logic of differences to the logic of equivalences in cultural policy has occurred in the context of the post-2012 institutional transformation, within which it became part of the hegemonic political project. Hence, to provide evidence for the above claim, the next section will examine several aspects of this institutional transformation of the cultural policy framework. Before that, I will briefly introduce its legislative background, which originates from the early 1990s.

8.2.1 *The Post-Soviet Legislative Framework of Cultural Policy*

Essentially, cultural policy in the Russian Federation is ruled by laws. These include (1) the fundamental federal law on culture (1992); (2) a set of nationwide sectoral laws; and (3) a number of regional legislations on cultural policy in 59 out of the

[4]The Ministry of Culture outlined the 'foundations of state cultural policy' (Izvetia 2014).

[5]See the special issue on cultural policy in the Iskusstvo journal (http://iskusstvo-info.ru/issues/kulturnaya-politika/)

[6]To address the institutional level of the problem, I understand the assemblage of different institutional entities of the civil society (i.e. research, academic, cultural, analytical and political actors) as an alliance of intellectual forces that struggle for intellectual leadership in policy production.

85 regions of the Russian Federation, which assume a local aspect of cultural development. In addition, 'many relationships in the sphere of culture are regulated by the Civil, Labour, Budget, Tax, Land and Urban Planning Codes of the Russian Federation' and other federal laws related to education, informational security and mass communications (Ministry of Culture 2014, 240). To become a law, all legislative initiatives must first pass three stages of parliamentary readings (i.e. be accepted twice by the Duma and by the Federal Council), then, be adopted by the Russian Government and, finally, be approved by the President of the Russian Federation. According to the Russian Constitution (1993, 104), the president of the state, Duma deputies, members of the Government, the Ministries of Culture and the Constitutional and the Supreme Arbitration Court all have equal authority to submit bills to the State Duma.

An initial normative framework of cultural policy was established by the first federal law 'Fundamentals of Russian Legislation on Culture', FRLC (Russian Supreme Council 1992). It prescribed the common reciprocal relationships between the state and other actors of the cultural sphere based on the principles of cultural and economic freedom.[7] These relationships were limited to four main targets that the law intended to tackle. In particular, it aimed (1) to 'protect the constitutional rights of Russian citizens to cultural activity'; (2) to create legal guarantees for free cultural activity and associations'; and to define (3) 'legal norms for relations between subjects of cultural activity'; and (4) 'principles of state cultural policy, legal norms of state support and guarantees of non-interference into creative processes' (Russian Supreme Council 1992: article 2). According to the FRLC, the key instruments of state cultural policy were four-year federal 'target' programmes of cultural development, government subsidies and tax benefits for the third sector and all cultural activities. However, many empirical studies (Kostina and Gudima 2007; Karpova 2009) have highlighted that the Russian Government repeatedly reduced the allocated budget for all 'target' programmes by half due to the budget cuts coming from the Ministry of Finance. Therefore, such a policy toolkit provided little opportunities for the diversification of local policies. The target programmes approved by the Russian Government were mainly oriented to support the state-run cultural sector and cultural heritage. Furthermore, the general recentralisation of governance that occurred within the 2004 administrative reform and a range of related centralising laws[8] practically cancelled the previously announced social

[7]To be precise, Article 11 of the FRLC (1992), states that '[e]veryone has the right to a free choice of moral, aesthetic and other values, [. . .] to the state's protection of cultural identity'. In addition, Article 46 outlines the economic freedom of 'cultural organisations', which have an unrestricted right 'to obtain gratuitous donations (grants, subsidies) from Russian and foreign legal entities and individuals, and international organisations'.

[8]The Federal Laws № 122 (2004) and № 94 (2005), and numerous amendments to the legislation on non-governmental organisations in 2006–2007, which aimed at increasing control over the public and third sectors as well as combating corruption, in fact, led to the elimination of the economic freedom of state-run cultural organisations (Russian Government 1996, 2004, 2005a).

guarantees and tax exemptions for cultural activity and the third sector (see Gudima 2007; Robertson 2009).

Nevertheless, the 1992 basic law on culture allowed the introduction of unprecedented democratisation and participation in policymaking, which progressed in line with post-Soviet decentralisation. First, the ideological content of culture was not limited to a particular, single idea imposed by the central government or declared in a law of high jurisdiction. In this respect, all regional authorities and republics had a right to develop their own 'programmes of cultural protection and development', sourcing intellectual leadership from numerous schools of thinking and professional units. Secondly, Article 28 of the 1992 FRLC proclaims that 'the state provides an opportunity for organisations that represent creative workers to participate in policy formulation'.

In theory, this mechanism of policy formulation assumed joint work between various experts or groups of interest and local governmental bodies (i.e. committees of the Federal Council, the State and regional Dumas as well as the Ministries of Culture). They were supposed to take into account the demands and needs of social or professional groups and formulate decisions at the municipal level. Then, if successfully argued for on the regional Duma's floor, such a political statement might become the subject of federal legislative activity and be put forward in the State Duma by political representatives or members of legislative branches.

On the whole, the basic post-Soviet legislation on culture clearly stipulated the introduction of political differences and a kind of network governance in the cultural sector. Nevertheless, the continuous process of legislative activities always implied an antagonism of two forces. On the one hand, the conservative forces of the Russian Government have intended to regulate, operate and maintain those cultural domains that are subordinated to the state apparatuses (i.e. Ministries of Culture) through financial and administrative control. On the other hand, the liberal forces dispersed across miscellaneous actors of the civil society have striven to expand the scope of legislation in terms of equality, social security and labour and economic rights for all actors in the art and cultural sphere irrespective of their affiliation with the state. The next sections describe two discursive formations of Russian cultural policy that were shaped by the liberal and conservative forces during their intellectual leadership.

8.2.2 The Fate of Cultural Governance in Putin's Russia

An analysis of the recent legislative initiatives (2007–2018) to change the basic law on culture (1992) and the political debates around it makes it possible to detect two ensembles of social relations, within which the conservative and liberal forces have exercised intellectual leadership within a particular regime of power relations. In practice, Russian cultural policy has developed in two major directions. Driven by competing assemblages of intellectual forces, its framework has evolved as (1) a political dimension of democratic debates and bottom-up initiatives and (2) administrative-regulative practices of the central government. The latter has eventually transformed into a Kremlin-run mechanism of rent distribution among loyal elites and, thereby, has entailed the relocation of the political will from the Parliament to the Presidential Administration.

This section examines the evolving network form of governance in cultural policy that was compatible with the post-Soviet political logic of difference. According to the results of my previous analysis (Romashko 2019), the process of decentralisation and regionalisation of post-Soviet cultural policy was mainly associated with the democratic project of the Russian Institute for Cultural Research. Under the leadership of Kirill Razlogov, this think-tank was a kind of pioneer in building mutual relationships between legislative authorities and non-governmental actors in society (see Razlogov and Butenko 2000).

In close cooperation with the State Duma, the federal and regional[9] Ministries of Culture and the European Council, the RICR had regularly initiated meetings and collaborative projects with local communities, professionals and scholars in order to make their side of the story heard at the political level. Throughout 1990–2012, this cluster of discursive practices was composed of a broad network of different association, unions, agencies and NGOs. They actively participated in cultural policy formulation by providing (1) relevant background for political argumentation and legal reasoning; (2) reliable evidence of the actual execution of laws and state guarantees; and (3) expertise on legislative initiatives (Fedorova and Kochelyaeva 2013). Typically, a large part of these bottom-up legislative proposals aimed to resist the ongoing limitation of rights, freedoms and social security in the cultural sector through the gradual budget squeeze and security policies of the mid-2000s, which were mentioned above in the previous section. Consequently, through a mechanism of political representation, this discursive formation succeeded in encompassing and orchestrating standard procedures and techniques of cultural policymaking, which ultimately constituted a domain of normativity and participation for various actors of the sector.

In April 2010, during the so-called 'Medvedev's modernisation government' (7 May 2008–7 May 2012), Kirill Razlogov, backed by the Duma's Committee on Culture, took a political moment to challenge the Parliament (Ivliev 2011). He claimed that cultural activity in Russia desperately needed a legal framework that would strengthen the protection of the constitutional rights and freedoms of all actors in the cultural sphere, including consumers and freelance creative labourers. He stressed three main problem areas (1) controversial issues related to the central government's attempt to 'regulate' and 'manage' the culture, 'beliefs, customs and traditions of people'; (2) a problem with the recognition of cultural diversity in Russia; and (3) difficulties with accepting the synthesis of cultural and human rights (Razlogov 2011: 36). As Razgolov stated, '[i]n our country, this problem is particularly acute, since, as you know, there are influential people who believe that the very concept of human rights is not applicable in our culture and our tradition, that

[9]For example, the Ministry of Art and Cultural Policy of the Ulyanovsk Region, Omskaya Oblast', the Republic of Karelia, etc.

we have other ideas about human rights' (Razlogov 2011, 37). At the end of his speech, he also concluded that the 'key problem' in Russia is 'the problem of recognizing the plurality of cultures, the problem of respect for another culture, the problem of its understanding... So, all *these differences*, they are *the very cultural life* that saturates all societies' (Razlogov 2011: 37–38, emphasis added). In November 2011, the first draft of the federal law 'on culture in the Russian Federation' was submitted to the State Duma (Ivliev et al. 2011). In line with the above-mentioned ideas, the law expressed consolidated bottom-up voices from regions and political demands of cultural labourers. It declared a considerably broader understanding of culture, in the sense that all forms of folk culture, art and creativity should be equally recognised as cultural activities that deserve support and protection (Institute of Economics and Social Policy 2011). The intention was to change the existing mechanism of state support[10] for culture through an economic and administrative liberalisation of the cultural sector.

An analysis of the primary considerations, reviews and comments on the draft (2011–2015), carried out and provided by several committees of the State Duma as well as regional Ministries of Culture and expert groups, shows that all actors accepted the concept of the law and its draft positively. Nevertheless, this legislative initiative failed to go through the first readings due to formal comments to the draft and a negative review from Vladislav Surkov, who was in charge of Putin's administration at the time (Russian Government 2011). Several academics who were involved in this legislative process admitted that there was 'no state's will to adopt it', since the Ministry of Culture indicated that 'the proposed legislation could be considered only after the adoption of the "Principles of State Cultural Policy (PSCP)"' (Gudima 2014, 41). Ultimately, in April 2018, the State Duma decided to reject the bill because:

> According to the results of the Presidential Council for Culture and Art's meeting held on 21 December 2017, President Vladimir Putin instructed the Presidential Administration of the Russian Federation, in collaboration with the Presidential Council for Culture and Art, to develop and present the concepts of the draft federal laws 'on culture' and on amendments to certain legislative acts in connection with the adoption of the federal law 'on culture' and, consequently, to ensure the development of these federal laws. Ultimately, *the draft federal law developed in accordance with the instructions of the President* of the Russian Federation *might happen to differ from* the draft law under consideration [the 2015 draft of the federal law 'on culture'], which, in the opinion of the Committee on Culture [of the State Duma], *is unacceptable.* (State Dumas Committee of Culture 2018; translated from Russian by the author, stress is added).

The extract above clearly demonstrates that in 2018 the authority of the presidential apparatus overrode the constitutional framework of cultural policymaking, or to put

[10]The FRLC (1992) was significantly limited by the Federal Law № 122 'concerning the common principles of the organisation of local government in the Russian Federation' (2004), which abolished Article 45, which was related to social security and assignments of cultural labour; Articles 27 and 28 on the status of creative workers and professional units; Article 53 on the interaction between cultural institutions and other enterprises etc. For more, see the latest edition of the FRLC (1992). Consultant. http://www.consultant.ru/document/cons_doc_LAW_1870/

it differently, the sovereign power of the Presidential Administration took over the role of the Parliament in cultural policy formulation. Thus, in order to understand the actual power relations behind the suspension of this legislative initiative, we should examine the genealogy of Kremlin-driven cultural policy—the nature and origins of its intellectual leadership—and the moment when it became hegemonic.

8.3 Consolidation of Intellectual Forces within the Kremlin's Russian World

During the second period of his presidency (2004–2007), Vladimir Putin appeared increasingly often in academic circles, round tables and forums of the most prominent intellectuals across the country. In these meetings, the Russian president expressed profound concern regarding the mission of culture, which in his own words is 'to make *"the people* out of *a mere population*"' (Putin 2006). Through this, the Kremlin designated culture as a terrain where a constitution of a new political agent—the people of the *Russian civilisation*—out of the *demos* has occurred. Expressing similar sentiments, Vladislav Surkov,[11] Vyacheslav Nikonov[12] and other influential figures of the AP, as well as numerous pro-Kremlin think-tanks and foundations,[13] have extensively succeeded in constituting a set of subject positions within the discursive formation of the 'Russian World' project. On the one hand, it has encompassed a number of administrative operations of money and power redistribution among Kremlin-affiliated entities and projects.[14] On the other hand, its symbolic dimension has expanded considerably at the expense of unlimited and unoccupied elements of the discursive field, which have regularly been converted into moments of the antagonistic and therefore hegemonic discourse of the establishment.

Initially, Surkov (2006) proposed a political process of 'nationalisation of the future' through the use of Russian 'culture as an organism of meaning formation and ideological influence'. Later, in his 2007 Address to the Federal Assembly, Putin defined the 'state sovereignty' of Russia through its 'cultural and spiritual distinctiveness' (*samobytnost'*) (Putin 2007). Further, followed by a round of applause, the president firmly stated that Russian is 'a true language of international communication' and should be 'popularised to secure a living space for the multimillion

[11]A former Deputy Head of the Presidential Administration.

[12]A member of the Public Chamber of Russia.

[13]Such as the 'Unity for Russia Foundation' (http://www.fondedin.ru/o-fonde.html), 'Russian Social and Political Centre' foundation (http://www.rppc.ru/), non-profit foundation 'Policy' (http://www.polity.ru/), discussion club 'Valdai' (http://ru.valdaiclub.com/) and 'Russian World Foundation' (https://www.russkiymir.ru/)

[14]For instance, the Russian World Foundation was established by Putin in 2007 (Russian President 2007).

"Russian World", which, of course, is much broader than Russia itself' (Putin 2007). In fact, a range of Kremlin statements rearticulated Shchedrovitskii's original conceptual framework of the 'Russian World' into a meaningful system of proto-conservative ideas, where 'sovereign democracy' (Surkov 2006) was politically linked to national culture, protectionist policies and state intervention in the cultural life of the population (for more, see Suslov 2018).

Finally, the Russian World narrative validated a specific set of Kremlin practices of intervention in the cultural terrain. It both affected the former instruments of cultural policy and generated a parallel toolkit of rent redistribution among subjects of the Russian World who performed the Kremlin's priorities and initiatives. For instance, the federal target programme 'Russian language (2006–2010)' was launched 'in order to strengthen the statehood, national security and prestige of the Russian Federation' (Russian Government 2005b). Federal targeted programmes were supplemented by a set of Kremlin initiatives, such as annual celebrations of the national thematic year or presidential grants in the sphere of culture. For example, during the 2007 'Year of Russian Language' (Russian President 2006), numerous international and national 'events in the field of culture, science and education' obtained federal financial assistance to deliver the political objectives of the Kremlin. Moreover, many state-affiliated NGOs and think-tanks were set up to implement a protectionist range of tasks to promote the Russian language and Russian national culture in accordance with Putin's message (Suslov 2018; Yatsyk 2019).

As a result, moments of the Kremlin's discourse on national identity became institutionalised into a meaningful system of governmental practices of the 'Russian World'. During the mid-2000s, the Russian World project spread via federal targeted programmes, institutions and policies. On the one hand, this intervention in the cultural domain was sufficient for the Kremlin to consolidate loyal intellectual forces. This way, the AP secured authority to speak on behalf of 'the people' after the 2012 crisis of Putin's legitimacy. On the other hand, after 2014 the 'Russian World' was rearticulated within a conservative political idea of 'sovereign democracy', which enunciated 'Russia's stance vis-à-vis the liberal democracies' (Suslov 2018, 9).

8.4 Closing Remarks on the Institutionalisation of State Cultural Policy

An institutional transformation of Russian cultural policy began in 2013. That year, the newly appointed Ministry of Culture rejected a national report on culture, which had been prepared by a team of experts in cooperation with several regional ministries and already endorsed by the European Council. In relation to this issue, Kirill Razlogov, one of the editors of this volume, noted that officials wanted him to 'improve' the final version of the text in line with Putin's quotations from the 2012 Valdai Club (Razlogov 2014a). Razlogov refused to comply with these instructions.

In response, the bureaucratic apparatus of the Ministry of Culture and the Russian Government were appointed to prepare and approve the national report on culture (Russian Government 2013). Thereby, the central government consolidated its supervision over the input and output of cultural policy all at once, which completely changed its framework in terms of procedures and methods of scientific research. Instead of providing an unbiased review of the real state of things in the cultural sphere and identifying its problem areas, all 'state reports on the state of culture in the Russian Federation'[15] celebrate the best practices of the 'Russian World project' and Putin's personal involvement in the formulation of cultural policy priorities. Thus, since 2013, each national report on culture has glorified Putin's seminal words. For instance, the 2018 Cultural Forum brochure started with Putin's words: '[i]t is extremely important to preserve our identity in the turbulent age of technological change, and here it is impossible to overestimate the role of culture, which is our national civilisational code and reveals creative principles in human beings' (Ministry of Culture 2018: 4, translated by the author).

Later in 2014, the Russian Institute for Cultural Research was dissolved as part of the implementation of the 'optimisation policy' of Putin's 2012 May Decrees (see Razlogov 2014b). It was replaced by the Presidential Council for Culture and Art appointed by Putin to take a leading role in cultural policy formulation. Consequently, in 2014–2016 the PCCA was commissioned to elaborate two nationwide legislative acts, namely, the 'Principles of State Cultural Policy' (Russian President 2014) and the 'Strategy of State Cultural Policy' (Russian Government 2016). Approved by the head of the country, without having been considered in the Duma, both papers were statutory and consistent with the conservative priorities of the Kremlin (see Romashko 2018). Both these so-called 'national strategic documents' attained a status of supreme power, revoking the previous federal and sectoral laws.

Imposing a totalising logic of equivalence on the further legislative as well as administrative process in the cultural sector, these official papers articulate 'culture' through the nodal points of the 'Russian World'. Consequently, the chains of equivalences include both the spiritual dimension of culture, in other words, spiritual bonds = Orthodox religion = Russian traditional values and non-Western morality, and its normative aspect, i.e. single cultural space = civilisational code = patriotism and historical identity = state sovereignty. In this manner, the meaning of culture is partially fixed, through an antagonism, to an empty signifier 'the West', which bears 'threats to national security in the field of culture, including the erosion of traditional Russian spiritual and moral values and the weakening of the unity of the multinational people of the Russian Federation' and makes 'never-ending attempts at falsification of the Russian history, at its revision' (Russian Government 2016: 6–7; 9).

[15]For example, see a number of Cultural Ministry reports from the period of 2014–2018 (https://www.mkrf.ru/activities/reports/)

In fact, the novel 'management of state cultural policy' (Russian Government 2015) produced a whole range of bureaucratic operations. Some of the most visible governmental practices were intended to bring about a general 'improvement in the management system of state cultural policy', mainly by focusing on two issues (Russian Government 2015). The first was the task of 'bringing *the legislation of the Russian Federation* in line with the goals and objectives *of state cultural policy*', which involved the process of elaborating a set of documents consistent with the president's annual list of instructions and the 2012 Presidential May Decrees (Russian Government 2015, 2016; Putin 2015).

The second task was to organise a structural basis for the operative work and actual management of Russian *state* cultural policy. In this respect, various state commissions, councils, committees and Kremlin-affiliated expert and working groups were commissioned to ensure the implementation of the 'principles of state cultural policy'. Subsequently, this created a need to 'improve the federal and regional legislation on culture' and to 'create structures at the federal and regional levels to ensure the implementation and monitoring of the goals and objectives of Strategy 2030 and the principles of state cultural policy' (Council of Federation 2017). For instance, between 2012 and 2018, the Russian Government adopted 51 federal laws in relation to culture and its regulation (Ministry of Culture 2018, 57). This is almost nine times more compared to the number of legislative acts accepted via the democratic mode of cultural policy during the equally long period of 2004–2011.

In general, this scope of rulemaking procedures served to justify the further morphologic growth of state-run organisations responsible for the implementation and control of targets, ideas and measures set out by the Presidential Decree № 808 on the PSCP (2014) and related acts. Moreover, it provided an institutional basis for the (1) monopolisation of power over cultural policy formulation within the presidential apparatus and (2) reduction of the political capacities of policymaking at the regional and local levels. To a certain extent, such a sovereign mechanism of decision-making is justified because the presidential instructions are authorised by the PCCA at its annual meeting. Hence, these decisions are not supposed to be questioned or challenged in the Parliament.

In sum, it can be said that state cultural policy became part of the hegemonic conservative project within the ideological limits of the Kremlin's 'Russian World'. It was carried out through the gradual empowering of the Presidential Council for Culture and Art and weakening of the democratic forms of governance as well as the representative capacity of the Parliament. The acceleration of these processes led to a moment in 2018 when the authority of the Presidential Administration completely substituted the former mechanism of governance and its logic of difference that conveyed various voices of the cultural sector.

Acknowledgments The research was supported by the Kone Foundation in 2018–2019. I would like to express my sincere gratitude to Jeremy Valentine, Miikka Pyykkönen, Andrey Makarychev and Mikko Jakonen for substantive help with the first draft of this chapter and their fruitful suggestions on its following versions. I would also like to acknowledge the editors of the volume for their critical comments that help me to develop my chapter to its final form.

References

Bogush G (2017) Criminalisation of free speech in Russia. Eur Asia Stud 69(8):1242–1256

Council of Federation (2017) Resolution 'concerning the implementation of the strategy of state cultural policy for the period until 2030 in subjects of the Russian Federation.' http://council.gov.ru/activity/documents/76702/. Accessed 15 October 2018

Fedorova T, Kochelyaeva N (2013) Cultural policies and trends in Europe. Russian Federation. Compendium. https://www.culturalpolicies.net/web/profiles-news.php?pcid=1390. Accessed 10 October 2018

Foucault M (1969) L'Archéologie du savoir. Paris: Editions Gallimard. English edition: Foucault M (2002) The archaeology of knowledge (trans: Sheridan A). New York: Routledge Classics

Foucault M (1975) Surveiller et Punir: Naissance de la prison. Paris: Editions Gallimard. English edition: Foucault M (1995) Discipline and punish: the birth of the prison (trans: Sheridan, A.). New York: Vintage Books

Gel'man V (2015) Authoritarian Russia: analysing post-Soviet regime changes. University of Pittsburgh, Pittsburgh, PA

Gramsci A (2000) The Gramsci Reader. Selected writings 1916–1935. Ed. David Forgacs. New York: The Your University Press

Grishaeva E (2015) Heretical virtual movement in Russian Live Journal blogs: between religion and politics. Digital Icons Stud Russian Eurasian Central European New Media 14:109–122

Gudima T (2007) Cultural policy: turning to the market or investing in people [Культурная политика: поворот к рынку или вложения в человека]. Cult Obs 2:20–25

Gudima T (2014) Analysis of drafts of 'Fundamentals of the State Cultural Policy' [Анализ проектов «Основ государственной культурной политики»]. J Strategic Priorities 3:40–52

Gudkov L (2015) Resources of Putin's conservatism. In: Leon A (ed) Putin's Russia. American Enterprise Institute, Washington, pp 52–72

Howarth D, Stavrakakis Y (2000) Introducing discourse theory and political analysis. In: Howarth DJ, Howarth DR, Norval AJ, Stavrakakis Y (eds) Discourse theory and political analysis: identities, hegemonies and social change. Manchester University Press, Manchester, pp 1–23

Institute of Economics and Social Policy (2011).The draft federal law 'on culture in the Russian Federation' (revised by the State Duma Committee on Culture of 26 October 2011). http://www.inesp.ru/special_projects/culture/info/#%D0%BF%D1%80%D0%B8%D0%BB%D0%BE%D0%B6%D0%B5%D0%BD%D0%B8%D0%B5_2. Accessed 1 November 2018

Ivliev GP (ed) (2011) Culture and legislation: on the materials of parliamentary hearings. State Duma Edition, Moscow

Ivliev GP, Drapeko EG, Kuschev VM, Stepanove ZM, Rastprguev NV, Zakharova CY (2011, April 26). The draft federal law 'on culture in Russian federation.' Rossiiskaya Gazeta.. https://rg.ru/2011/10/26/kultura-sitedok. html. Accessed 1 November 2018

Izvetia (2014, April 20) The Ministry of Culture outlined the 'foundations of state cultural policy'. https://iz.ru/news/569016. Accessed 15 October 2018

Kalinin I (2015, January 28) Culture matters: why the Kremlin wants to be the keeper of Russia's cultural heritage. Calvert J. https://www.calvertjournal.com/opinion/show/3608/Culture-matters-Russia-cultural-policy-Ilya-Kalinin. Accessed 15 October 2018

Karpova G (2009) State regulation and public priorities in the sphere of cultural policy in Russia [Государственное управление и общественные приоритеты в сфере культурной политики России]. J Social Policy Res 7(1):7–20

Kazharski A (2019) Eurasian integration and the Russian world: regionalism as an identitary enterprise. Central European University Press, Budapest–New York

Kostina A, Gudima T (2007) Cultural policy in contemporary Russia: correlation between ethnic and national. [Культурная политика в современной России: соотношение этнического и национального]. Moscow: LGK

Kremlin (2001) Council for culture and art. http://en.kremlin.ru/structure/councils. Accessed 8 September 2018

Kremlin (2013, October 2) Minutes of the meeting of the council for culture and art. Moscow. http://kremlin.ru/events/president/news/19353. Accessed 8 September 2018

Laclau E, Mouffe C (2001) Hegemony and socialist strategy. Verso, London

Ministry of Culture (2014) State report on the state of culture in the Russian Federation. https://www.mkrf.ru/activities/reports/report2014/. Accessed 3 November 2018

Ministry of Culture (2015) Principles of state cultural policy of the Russian Federation. https://www.mkrf.ru/upload/mkrf/mkdocs2016/ OSNOVI-PRINT.NEW.indd.pdf. Accessed 3 November 2018

Ministry of Culture (2018) Culture is a national priority. Fact and figures 2012–2018. St. Petersburg: 7th International Cultural Forum. https://www.mkrf.ru/upload/iblock/e24/e2425955611baa7d233df53059f83e6d.pdf. Accessed 3 November 2018

Moroz O (2016) Strategies of Russian state cultural policy: investigation experience. [Стратегии российской государственной культурной политики: опыт расследования]. J Reserve Stock [Неприкосновенный запас] 3(107). https://www.nlobooks.ru/magazines/neprikosnovennyy_zapas/107_nz_3_2016/article/12002/

Noble B, Schulmann E (2018) Not just a rubber stamp: parliament and law-making. In: Treisman D (ed) The new autocracy: information, politics, and policy in Putin's Russia. Brookings Institution Press, Washington, DC, pp 49–82

Putin V (2006, November 29) Opening speech at a meeting with the creative intelligentsia dedicated to the 100th anniversary of the birth of Dmitry Likhachev. Kremlin. http://kremlin.ru/events/president/transcripts/23930. Accessed 3 November 2018

Putin V (2007) Address to the federal assembly. Moscow: Kremlin. http://www.kremlin.ru/acts/bank/25522. Accessed 3 November 2018

Putin, V. (2015). List of instructions for the joint meeting of the State Council and the Council for Culture and Art.. http://www.kremlin.ru/acts/assignments/orders/47511. Accessed 3 November 2018

Razlogov K (2011) Report on the parliamentary hearings 'concerning the project concept of the new basic federal law on culture' on 19 April 2010. In: Ievliev G (ed) Culture and law: materials of the parliamentary hearings. State Duma, Moscow, pp 33–44

Razlogov K (2014a) Interview: 'What is good for art is not always good for society'. Art J, *3*(590). http://iskusstvo-info.ru/kirill-razlogov-to-chto-horosho-dlya-iskusstva-daleko-ne-vsegda-horosho-dlya-obshhestva/. Accessed 10 November 2018

Razlogov K (2014b, February 12) Schizo-Reality and the 'New Barbarians': Paradoxes of the 'Mettlesome Optimisation' of cultural studies. Novaya Gazeta.https://www.novayagazeta.ru/articles/2014/02/01/58178-kirill-razlogov-shizorealnost-i-171-novye-varvary-187. Accessed 1 November 2018

Razlogov K, Butenko I (eds) (2000) Culture and cultural policy in Russia [Культура и культурная политика в России]. Moscow Public Research Foundation, Moscow

Robertson G (2009) Managing society: protest, civil society, and regime in Putin's Russia. Slav Rev 68(3):528–547

Robinson N (2017) Russian neo-patrimonialism and Putin's 'Cultural Turn'. Eur Asia Stud 69 (2):348–366

Romashko T (2018) Biopolitics and hegemony in contemporary Russian cultural policy. Russian Politics 3(1):88–113

Romashko T (2019) Russian cultural policy: from European mode of governance towards conservative hegemony. In: Hoffmann T, Makarychev A (eds) The EU and Russia: spaces of interaction in times of crisis. Routledge, London, pp 27–51

Ross C (2015) State against civil society: contentious politics and the non-systemic opposition in Russia. Eur Asia Stud 67(2):171–176

Russian Constitution (1993, December 25) Rossiiskaya Gazeta (trans: Garant-Service). Moscow: Garant-Internet. http://www.constitution.ru/en/10003000-01.htm. Accessed 3 November 2018

Russian Government (1996) Federal Law № 7 'on non-commercial organisations'. Consultant. http://www.consultant.ru/document/cons_doc_LAW_8824/. Accessed 1 November 2018

Russian Government (2004) Federal Law № 122 'on introducing changes in legislative acts of the Russian Federation and annulment of certain legislative acts of the Russian Federation in connection with adoption of Federal laws "about modification and additions in the Federal law "on General principles of organization of legislative (representative) and Executive state authorities of constituent entities of the Russian Federation" and "about General principles of organization of local self-government in the Russian Federation" (with changes and additions)'. Garant-Internet. http://base.garant.ru/12136676/. Accessed 1 November 2018
Russian Government (2005a) Federal Law № 94 'about placement of orders for deliveries of goods, performance of works, rendering of services for the state and municipal needs'. Consultant. http://www.consultant.ru/document/cons_doc_LAW_54598/. Accessed 12 November 2018
Russian Government (2005b) Decision № 833 'on the federal target programme "Russian language (2006–2010)"'. http://fcp.economy.gov.ru/cgi-bin/cis/fcp.cgi/Fcp/ViewFcp/View/2010/189/. Accessed 3 November 2018
Russian Government (2011) Official review № 2.12–17/1045 'on the draft Federal Law № 617570–5 "on culture in the Russian Federation"', introduced by deputies of the State Duma E. G. Drapeko, Z. M. Stepanova and G. P. Ivliev [Официальный отзыв № 2.12–17/1045 от 2 ноября 2011 г. на проект федерального закона № 617570–5 'О культуре в Российской Федерации', внесенный депутатами Государственной Думы Е.Г. Драпеко, З.М. Степановой и Г.П. Ивлиевым]. Moscow: Kremlin
Russian Government (2013) Federal Law № 63 'on amendments to the law of the Russian Federation "Fundamentals of the legislation of the Russian Federation on culture"'. Kremlin, Moscow
Russian Government (2015) Instructions 'on the enforcement of the orders of the President of Russia on the results of the joint meeting of the State Council and the presidential Council for Culture and Art'. http://government.ru/orders/selection/404/16718/. Accessed 2 October 2018
Russian Government (2016) Decision № 326-R 'strategy of the state cultural policy'. http://static.government.ru/media/files/AsA9RAyYVAJnoBuKgH0qEJA9IxP7f2xm.pdf. Accessed 10 November 2018
Russian President (2006) Decree № 1488 'on holding the Year of Russian language'. Moscow: Kremlin. http://kremlin.ru/acts/bank/24798. Accessed 2 October 2018
Russian President (2007) Decree № 796 'on the foundation of the Russkiy Mir Foundation'. Moscow: Kremlin. http://kremlin.ru/acts/bank/25689. Accessed 15 October 2018
Russian President (2014) Decree № 808 'on the approval of the foundations of state cultural policy'. Moscow: Kremlin. http://kremlin.ru/acts/bank/39208. Accessed 15 October 2018
Russian President (2015, December 31) Decree № 683 'on the Strategy of National Security of the Russian Federation'. Rossiiskaya Gazeta. https://rg.ru/2015/12/31/nac-bezopasnost-site-dok.html. Accessed 1 November 2018
Russian Supreme Council (1992) Federal Law № 3612–1 'Fundamentals of Russian Legislation on Culture'. Consultant. http://www.consultant.ru/document/cons_doc_LAW_1870/. Accessed 15 October 2018
State Dumas Committee of Culture (2018, April 10) Resolution № 3851–7 GD 'on rejection of the Bill № 617570–5'. System of Ensuring Legislative Activity of the State Automated System. https://sozd.duma.gov.ru/bill/617570-5. Accessed 2 September 2018
Surkov V (2006, November 20) Nationalization of the future: paragraphs pro Sovereign democracy. Expert 43(537). https://expert.ru/expert/2006/43/nacionalizaciya_buduschego/. Accessed 15 October 2018
Suslov M (2018) Russian world' concept: post-Soviet geopolitical ideology and the logic of 'spheres of influence. Geopolitics 23(2):330–353
Turgaev A, Vostryakov L, Brezhneva V (eds) (2017) Textbook fundamentals of the state cultural policy of the Russian Federation. Ministry of Culture, Moscow-SPb
Turoma S, Ralitainen S, Trubina E (2018) At the intersection of globalisation and 'civilisational originality': cultural production in Putin's Russia. Cult Stud 32(5):651–675

Vostryakov L, Turgaev A (2018) New model of state cultural policy of Russia. Bull State Univ Cult St Petersburg 2(36):6–16

Yatsyk A (2019) Russian world(s) in Vienna: agents, compatriots, and people. In: Hoffmann T, Makarychev A (eds) The EU and Russia: spaces of interaction in times of crisis. Routledge, London, pp 71–90

Tatiana Romashko is a grant researcher and a doctoral student at the University of Jyväskylä. The scope of her interests is composed of Russian cultural policy and Finnish–Russian cross-border relations. Tatiana has extensive experience in teaching. She came to the University of Jyväskylä in 2017 from Russia in response to an invitation to teach on the Master's Programme in Cultural Policy. Before that, Tatiana worked as a senior lecturer at Herzen University and other various universities of St. Petersburg in Russia.

Chapter 9
Manifestos of Rupture and Reconciliation: Do-it-Yourself (DiY) Music Practices, Ethics and the Quest for Authenticity in the Cultural Industries

Evangelos Chrysagis

Abstract This chapter considers three manifestos by UK-based music promoters and record labels that had influenced the ideas and practices of my interlocutors in Glasgow at the time of my ethnographic fieldwork on Do-it-Yourself (DiY) music practices (2010–2011). In exploring these statements, I highlight their function: what do these manifestos do, and how? I focus on the content of the statements, their formal qualities and the rhetorical techniques used by the authors. In doing so, I underscore the ways in which these texts project a matrix of ethical values pertinent to work in creative economies and convey an underlying quest for authentic conduct in the cultural industries. In an era when creativity has come to signify an economic asset framing market-oriented discourses, the three statements demonstrate that DiY stands as a useful example of an ethical and authentic mode of self-expression. They further show that contemporary manifestos may still retain the passionate rhetoric and revolutionary sensibilities of avant-garde manifestos, but in many instances they seek to reconcile the tension between creativity and commerce in the cultural industries.

Keywords Manifestos · Do-it-Yourself (DiY) · Ethics · Authenticity · Conduct · Etiquette

> What interests me about the manifesto is that it's a defunct format . . . For that very reason it's compelling . . . Things that don't work have great potential.
>
> (McCarthy cited in Obrist 2010, 63)

E. Chrysagis (✉)
University of Edinburgh, Edinburgh, UK

I. Kiriya et al. (eds.), *The Industrialization of Creativity and Its Limits*, Science, Technology and Innovation Studies, https://doi.org/10.1007/978-3-030-53164-5_9

9.1 Introduction

At a time when many regard the manifesto as a thing of the past, others see 'a new boom time for the manifesto' (Reynolds 2001, n.p.). While this might be true, especially owing to the visibility offered by the Internet, the golden era of popular music manifestos seems to be long gone (Bemrose 2015; Jelbert 2010; Kingsmill 2014; Mankowski 2017). However, music practitioners still passionately pen manifestos, and certain scholars have explored their rhetorical strategies and the texts' relationship to political manifestos and the avant-garde. Brian Fauteux (2012), for instance, examines a manifesto by the Swedish punk/hardcore band Refused in relation to the LP album in which it appeared. Fauteux exposes the links between music, art and politics in the manifesto by discussing its central themes of 'class and cultural hierarchies', 'media ownership in the cultural industries' and 'reclaim[ing] art and culture for the people', among others (ibid., 467).

Building on Fauteux's insights, this chapter considers three manifestos by UK-based music promoters and record labels: London's Upset The Rhythm, Bradford-based Obscene Baby Auction and Glasgow's now-defunct Nuts and Seeds. As I shall demonstrate, all three music actors had influenced the ideas and practices of my interlocutors in Glasgow at the time of my ethnographic fieldwork on Do-it-Yourself (DiY) music practices (2010–2011). While the politicised nature of the manifesto by Refused can find a parallel in these statements, I am mainly interested in highlighting their function: that is, what do these manifestos *do*, and *how*? To this effect, I focus on the content of the statements, their formal qualities and the rhetorical techniques used by the authors. In doing so, I underscore the ways in which these texts project a matrix of ethical values pertinent to work in creative economies and convey an underlying quest for authentic conduct in the cultural industries. Despite the writers' ambivalence towards the term 'DiY', I suggest that the ethos and the forms of conduct they describe are firmly embedded within the tradition of DiY music-making.

Another form of authenticity at play here is the authenticity of the statements *as* manifestos. According to Janet Lyon, 'to write a manifesto is to participate symbolically in a history of struggle against dominant forces' (1999, 4). The three texts demonstrate that contemporary manifestos may still retain the passionate rhetoric and revolutionary sensibilities of avant-garde manifestos, but in many instances they employ forms of expression that seek to reconcile the tension between creativity and commerce in the cultural industries. This reflects the fact that the manifesto as a genre has been constantly evolving alongside capitalism and its own history of transformation (Puchner 2002, 452–453).

In the remainder of the chapter, I first provide an ethnographic overview of the relationship between the three music actors and my Glasgow-based research participants. Then I turn to the history of the manifesto to trace the 'manifestic' qualities of a text, which will enable me to embed the statements by Upset The Rhythm,

Obscene Baby Auction and Nuts and Seeds within the history of the genre.[1] The content of the statements is analysed in a subsequent section, which culminates in the final part of the chapter. There, I argue that the three manifestos delineate particular forms of etiquette, and that we can evaluate these modes of conduct as both ethical and authentic.

9.2 Ethnographic Context

During my fieldwork on DiY music-making, I closely followed the creative practices of Cry Parrot, a live music promoter, and Winning Sperm Party, a record label that also hosted music events. Both actors, alongside the noise-rock band Divorce, became valuable case studies (Chrysagis 2016, 2017, 2019). Cry Parrot regarded Upset The Rhythm, which started putting on gigs in 2003 and releasing records in 2005, as 'the point of reference for DiY music in the UK'. Cry Parrot looked up to the London-based promoter, and would regularly host musicians from the latter's record label, such as John Maus and PLUG (ibid. 2017, 141–142). Upset The Rhythm's manifesto, published on its dedicated website, demonstrated that it had managed to transcend the localism usually associated with DiY music, and that was particularly appealing to Cry Parrot.

Winning Sperm Party, on the other hand, had suggested that Andy Abbott, an artist, writer and musician based in West Yorkshire, would be 'a good person to talk to about DiY'. Abbott was in a band from Leeds called That Fucking Tank, and Winning Sperm Party had hosted the band for gigs in Glasgow in the past. He was also a founding member of Obscene Baby Auction, a Leeds-based music collective and record label that was set up in 2001 and later moved by Abbott to Bradford. I was told that Obscene Baby Auction and Winning Sperm Party were 'similar' but, while Abbott was outspoken and articulate about his ideas on DiY activity, Winning Sperm Party was reluctant to put forward a specific agenda in relation to DiY (Chrysagis 2019, 7). It was clear that Abbott had influenced both their attitude towards DiY and their approach to practical matters, such as refraining from live music activities on weekdays and concentrating on weekends to ensure a better audience turnout. While I did not have the opportunity to meet Abbott during fieldwork, his manifesto 'On "DIY"' provides a glimpse into the views that informed the practice of Obscene Baby Auction.

Abbott also collaborated with members of Nuts and Seeds. In fact, Giles Bailey, who went on to form Nuts and Seeds in Glasgow when he moved there from Leeds in the autumn of 2002 to study at the Glasgow School of Art (GSA), was a co-founder of Obscene Baby Auction, along with Abbott and Shakeeb

[1]The relationship between manifestos and *parrhesia*—the manifesto's 'passion for truth-telling' (Lyon 1999, 14)—requires extensive treatment that cannot be accommodated in the present chapter.

Abu-Hamdan.[2] Nuts and Seeds became active in late 2002, and Bailey, who initially ran Nuts and Seeds on his own, would occasionally receive requests from touring bands playing in Leeds to book them for gigs in Glasgow (Lowndes 2010, 401). Gradually, Nuts and Seeds evolved into a music collective that comprised several GSA students. The collective released records in addition to putting on music events, but its prolific activity came to an end when core members, including Bailey, decided to move out of Scotland. This happened shortly after my fieldwork began, but the influence of Nuts and Seeds was already apparent in younger music actors such as Winning Sperm Party and Cry Parrot. Such was the impact of Nuts and Seeds on Glasgow's DiY music network that Cry Parrot was initially known as 'Junior Nuts and Seeds' (Chrysagis 2017, 143). As I will show, Nuts and Seeds had laid out their ideas and intentions in a succinct statement originally published on their MySpace page. Their manifesto reflects attitudes that both Cry Parrot and Winning Sperm Part subsequently endorsed as DiY music promoters.

9.3 What Is a Manifesto?

Before delving into the three statements, a brief overview of the manifesto genre is required to identify its formal characteristics. Contrary to its common association with revolutionary politics and subversion that emerged with Marx and Engels' *Communist Manifesto*, the manifesto (from the Latin *manifestare*—to reveal, make visible) initially constituted a form of communication for the ruling classes, such as the state and clergy, to make their decisions known. While such declarations were rooted in unquestioned forms of authority, thus immediately leading to action, '[t]he revolutionary manifesto will break the conjunction of authority, speech, and action … and instead create a genre that must usurp an authority it does not yet possess' (Puchner 2006, 12). As Martin Puchner argues, there was also 'a second lineage within the prehistory of the manifesto, one that derives from the religious practice of revelation or manifestation' (ibid.).

From its religious meaning of divine revelation and the declarations by those in power to make their intentions publicly known to political statements and the avant-garde texts of the twentieth century, the history of the manifesto shows that its definition has been a retrospective one. Indeed, 'most texts that are now, post-Marx, called manifesto did not label themselves in this way' (ibid.). The manifesto emerges as 'an extremely plural and open form' (Yanoshevsky 2009, 263), 'an alternative genre' that 'can *always* be redefined' (Caws 2001, xxviii). Lyon claims that attempting to produce 'a definitive profile of "the manifesto," … would be sharply

[2]See http://www.yvonnecarmichael.com/obscenebabyauction/index.php/a-history/2/. Accessed 15 October 2019.

limiting', because 'it would obscure the particular historical conditions that make possible ideological readings of individual manifestoes', and would disregard the fact that 'the term "manifesto" has itself taken on wide valences in our culture' (1999, 12). Laura Winkiel further reminds us that we should perceive the manifesto as a transnational genre, which can help us trace the 'uneven developments of modernity worldwide' (2008, 7).

Despite its open-ended and ever-changing form, it *is* possible to point towards specific characteristics of the manifesto—the 'manifestic' qualities of a text—and how it exerts its force and authority. The list is not exhaustive, however, and these elements can take many different forms. For Puchner (2002, 2006), manifestos exhibit a tension between 'performativity' and 'theatricality'. Following J. L. Austin, he observes that political manifestos engage in performative utterances that effect change. By contrast, avant-garde manifestos—which constitute a transition from the political function of manifestos to an artistic one that still retains its political resonance—relied on theatricality for their efficacy, such as hyperbolic speech and a mode of delivery that suited avant-garde venues. Yet, as Puchner explains, to some extent, both types of manifestos mobilised performative and theatrical components in their effort to assert their authority. Additional features are 'a moment of rupture', the 'enumeration of grievances' and the manifesto's 'epigrammatic style' (Lyon 1999, 3). To these we could add the manifesto's 'versatility', 'violent position' and 'a flagrant commanding relationship ... between its producer and his or her audience' (Yanoshevsky 2009, 261, 263). Manifestos delineate two further relationships: they conjure up an identity for the writer(s) in relation to an explicitly defined or implicitly conceived 'other' (Lyon 1999, 16), and this identity is reinforced by the use of the pronoun 'we', serving to legitimise the positions expressed in manifestos (ibid., 23–26). Considering that most contemporary manifestos are products of private rather than collective endeavours (Puchner 2002, 455), the use of 'we' appears to be highly controversial—indeed 'an inherently colonizing construction' (Lyon 1999, 26). Another formal property of manifestos is what Lyon terms 'a resounding invocation of an apocalyptic present tense' that incites to action *now* (ibid., 30). For Puchner, the history of the manifesto after the *Communist Manifesto* has been characterised by such 'impatience': 'the attempt to undo the distinction between speech and action, between words and the revolution' (2006, 22), or as Mary Ann Caws writes, 'between what has been done and what will be done, between the accomplished and the potential' (2001, xxi). The rupture with the past and a sense of urgency in embracing the new are particularly prominent in modernist avant-garde texts. As Winkiel points out, such a break reflected a 'Eurocentric notion of history that sees it advancing unproblematically forward, steadily improving' (2008, 7), which was very different from the perception of history in colonial contexts.

What is the purpose of writing a manifesto in the contemporary moment, when the genre is considered obsolete, a relic of modernism and a 'defunct format', according to the epigraph? To argue that writing a manifesto in the twenty-first century is a retroactive gesture resulting in a 'late capitalist-pastiche' is highly problematic, because 'it presumes, by implication, a genuine, authentic manifesto that precedes this pastiche' (Puchner 2002, 455), but Puchner's careful examination of avant-garde manifestos shows that such a 'pure' manifesto does not exist. 'Writing manifestoes', Luca Somigli notes, 'remains a privileged way for dissenting or marginalized voices to speak out, to affirm their presence, to reach out to like-minded individuals and invite them to band together for a common cause' (2003, 22). In what follows, I discuss the statements by Upset The Rhythm, Obscene Baby Auction and Nuts and Seeds, emphasising the manifesto's contemporary significance, its evolving form and the ways in which the three statements have been shaped by the history of the genre.

9.4 What Is in a Manifesto?

9.4.1 Upset the Rhythm

About Us[3]

Upset The Rhythm is a record label and live music promoter based in London, UK. Since 2003, we've been interested in developing a program of eclectic, innovative and thought-provoking music events across the capital. During this time we've enjoyed working with musicians from all over the world, including defining shows for Omar Souleyman, Asiq Nargile, Islam Chipsy and Group Doueh, alongside concerts for more well known acts like Sleaford Mods, Future Islands, Deerhoof, Wolf Eyes and Oneohtrix Point Never. Committed to breaking down barriers between musicians and audiences, Upset The Rhythm has worked with many exciting performers from all walks of life, from hosting the excellent, learning-disabled hiphop group The Fish Police to debuting the electrifying field recordings, jazz sax and poetry of Matana Roberts. We like working with artists of all ages, nationalities, abilities and genders who gather loosely under the umbrella of 'experimental music', as this takes us closer to what makes music most transformative and inspiring.

To date Upset The Rhythm has put on over 800 shows, with some of the largest being two sold out dates at London's Hippodrome, headlined by Sunn O))) and Liars, as part of the live music program for the 2006 Frieze Art Fair. The following year we set up one of WIRE Magazine's 25th birthday parties, whilst 2008 saw us host a label showcase at the SXSW festival (Austin, Texas) featuring John Maus, Lucky Dragons, Death Sentence: Panda!, No Age and High Places. We've since held similar UTR label parties in New York, Los

(continued)

[3]Statement retrieved from http://www.upsettherhythm.co.uk/about.shtml. Accessed 15 October 2019.

Angeles and San Francisco, as well as all across the UK. Over the years Upset The Rhythm has been lucky enough to collaborate with many art galleries on events including our YES WAY festival of UK music and art (with Auto Italia South East, 2009–2011), John Maus at the Serpentine Gallery, Lucky Dragons at SPACE and most recently with Artsadmin on their London takeover of Mons' 'Capital of Culture' celebrations (2014). 2010 found us working with artist David Shrigley on his 'Worried Noodles' charity event at The Scala, headlined by Hot Chip. 'Spaghetti Tree', a weekend event at Peckham's Bussey Building coinciding with April Fools Day headlined by No Age and Dan Deacon, followed in 2012. Whilst 2013 saw us focus our attentions on 'Yard Party', a three-day music festival in a theatre in Hackney Wick encompassing an assortment of acts, from the sublime folk guitar stylings of Michael Chapman to the industrial world-techno of Cut Hands.

2015 proved to be our busiest year yet, most notably setting up a multiple site-specific residency for underground music legend Richard Youngs in Tower Hamlets, involving the Balfron Tower and Mile End Ecology Pavilion. We also spent the year curating a series of rare one-off performances from '1980s music visionaries' involving Martin Newell, Rose McDowall, Maximum Joy, Normil Hawaiians and The Space Lady. 2015, also saw UTR host Future Islands for two swiftly, sold-out shows at The Roundhouse following on from their breakthrough year. However, Upset The Rhythm is also very much dedicated to London's more intimate, DIY and experimental venues. However small or large the show is it remains meaningful that each event has a tailored quality to it, with the aesthetic being just so, delivering a high quality experience. Our ideas for curating events are only limited by our collective imagination and two good examples of notable approaches include organising an a cappella ensemble performance on the roof of a Norman tower as well as a future-facing a/v quad-sound electronics performance in a disused car show room. Turning unusual spaces into one-off music venues is another of our keen interests and sees us putting on events in buildings as diverse as tin tabernacles to community centres.

Our record label began in the summer of 2005 as a natural extension of the friendships we make through our live shows. The label is another way for the artists we enjoy working with to exercise their creative freedom and for us to lend our support. So far we have released in excess of 80 records, with artists as different as John Maus and Pega Monstro. We've also been tirelessly keen to reflect the UK's own abundance of DIY music, working with bands like Sauna Youth, Trash Kit and The Pheromoans on multiple releases. Last year also saw us begin a reissue project with 80s outsider punks Normil Hawaiians to much fanfare. Our releases are available digitally, as well as on LP, CD, 10″ and 7″ and we find ourselves fortunate enough to have our records distributed throughout the world courtesy of SRD. Where we can, we work with other like-minded promoters to organise European tours for the artists on our label and for bands we are particularly passionate about.

(continued)

Statement of Intent

With both our live shows and our records, we provide a platform for an array of artists from the international underground, whilst showcasing and supporting the UK's own fertile musical community.

We are a collective that is passionate about exciting and interesting music, and we enjoy working with the musicians that we love.

We hope to put on shows that are thoughtful, fun and enjoyable for both the audience and the performer.

We treat both our artists and our audience with respect - paying musicians well, keeping ticket prices comparatively low, and ensuring profits from individual shows or records are used to fund future ventures.

Upset The Rhythm would not exist without the artists we work with or our audience, to both we are eternally grateful.

Upset The Rhythm had managed to build an international following and establish relationships with a wide range of music actors in the UK and overseas. In the eloquently written statement this is reflected by the explicit aim to host bands 'from all over the world', an ethical commitment to inclusivity ('breaking down barriers between musicians and audiences ... working with artists of all ages, nationalities, abilities and genders') and the experimentation with different music genres ('We like working with artists ... who gather loosely under the umbrella of "experimental music"') and venues ('Turning unusual spaces into one-off music venues is another of our keen interests').

Upset The Rhythm's prolific output seemingly contrasts with the conventions of DiY music and the assertion that grassroots sociality, friendship and personal relations are the core values pervading the collective's practices. In the 'About Us' section, Upset The Rhythm does not *explicitly* identify with 'DiY', which is only mentioned twice in the text. The term is never associated with the authors but with 'venues' and 'music' in general ('Upset The Rhythm is also very much dedicated to London's more intimate, DIY and experimental venues'; 'We've also been tirelessly keen to reflect the UK's own abundance of DIY music'). The writers seem to recognise this tension in the middle of the third paragraph, where they introduce their commitment to DiY with a sharp contrast after recounting several commercially successful endeavours: '*However*, Upset The Rhythm is also very much dedicated ...' (emphasis added). Drawing a distinction between DiY music venues and 'sold-out shows at The Roundhouse' might be intuitive, but it also means that Upset The Rhythm's view of DiY music appears to be associated with smallness, locality and obscurity. Eventually, the distinction is replaced by a focus on 'quality' ('However small or large the show is it remains meaningful that each event has a tailored quality to it ... delivering a high quality experience').

The ambivalent stance towards DiY disappears in the 'Statement of Intent', which outlines Upset The Rhythm's modus operandi. Passion for music and a strong focus on ethics ('We are a collective that is passionate about exciting and interesting music'; 'We treat both our artists and our audience with respect') create a rupture with established commercial music practices—hence the detailed explanation regarding financial arrangements ('paying musicians well, keeping ticket prices comparatively low, and ensuring profits from individual shows or records are used to fund future ventures'). Here, the 'other' is not explicitly defined in the text, but implied by what Upset the Rhythm is *not*.

Returning to the 'About Us' section, it can be argued that name-dropping and the brief descriptions of past music events detailing Upset The Rhythm's numerous collaborations constitute self-promotion. Surely manifestos cannot accommodate any form of advertisement at their core? Yet what would it mean to conceive of 'advertisement perhaps not the absolute perversion of the manifesto, but only its latest transformation?' (Puchner 2002, 455). Indeed, self-promotion has been a well-honed strategy even for early avant-garde manifestos. As Puchner notes, 'futurist and other manifestos frequently borrowed techniques from advertisement to perfect the art of calling attention to themselves. A tendency toward advertisement, we must acknowledge, has been part of the manifesto since its adaptation by the avant-garde in the early twentieth century' (ibid., 460). To assume that Upset The Rhythm's manifesto is not *really* a manifesto because of its self-promotional dimension stumbles upon the fact that such techniques were already present in avant-garde texts that largely epitomised the formal characteristics of the manifesto genre.

Simultaneously promoting DiY music and keeping it at arm's length is in itself an advertisement strategy: it allows Upset The Rhythm to avoid the stigma of amateurism associated with the term 'DiY' (see also Chrysagis 2017, 149–151), thus enabling the collective to host bigger events. At the same time, it helps Upset The Rhythm accumulate 'subcultural capital' (Thornton 1995) through its association with national and international DiY music networks. As we have seen, implicitly admitting the uneasy coexistence between commercial and DiY music has not prevented the writers from trying to reconcile this tension by recourse to 'quality'. Rhetorically, this is achieved through the deployment of an agreeable tone and moderate language, which differ considerably from the militant positions and exaggerated style of avant-garde manifestos.

9.4.2 *Obscene Baby Auction*

On 'DIY'[4]

Loath as I am to put forward a definition of DIY in the fear that it might be interpreted as an attempt to fix its meaning, I feel it necessary to write a few

(continued)

[4]Statement retrieved from http://www.yvonnecarmichael.com/obscenebabyauction/index.php/on-diy/. Accessed 15 October 2019.

words here on the nature of activity that Obscene Baby Auction engages in, supports and with which it shares some affinity. This is particularly pressing in the current context (2011) where 'DIY' as a term has, some would have it, been successfully recuperated and co-opted by state and market forces alike (see David Cameron's 'Big Society', the substitution of 'indie' for 'DIY' in gip-inducing style mags/blogs and so on). For me the term is worth defending and still has some potency but only with a few qualifiers.

When I talk of DIY/self-organised/independent/underground/non-capitalist activity I'm referring to activity done for love not money; that is, not as a means to an end, or a stepping-stone in a project of self-advancement. Rather, I am thinking of a pursuit that is engaged in for the sheer pleasure of doing the thing. It should be quite clear that this activity is a world apart from the entrepreneurial or careerist logic that underpins a lot of so-called DIY endeavours where doing something independently, not-for-profit, or for oneself is understood purely as a necessary first stage on the road to 'making it'. This latter form of pragmatism ("No-one else is going to do it for me so I'll make my own destiny") is the starting point from which a lot of 'radical' DIY activity can emerge, but a break with capitalist desires that instigate it is required in order to avoid simply reinforcing the neoliberal, competitive, market-led narrative of our times.

The fact of the matter is that DIY activity when engaged in for its own sake is more fun and more pleasurable than profit-motivated pursuits and opens up a world of possibilities that would normally remain foreclosed. Clearly, playing or enjoying music in 'autonomous' spaces and trying to create more inclusive, accessible and 'authentic' arenas in which music can be appreciated is not, alone, going to change the world. It can, however, offer a glimpse of an alternative to the individualist, cut-throat, and ultimately alienating and boring world of business-as-usual.

This rupture in the ideology that has been ingrained in those of us that have been through the state education and work system—where we are told that if you are good at or enjoy something then the logical step is to specialise in that field in order to compete to make money from it is of no small significance but happens all the time, often unrecognised or overlooked. It can happen when a group of friends get together and make food to share freely with one another, or when a collective form a band just to make some noise and hang out together, or when a party is thrown for the hell of it. The list goes on.

The rupture is not exclusively but infinitely more likely to occur in collective experiences of 'doing together' and, when taken seriously and shown fidelity to, opens up onto a horizon of new possibilities that infer a total upheaval in the political and economic landscape in which we currently operate. As such, 'real' DIY activity is antagonistic to capitalism, not always in the sense that it directly opposes it, but that it does without and creates an

(continued)

alternative within and beyond it, and in so doing challenges capitalism's purported totalisation or all-pervasiveness.

So, it is my conviction that for all its lifestyle politics and indulgent shortcomings (the fact that it is based in having a good time and is often not just a little cliquey) DIY music is a political project and one worth discussing in such terms. There is a responsibility in the current climate for us to recognise, unpick, complicate, experiment with and progress the radical qualities of DIY activity. The alternative is that it gets swamped in a wave of empty and market-oriented rhetoric and becomes the next in a succession of labels such as 'rock and roll', 'counter culture', 'punk' or 'indie' to be drained of most if not all of its potency and fed back to us as a consumable and harmless aesthetic to try on and discard next week when tastes change.

In order to resist this age-old cycle of recuperation it is necessary to keep DIY 'moving', to not allow it to settle in to a comfortable, congratulatory and uncritical self-perception nor to calcify in tried and tested 'safe' spaces, yet at the same time to recognise what is special or unique about it and to defend and build on its assets, to create blockages and manifestations that can resonate with other non-capitalist experiments in fields beyond weird and sometimes noisey rock music. Of utmost importance, though, is to have fun doing it.

Andy Abbott, 2011

Further Reading

Karl Marx—Capital
Raoul Vaneigem—The Revolution of Everyday Life
Hardt and Negri—Commonwealth
Richard JF Day—Gramsci is Dead
John Holloway—Crack Capitalism
The Free Association—Moments of Excess

The text has all the formal characteristics of a manifesto: it creates a sense of urgency, with a focus on the present ('This is particularly pressing in the current context'), while inciting to action in order to salvage DiY and defend its true meaning, which has 'been successfully recuperated and co-opted by state and market forces alike'—identified here as the 'other'. Later on in the statement, two paragraphs begin with a reference to 'rupture', a sine qua non of manifestos ('This rupture in the ideology that has been ingrained in those of us that have been through the state education and work system'; 'The rupture is not exclusively but infinitely more likely to occur in collective experiences of "doing together"').

It must be noted that the focus on DiY and the fact that the manifesto was written exclusively by Abbott means that the text is not about Obscene Baby Auction per se. This is clear enough from the title. Defending the term, then, entails bringing into view the manifold practices and initiatives already taking place under the rubric of 'DiY'.

Still, passionately advocating an idea that has not yet taken on specific meaning runs the risk of facilitating rather than foreclosing the process of co-optation, although rhetorically the manifesto attempts to do the exact opposite. For instance, in the second paragraph, DiY is conflated with other terms without explanation ('When I talk of DIY/self-organised/independent/underground/non-capitalist activity'). One is left wondering how this is radically different from 'the substitution of "indie" for "DIY" in gip-inducing style mags/blogs', mentioned earlier in the text as forming part of the current predicament, or how it prevents DiY from becoming 'the next in a succession of labels such as "rock and roll", "counter culture", "punk" or "indie" to be drained of most if not all of its potency'. To be sure, the context is different and Abbott *does* outline both the characteristics of 'authentic' DiY activity ('not as a means to an end'; 'a pursuit that is engaged in for the sheer pleasure of doing the thing'; 'independently, not-for-profit, or for oneself') and some of its shortcomings ('lifestyle politics'; 'having a good time'; 'not just a little cliquey'), but a great deal of other ventures not labelled 'DiY' would fit these descriptions. What needed further elaboration is the final sentence, in which the author, seemingly contradicting his criticism about DiY's self-indulgence, claims that: 'Of utmost importance, though, is to have fun doing it'. The focus on lived experience, I believe, is a dimension of DiY practice that cannot be replicated and commodified. As George McKay puts it, DiY 'is predicated on such authenticity, such commitment, such rooted realness of action' (1998a, 32).

In this sense, a manifesto on DiY that constitutes 'an attempt to fix its meaning' would be a paradox. The text celebrates and passionately defends DiY, but Abbott recognises from the outset the need to avoid a static interpretation. This deliberate contradiction is consistent with the shifting nature of DiY practice, but also resonates with early avant-garde, which that presented themselves as manifestos proper, while simultaneously critiquing and subverting the genre's conventions. The example par excellence is Tristan Tzara's *Dada Manifesto 1918*, which is written in manifesto form but, in it, Tzara declares that 'in principle I am against manifestos, as I am also against principles' (Danchev 2011, 137). We can say that *On DiY* is a manifesto that 'oscillates between continuing to be a manifesto and becoming a parody of one' (Puchner 2002, 460).

9.4.3 Nuts and Seeds

About us[5]

The door prices are kept affordable and the bands are paid well in order to support a sustainable and ethical network for live music. Costs are kept low

(continued)

[5]Statement retrieved from http://www.myspace.com/nutsseeds. Accessed 27 May 2012.

> and bands are fed, paid and given a decent place to sleep. All the money made on the door goes to covering costs and paying the bands and consequently there are no guest lists. Every effort is made to keep music inclusive, cheap, anti-elitist and fun. Nuts and Seeds frown upon the following: Attempts to enter gigs without paying the door fee (rarely in excess of 4 pounds) because you work for music press/a record label/music publishing organization etc. Deluded aspirations to major label stardom leaving the magnanimous and good willed trampled in your wake. Taking down our posters. Nuts and Seeds will not take down your posters.

Although the term 'DiY' is not mentioned anywhere in the statement, the text reads as a manifesto for organising DiY gigs. In typical manifesto fashion, Nuts and Seeds focuses on the critical juncture between here and now through the use of present tense and the highly personal tone of the final sentence ('Nuts and Seeds will not take down your posters'), targeting certain Glasgow-based commercial promoters and the practice of either taking down DiY posters or placing their own posters on top of them (Chrysagis 2016, 299–300).

The first part of the manifesto outlines the actual tasks involved in hosting touring bands and describes Nuts and Seeds' approach to live music ('affordable', 'sustainable' and 'ethical'; 'Costs are kept low and bands are fed, paid and given a decent place to sleep'). Financial transparency is also important: 'All the money made on the door goes to covering costs and paying the bands'. For Nuts and Seeds, music should be 'inclusive, cheap, anti-elitist and fun', despite the recognition that it is not always possible to keep it that way ('Every effort is made ...'). This agonistic dimension that leaves room for failure is overshadowed by the second part of the statement, with its highly critical tone and ethically charged attack to practices that Nuts and Seeds rejects outright. Entering gigs 'without paying the door fee', '[d]eluded aspirations to major label stardom' and '[t]aking down our posters' are all considered major transgressions. This is an intensely moral rupture with the practices of specific, commercially minded promoters, as well as bands and audience members who do not share the collective's ethos.

In less than 150 words Nuts and Seeds manages to sketch what is involved in putting on DiY gigs. Yet this is not an operational guide for music practitioners, such as *Don't Make a Scene* (2014), to which members of both Upset the Rhythm and Obscene Baby Auction, as well as Cry Parrot, contributed with relevant thoughts and advice. Rather, the manifesto describes appropriate behaviour for promoters, bands and audiences alike. Its highly critical tone, combined with the rhetorical use of hyperbole echoes the 'violence and precision' of early avant-garde manifestos (Perloff 1984). While Nuts and Seeds consisted of artists, the collective did not draw on the avant-garde notion of the manifesto as a performance that blurred the boundaries between art and criticism. Nevertheless, the polemical tone and theatricality of certain statements ('Deluded aspirations to major label stardom leaving the magnanimous and good willed trampled in your wake') find clear parallels in the history of the genre.

9.5 After the Manifesto

Upset The Rhythm's manifesto deploys a reconciliatory tone that encompasses both commercial practices and DiY music pursuits. The manifestos by Obscene Baby Auction and Nuts and Seeds, by contrast, perform a rupture with established practices, suggesting alternative ways of making and consuming music and novel ways of relating between music practitioners and audiences. All statements texts thus serve a double function, despite the common perception that 'artists' manifestos typically define themselves *against*. ... To specify what they are *for*, on the other hand, is a good deal more difficult' (Danchev 2011, xxv). As we have seen, the three texts embrace contradiction, and to some extent self-parody, but Fauteux argues that 'a sense of haste and carelessness is often an attribute of the manifesto, which may result in a confusion of the manifesto's political motives' (2012, 473). This is because art manifestos, although always political in some sense, are mainly geared towards creating a break with *aesthetic* practices, in the tradition of the avant-garde manifesto, which 'adapts this desire for a revolutionary event and imports it into the sphere of art' (Puchner 2002, 451).

Yet 'revolution'—the rupture that manifestos seek to impose—'raises questions about what follows this break' (Fauteux 2012, 477). As Puchner aptly notes, '[w]hile the manifesto often seeks to break with the status quo, it also tends to create a new dogma' (2002, 456). From the preceding section, it becomes apparent that an ethical and authentic behaviour in the cultural industries is the main theme running through the texts. If manifestos aim to establish a normative order, how can we accept that the forms of conduct outlined in the three statements are both ethical and authentic?

Behaviour that is informed by specific etiquette would seem to obscure the transparent relationship between what one 'does' and what one 'means', and is thus 'a barrier to authenticity' (Yeung 2010, 241). According to Shirley Yeung, rather than perceiving etiquette merely as calculated demeanour or deceptive performance, we could see it as the means by which individuals *acquire* the desired virtues that inform their conduct. This conduct will become 'natural' and 'authentic' through ongoing practice: 'I suggest that at the heart of a seemingly external etiquette lies, quite simply, ethics—that is, the imperative to align principle with habitual practice in bringing about, paradoxically, one's own virtue and sincerity through disciplined effort' (ibid., 243). This process holds 'the promise of both virtuous authenticity and authentic virtue' (ibid., 244). In principle, as a strict and teleological adherence to a set of guidelines, etiquette is inauthentic. As Yeung argues, however, etiquette involves a good deal of unpredictability, improvisation and judgement. To the extent that it engenders ethical sensibilities, etiquette presents an end in itself; then, one indeed 'means what one does' (ibid., 245).

The three manifestos conjure up authentic forms of behaviour that nurture ethical values in the context of cultural work, but they do not explain how these modes of conduct can be authenticated in relation to a diverse history of DiY in the cultural industries. Although there are many examples across different domains for current practitioners to draw on (e.g. Day 2017; Lowndes 2016; McKay 1998b), there is no coherent 'tradition' against which present practices can be verified and evaluated, which can also explain the authors' ambivalence towards the term 'DiY'. Perhaps, then, it would make no sense to refer to DiY as a form of 'tradition', because traditions are either readily verifiable by harking back to an original ideal or a modern fiction and invention (Hobsbawm and Ranger 1983). After all, the more one attempts to authenticate something with reference to a past ideal, the more likely it is that this will be a fake or pale imitation (Lindholm 2008, 20). Still, we could perceive tradition as a set of practices and discourses that link past and present, and which highlight forms of knowledge that animate and sustain these modalities into the present (Mahmood 2005, 113–117). Thus defined, DiY 'tradition' emerges as a form of *engagement* with DiY's practical and discursive constituents, rather than an unchanging structure or a set of rules. The orientation of the three manifestos towards the here-and-now but also the future-in-the-present does not excise the relevance of existing knowledge and experience. In other words, DiY tradition is sustained through the continuous adjustment and alignment of past practices in accord with present needs and concerns. 'Thinking with tradition', writes Anand Pandian, allows us to get 'a sense of the contemporary moment as rooted in the inherited forms of the past but also bearing the seeds of many possible futures' (2008, 477). As the Obscene Baby Auction manifesto states, the 'rupture' has already occurred—it 'happens all the time'.

Perceiving tradition as a repertoire of malleable practices and discourses that have present significance becomes particularly relevant to the reconsideration of the manifesto genre. The meaning of tradition as a continuum between past, present and future converts the manifesto from 'a genre of action' to 'a genre of reflection': many contemporary texts 'look backwards' and 'speak out for a return', bringing the classical manifesto's 'futurist performativity' into question (Puchner 2002, 453, 458). It follows that tracing the manifesto's evolution and transformation is key to the evaluation of contemporary texts *as* manifestos. Thus, what makes the three statements 'manifestos' has less to do with their capacity to faithfully reproduce specific features of avant-garde texts and more with their ability to embody the manifesto's distinctive and diverse lineage in a contemporary form.

9.6 Conclusion

In an era when creativity has come to signify an economic asset framing market-oriented discourses, the three manifestos demonstrate that DiY, despite the all-pervasiveness of capitalism, or maybe because of it, stands as a useful example of an ethical and authentic mode of self-expression. As Charles Lindholm puts it, 'the quest for a felt authentic grounding becomes increasingly pressing as certainty is eroded and the boundaries of the real lose their taken-for-granted validity' (2002, 337). The manifestos discussed in this chapter attest to an urgent need for a 'felt authentic grounding' in creative economies; a grounding that, for the most part, privileges collective experience over business models and individualistic aspirations.

For example, Nuts and Seeds were dedicated to supporting 'a sustainable and ethical network for live music'. Likewise, for Obscene Baby Auction, 'experiences of "doing together"' create 'a horizon of new possibilities', and '"real" DIY activity is antagonistic to capitalism, not always in the sense that it directly opposes it, but that it does without'. As Abbott further notes, though, DiY may have lost its powerful meaning, becoming a 'hip' term and, I would add, a byword for 'creativity' that conceals widespread problems faced by DiY practitioners in the cultural industries, such as financial precarity and self-exploitation (Threadgold 2018). As a result, DiY's explicit collaboration with capital emerges as a necessary evil for many artists operating in an increasingly alienating and competitive environment. The manifesto by Upset The Rhythm is a case in point, seeking to bridge the gap between DiY music practices and commercial objectives. Yet this is a false distinction, because it underplays the *intrinsic* relationship between DiY and the music industry:

> Although DIY music is often construed as "grassroots," I argue that its rituals and forms originate from within mainstream popular culture, and that DIY remains enthralled by music industries phenomena even as it attempts to bypass or reconfigure them. This results in specific tensions which are not only irresolvable but are fundamental to, and indeed constitutive of, DIY music. (Jones 2019, 1)

The fundamental link between DiY, media infrastructures and mainstream popular music demonstrates that what happens after the 'break' is not necessarily 'revolutionary'. To claim, however, that commercial strategies, such as self-advertisement, go against the subversive thrust of the three statements would disregard both the history of the manifesto and the fact that manifestos have been products of capitalism and its own history of change.

The three manifestos aim to foster authentic and ethical forms of behaviour that are consistent with the diverse history of DiY music practices, but one could argue that the statements raise the question of *who*, rather than *what*, 'is being authenticated' (Moore 2002, 210). In *The Ethics of Authenticity*, Charles Taylor proposes that '[t]he struggle ought not to be *over* authenticity, for or against, but *about* it, defining its proper meaning', which 'at its best'—when it expands ethical horizons beyond the self—'allows a richer mode of existence' (1991, 73–74). In this sense, the 'authenticity' of manifestos, of their authors and of DiY music practices becomes subservient to the forms of life they evoke, embody and make possible. Perhaps indulging in the collective pleasures of DiY *is* a richer, even radical, mode of existence. All three manifestos underscore the 'fun' dimension of music events: 'We hope to put on shows that are thoughtful, fun and enjoyable' (Upset The Rhythm); 'DIY activity when engaged in for its own sake is more fun and more pleasurable than profit-motivated pursuits' (Obscene Baby Auction); 'Every effort is made to keep music inclusive, cheap, anti-elitist and fun' (Nuts and Seeds). This is where we can grasp the essence of DiY: 'Of utmost importance', as Abbott exclaims, 'is to have fun doing it'.

References

Bemrose B (2015) Life lessons we can learn from music's great band manifestos. https://www.nme.com/blogs/nme-blogs/life-lessons-we-can-learn-from-musics-great-band-manifestos-761317. Accessed 15 October 2019

Caws MA (ed) (2001) Manifesto: a century of isms. University of Nebraska Press, Lincoln, NE

Chrysagis E (2016) The visible evidence of DiY ethics: music, publicity and technologies of (in)visibility in Glasgow. Vis Cult Br 17(3):290–310

Chrysagis E (2017) A sense of togetherness: music promotion and ethics in Glasgow. In: Chrysagis E, Karampampas P (eds) Collaborative intimacies in music and dance: anthropologies of sound and movement. Berghahn Books, Oxford, pp 139–160

Chrysagis E (2019) When means and ends coincide: on the value of DiY. J Cult Econ. https://doi.org/10.1080/17530350.2019.1646158

Danchev A (ed) (2011) 100 artists' manifestos: from the futurists to the stuckists. Penguin, London

Day A (ed) (2017) DIY utopia: cultural imagination and the remaking of the possible. Lexington Books, Lanham, MD

Don't make a scene: a field guide to putting on DIY gigs (2014) St. John R, Owl B (comps). http://www.robstjohn.co.uk/wp-content/uploads/2015/11/Dont-Make-a-Scene-2014.pdf. Accessed 15 October 2019

Fauteux B (2012) "New noise" versus the old sound: manifestos and *The Shape of Punk to Come*. Pop Music Soc 35(4):465–482

Hobsbawm E, Ranger T (eds) (1983) The invention of tradition. Cambridge University Press, Cambridge

Jelbert S (2010) We mean it, maaan!: the lost art of the pop manifesto. https://www.theguardian.com/music/2010/apr/29/pop-manifestos-manics-malcolm-mcclaren. Accessed 15 October 2019

Jones E (2019) DIY and popular music: mapping an ambivalent relationship across three historical case studies. Pop Music Soc. https://doi.org/10.1080/03007766.2019.1671112

Kingsmill K (2014) The lost initiative of a band manifesto. https://www.smh.com.au/entertainment/music/the-lost-initiative-of-a-band-manifesto-20140515-38bt2.html. Accessed 15 October 2019

Lindholm C (2002) Authenticity, anthropology, and the sacred. Anthropol Q 75(2):331–338

Lindholm C (2008) Culture and authenticity. Blackwell Publishing, Oxford

Lowndes S (2010) Social sculpture: the rise of the Glasgow art scene. Luath Press, Edinburgh

Lowndes S (2016) The DIY movement in art, music and publishing: subjugated knowledges. Routledge, New York, NY

Lyon J (1999) Manifestoes: provocations of the modern. Cornell University Press, Ithaca, NY

McKay G (1998a) DiY culture: notes towards an intro. In: McKay G (ed) DiY culture: party & protest in nineties Britain. Verso, London, pp 1–53

McKay G (ed) (1998b) DiY culture: party & protest in nineties Britain. Verso, London

Mahmood S (2005) Politics of piety: the Islamic revival and the feminist subject. Princeton University Press, Princeton, NJ

Mankowski G (2017) "Be pure, be vigilant, behave": what did post-punk manifestos aim to achieve? In: Dines M, Way L (eds) Postgraduate voices in punk studies: your wisdom, our youth. Cambridge Scholars Publishing, Newcastle upon Tyne, pp 25–40

Moore A (2002) Authenticity as authentication. Pop Music 21(2):209–223

Obrist HU (2010) Manifestos for the future. In: Aranda J, Wood BK, Vidokle A (eds) What is contemporary art? (e-flux journal). Sternberg Press, Berlin, pp 58–69

Pandian A (2008) Tradition in fragments: inherited forms and fractures in the ethics of South India. Am Ethnol 35(3):466–480

Perloff M (1984) 'Violence and precision': the manifesto as art form. Chic Rev 34(2):65–101

Puchner M (2002) Manifesto = theatre. Theatr J 54(3):449–465

Puchner M (2006) Poetry of the revolution: Marx, manifestos, and the avant-gardes. Princeton University Press, Princeton, NJ

Reynolds S (2001) Manifesto destiny. https://www.villagevoice.com/2001/05/15/manifesto-destiny-2/. Accessed 15 October 2019
Somigli L (2003) Legitimizing the artist: manifesto writing and European modernism 1885–1915. University of Toronto Press, Toronto
Taylor C (1991) The ethics of authenticity. Harvard University Press, Cambridge, MA
Thornton S (1995) Club cultures: music, media and subcultural capital. Polity Press, Cambridge
Threadgold S (2018) Creativity, precarity and illusio: DIY cultures and 'choosing poverty'. Cult Sociol 12(2):156–173
Winkiel L (2008) Modernism, race and manifestos. Cambridge University Press, Cambridge
Yanoshevsky G (2009) Three decades of writing on manifesto: the making of a genre. Poet Today 30(2):257–286
Yeung S (2010) Natural manners: etiquette, ethics, and sincerity in American conduct manuals. In: Lambek M (ed) Ordinary ethics: anthropology, language, and action. Fordham University Press, New York, NY, pp 235–248

Evangelos Chrysagis holds a PhD in social anthropology from the University of Edinburgh. His doctoral research explored the intersection of 'Do-it-Yourself' (DiY) music practices and ethics in Glasgow. Evangelos is co-editor of *Collaborative Intimacies in Music and Dance: Anthropologies of Sound and Movement* (Berghahn 2017), a book that examines music and dance from a cross-cultural perspective. His latest publication is an article for the *Journal of Cultural Economy*, entitled 'When means and ends coincide: on the value of DiY' (2019).

Part III
Industrialization: Creative Markets and Technologies

Chapter 10
Creative Industries, a Large Ongoing Project, Still Inaccurate and Always Uncertain

Bernard Miège

Abstract Though first developed in the mid-1990s, creative industries are still in their grand project stage. This chapter's central hypothesis is that lumping the creative and cultural industries into the same category cannot be regarded as more real or effective than the emergence of a single category, i.e., creative industries, as advertised by professionals, experts, and policy makers. While the constituent elements of the cultural industries are by now relatively well known, this is not yet the case for the creative industries, which remain highly heterogeneous. It is therefore possible to list the similarities and dissimilarities between these two industries and even to identify numerous structural differences between them, even as they still appear in 11 market segments drawn from the 27 member states of the European Union, the data of which were available in 2014. If we accept this, the quantitative pre-eminence of cultural industries is not about to end.

Keywords Communication industries · Creative industries · Cultural industries · Political economy of communication

10.1 Introduction

This chapter is linked to several years of individual and collective works related to the changes and essential mutations to informational and cultural industries (ICULT) due to the emergence and development of creative industries (ICREA).[1] In particular, this chapter is linked to the *The Industrialization of the Symbolic: Creative Industry Goods in the Context of Cultural Industries*, a 2013 book I wrote with Philippe Bouquillion and Pierre Moeglin. This chapter focuses on the continuous extension of the industrialization of new symbolic goods that are inserted or

[1]The author takes these abbreviations from the terms in French language.

B. Miège (✉)
Emeritus, Gresec, University Grenoble Alpes, Saint-Martin-d'Hères, France
e-mail: Bernard.Miege@univ-grenoble-alpes.fr

I. Kiriya et al. (eds.), *The Industrialization of Creativity and Its Limits*, Science, Technology and Innovation Studies, https://doi.org/10.1007/978-3-030-53164-5_10

aggregated into consumer goods. At the same time, it is necessary to indicate that most of my work as a researcher has focused on ICULT (Miège 1989, 2011a, b, 2017, 2018; Collectif 2012) and on the anchoring of information and communication technologies in contemporary societies.

I first point out why the study of ICREA remains difficult and complex, and then I discuss the differences that persist between ICULT and ICREA. At the end of this chapter, I raise the fundamental questions we should be asking today.

10.2 Twenty Years After its Launch, This Great Project Still Confounds

What is the source of the difficulties to understand the cultural and creative industries? To start with, the terms "major project," "great project," or "global project" were applied to large-scale programs in the late 1980s that were concerned with the computerization of companies and the development of telecommunications. These terms also learnt themselves to describing the prospects of the information superhighway of the mid-1990s.

Based on a technological component and increasingly organized a globalized context, often with the assistance of international organizations, these major projects succeeded one another. In their succession, they mobilized programs with variable potential in which the social, the cultural, and the communicational were directed by technology. However, technology was far from the main driving force behind these projects.

Having emerged two decades ago in Great Britain under specific conditions (with the objective being mainly the restructuring of industrial areas in deep economic decline), the idea of the major project first spread to other English-speaking countries, and has now spread across much of the planet but with goals that differ according to time and place. In very general terms, in Africa, for example, the emphasis is mostly on popular music, cultural tourism, and clothing. In India, it is on crafts. In China, it is on software. In Brazil, it is on architectural design. In European countries, it is on the expansion of luxury goods. Throughout the world, these projects are generally concerned with design, but they take varying approaches. Given that we live in a politically and economically pluralized world, this diversity is unsurprising.

Furthermore, international meetings and discussions between experts have been difficult to organize, and no global agreement yet exists on the list of activities associated with ICREA. There is therefore a great heterogeneity that characterizes ICREA, and sometimes these so-called industries have little to do with industrial production (there can, however, be synergies between neo-artisanal productions on a local basis). Despite this, we can admit that this is a global project, although predictably, it excludes the poorest countries.

Indeed, this politico-industrial project has been marked by the conjuncture of many disciplines and currents of thought. Initially, the superstars of the field were the liberal economists of culture, such as David Throsby (2001) or Richard E. Caves (2000), who are specialists in management science, and geographers, urban planners, and graphic designers. It is also necessary to consider the decisive role of internationally renowned experts and public thinkers of modernity in the ICT world, such as Henry Jenkins (2006), an expert on convergence, Richard Florida (2002), an expert on the creative class, Scott Lash and Celia Lury (2007), experts on global culture, and Jeremy Rifkin (2000), an expert on access and collaboration. Subsequently, the field has been influenced by authors that focused on the symbolic character of creative goods.

To be sure, finding coherence in this political, industrial, and cultural melting pot is a challenge. It is even more difficult to interpret the aims of the project's initiators as transversal, inter-sectorial, and focused on the local and the location of creative activities (we can think of, for instance, the label "creative cities"). For a single researcher such as myself, accounting for all these dimensions is impossible. Thus, my chapter departs from the political economy of communication (Mosco 1996), and I limit myself to the theoretical and methodological perspectives of information and communication studies.

From there, we must explore what it means for a project to be focused on the management of creativity. Creativity is a symbolic dimension long sought in many productive operations. It was motivated by psychological incentives enacted throughout the production process, for example, but with confusing results. With ICREA, the objective is to produce a category of goods that can be identified as creative from conception to consumption. The difficulty is that this recognition does not rest on clearly recognizable material characteristics (Bouquillion and Combès 2012). Hence, the importance given to the management and marketing of creative dimensions. We can argue that creative goods are those that are managed as such; this, as we shall see, is an essential difference they have with ICULT goods.

Other aspects also form part of the project. For instance, a certain amount of initiative is expected in creative work, as is the accentuation of its flexibility and the idea (real or simulated) of giving power to consumers, who are framed as "users." Together with Philippe Bouquillion, and Pierre Moeglin: (2013), I have shown that these different elements can be found in three paradigms that constitute industrialized symbolic goods. These paradigms are:

- The paradigm of creation (in which culture extends to all what is presented as creative).
- The paradigm of collaboration (in which individuals collaborate in creation).
- The paradigm of convergence (in which all content is equivalent).

Another fundamental feature of creative productions is their alignment with the digital economy. What is surprising is that ICREA is now largely connected to the development of digital techniques, which have been booming since the beginning of the present century but have different origins and driving forces. If the creative economy is now dealing with the digital economy, it is a mistake to confuse them and put them on the same level. The creative economy is, in fact, a little older than the digital economy; the social actors who propel it are different; and it is undoubtedly less dynamic. Further, digital platforms are only a secondary element in the exploitation of many creative products, such as in the arts and crafts and haute couture sectors.

In addition, a specific trait of creative products can be found at the center of the United Nation's agenda; this development dates back to the first decade of this century. Also, despite some procrastination, ICREA (increasingly confused with the creative economy) remains at the center of most nations' agendas, not just the most powerful. Creativity and culture clearly contribute to economic and social development, especially at the local level, as well as dialogue between peoples; this was the message of the 2013 *United Nations Creative Economy Report* published by UNE SCO. ICREA is also linked to a new post-2015 sustainable development agenda that recognizes the importance of culture as a catalyst and driver.

In Europe, culture represents an extensive economic asset and a valuable source of creativity and innovation. According to the European Parliament's 2016 report on European Union cultural and ICREA policies, cultural and creative industries have become high-capacity drivers for economic growth. Beyond their significant economic contribution, they have built a bridge between arts, culture, business, and technology, the potential of which remains poorly exploited. In turn, in Africa, U NESCO has undertaken training incentives to inform interested governments.

10.3 Persistent Differences Between ICREA and ICULT

These two categories are increasingly associated and even grouped together, which is a way of insisting on what they have in common and even imposing the idea of a unified category. Yet, they remain dissimilar (Table 10.1). We will begin by pointing out what is at the heart of each category, and then we will identify the similarities and dissimilarities.

10.3.1 The Heart of ICULT

We can identify five features in relation to ICULT. The first is the notable diversity of its cultural products, and it is interesting to distinguish between

- Reproducible products that do not require the involvement of informational and cultural workers in their production (these are essentially technical products that allow access to cultural and informational organizations).
- Reproducible products that do require the involvement of cultural and informational workers in their production, such as books, compact disks, movies, and

Table 10.1 Cultural industries versus creative Industries

Book publishing	The fashion industry (and high fashion)
News and information	Luxury goods industries (more than 30)
Cinema and audiovisual	Arts and crafts
Recorded music	Design in furniture and furnishings
Video games	Architecture
Info-mediation	Design in advertising

television programs (these products are at the heart of industrialized cultural merchandise).

- Semi-reproducible products that presuppose the intervention of artists, though their reproduction is limited by technically or socially distinctive processes, such as lithographs and limited reproductions of fine art.
- Commodities unrelated to the cultural industries, such as music hall concerts and unique pieces of art.

This typology gives a central position to the notion of reproducibility, which is also considered the industry's primary characteristic.

The second feature is the unpredictable or uncertain character of cultural or informational use values generated by industrialized cultural production, which is one of the latter's structural identifiers. In order to control the effects of such phenomena, the industries put together a set of safeguards and calculate the cost per series or catalogue (qualified as tube and catalogue dialectic), rather than per product. These original traits are somewhat structural—they justify a separate treatment for cultural and informational industries among other industrial fields, not as an archaic field but as an irreducible one, at least until now, relative to traditional forms of industrialization.

The third feature is resorting to artistic and intellectual workers for conception, and their products mostly operate according to artisan modalities that are supposed to guarantee autonomy in creation. It is important to underline the reoccurring particularities of payment modalities for most of those taking part in the conception of products. Most of them are compensated outside the traditional wage system, although this is a norm to which most workers in industrial societies are subject. This trait is not a remnant from another era; instead, it is a settled character that allows the flexible managing of strong artistic and intellectual workforces that need to adapt at any moment to multiple new demands related to genres, forms, and standards.

The fourth feature is the presence of two fundamental models (generic): the editorial model (originally concerning the editing of books, discs, and movies) and the flow model (originally connected to mass radio and television) are at the base of the exploitation of industrialized cultural merchandise (from creation to consumption). A model could also be considered an ideal type. However, contexts vary and cannot be purely considered as belonging to one model or the other. Moreover, we can observe various possible declensions.

The fifth feature is a moderate internationalization that partially respects national cultures and the private interest of firms that contribute to their organization.

10.3.2 *The Heart of ICREA*

Clearly, the same approach is more difficult to follow with ICREA, as it is even beyond the reach of some of their actors, such as those in architecture, advertising, and e-design, for the reasons set out below:

- The creative dimension of economic activities in ICREA cannot be placed on the same level as the social-symbolic and imaginary dimensions that constitute the foundation of ILCUT; in any case, the social recognition—and therefore legitimacy—of this creative dimension is less assured and more diffuse than those associated with ICULT, even if this varies across sectors. Creativity is a value that is essentially attached to production and economic activity.
- There is great heterogeneity among the various productive activities that this chapter classifies as ICREA. Most of the time, these activities are not individualized and remain mixed with others. It has already been pointed out that this is the situation for design and architecture, but it is necessary to add the advertising and fashion industries as well, including haute couture and, increasingly, more of the clothing industry in general.
- It is difficult to identify legal norms, professional references, or modalities of functioning that may easily allow the inclusion of the industries of luxury, design, arts, and crafts.

Therefore, under the current conditions, we can only place ICULT and ICREA side by side—as opposed to merging them—and identify a few common characteristics and many dissimilarities. While similarities and trends toward rapprochement exist between ICULT and ICREA (the main ones being incentives for creativity and the call for collaborative work in the design phase), these findings leave aside a whole series of differences that persist most clearly as legal systems (on the one hand copyright law; on the other, trademark law and intellectual property rights) and remain well differentiated. Indeed, the consistency of the products is analogous, but this analogy mainly concerns semi-reproducible products, which remain a minority type within ICULT, and quite rarely applies to reproducible products (the so-called mass products that constitute only a part of the production process). Nevertheless, it is possible to compare the socioeconomic sectors of ICULT (left column) and the activities of ICREA (right column) and observe that important macroeconomic disproportions that remain between them (Table 10.1).

Despite obvious methodological shortcomings, significant information and knowledge elements in various global data are available, especially in a comprehensive 2014 study entitled *Creating Growth: Measuring Cultural and Creative Markets in the EU*, produced by GESAC (Groupement Européen des Sociétés d'Auteurs et Compositeurs—European Grouping of Societies of Authors and Composers, a

Table 10.2 Cultural and creative market segments

Cultural and creative market segment	Employment (100,000)	Turnover in billion euros	Observations
Books	646	36.3	Includes libraries
Newspapers and magazines	483	70.8	Includes press agencies
Music	1168	25.3	Includes performing arts and nonprofit sector
Performing arts	1234	31.9	
Television	603.5	90	Includes creation, production, postproduction, and pay-per-view
Film (excluding performing arts)	641	17.3	Includes production and distribution as well as DVD and VOD
Radio	97	10.4	None
Video games	108	16	Includes online
Visual arts	1231	127.6	Includes galleries, photographic activities, design, arts and crafts, museums
Architecture	493	36.2	Includes monitoring of construction
Advertising	818	93	Includes commercial communications agencies

European group of 32 creative societies whose mission is to promote and protect authors' rights in Europe in the fields of music, audiovisual, visual arts, and literary and dramatic works)[2] and supported and endorsed by the European Union. GESAC is a professional federation and not a statistical institute; however, in the absence of statistical data, its investigation deserves consideration, subject to subsequent verification. This is an initial approach, and I will certainly point out some obvious limitations.

Overall, the 11 cultural and creative market segments represent 4.2% of the European Union's gross national product, with 7060 million jobs and 540 billion euro in turnover. Important conclusions can be drawn about the relationship between ICULT and ICREA. Table 10.2 displays the breakdown of these 11 segments.

Here, despite the non-correspondence of the statistical categories summarized by my questions, four central conclusions can be established. Each is rich in lessons and significantly illuminates the salient trends of these two types of industries:

- There is no correlation between jobs and market turnovers in connection with capital intensity.
- The emergence of ICREA's socioeconomic sectors and the disputed or disputable empowerment of some of them has been difficult to quantify? e.g., design).
- Always very dominant position of historical cultural and socioeconomic sectors essentially related to ICEA, according to the indicators used.

[2]http://www.creatingeurope.eu/en/wpcontent/uploads/2014/11/study-full-fr.pdf.

- ICULT have been deconstructed in favor of ICREA, which is a major objective of the great project and has been openly affirmed by experts and political decision makers (though this is not a guaranteed trend, especially as long as copyright continues to be recognized in ICULT and as long as they are not challenged by the other modalities of the law of intellectual property).

10.4 Some Current Issues

These are questions as much for the production and consumption of cultural and creative goods as they are for research (but with different formulations), and they come with the risk of mistaking emerging elements for future trends.

First, we must ask ourselves if the disruptive emergence of the communication industries (especially the Big Five: Google, Amazon, Facebook, Apple, and Microsoft) (Miguel de Bustos 2017)—in diverse conditions, given that Chinese conglomerates are not highly globalized—will lead to decisive changes in ICULT and ICREA.

In just over 10 years, the communication industries have indisputably gained a globally dominant position. However, the transformations that they produce do not call into question industries that specialize in content, as many may think; indeed, they are mainly involved in the promotion of cultural and informational goods: the making of their reputation, the circulation of consumer reactions and expectations (consider big data), and their diffusion. In other words, what has ensured their rapid rise to dominance is the fact that they have imposed themselves on the intermediation phase.

Until now the Big Five have paid little attention to the production of content, as they prefer to let other industries take the risks. However, if this aspect is now still prevalent, recent initiatives show that this disaffection with content is probably not definitive, and they are trying increasingly to produce blockbusters.

The new configuration between ICULT and ICREA has not been without immediate consequences. The main victims have been the industries already in decline, such as the daily press. Other industries have responded by progressively implementing new modalities (e.g., recorded music), and many of them have already taken advantage of the presence of social media and digital techniques (for instance, in the development of broadcasting, cinema, or television series). Among the major cultural and media groups in the world, only The Walt Disney Company is experiencing difficulties competing with other large corporations. This shows what has come to be and where the major challenges are.

As for the ICREA, because of their diversity and heterogeneity, they are relatively unaffected by such developments, despite their dynamics. This is why digital platforms may only affect them secondarily for the time being.

Second, one must also ask whether we are moving toward an increase in the power of users/consumers. With the advent of social media and the development of digital technologies, many initiatives are now left to consumers who can quickly influence the reception of cultural products, intervene in their design, participate in their financing, and promote the commodification of little-known minority expressions (it is only in this sense that the idea of the long tail can be understood). For Chris Anderson (2006), products that are in low demand or have meagre mass appeal can experience a boost in market share and even become best sellers, if distribution channels can offer enough choices. The following questions then arise: is this empowerment really a new force, and why does this supposed force not disclose new modalities of functioning to cultural markets? Most likely, it is in this second alternative that we must now place ourselves in. With this proposal, we are dealing with a manifestation of what we have previously presented as the paradigm of collaboration.

Similarly, the possibility for amateurs to participate in all manner of cultural production and make their products known must not only be analyzed as favoring the enlargement of creators. Rather, for the content industries, this is also a way to widen the pool of artists, allowing for a regular renewal of themes, genres, and forms while appealing to creative work, with low remuneration and unsatisfactory working conditions. This is merely the reinforcement of an already long trend together in ICULT and in ICREA, and with it, we are dealing with a manifestation of what we have presented as the paradigm of creation.

Third, these developments have led to an increasingly industrial perspective on cultural policies. In France and other European countries, for example, the objectives of cultural policy are changing: public subsidies are increasingly disseminated to anything that supports industrialization, especially through digital techniques. We find the same trend in local initiatives. However, public policies have great difficulty positioning themselves in the relationships of the communication industries and the Cultural Industries, and even more so the Cultural Industries, and thus, they essentially contribute to Cultural Industries' adaptation to the strategies of the global corporations, as they are powerless before the strategies—including the financial strategies—of these companies.

Fourth, are we moving toward an enhancement of industrial property rights to the detriment of copyright? Beyond this question, we find a challenge of prime importance: on the one hand, with industrial property rights (patents, trademarks, designations of origin), the interests of industrial actors are directly and often exclusively taken into account; on the other hand, with the rights of literary and artistic property, such as copyright and neighboring or related rights (neighboring rights are granted to performers, phonograms producers, videogram producers, and audiovisual communication companies), the beneficiaries are only the publishers and the different categories of artists, with great inequalities between them. Many pressures tend to bring the two systems closer together, but the most powerful of the new actors (the Big Five) and ICREA are active in favor of industrial property rights, which are much less restrictive for them and are traditional in the computer industries. This challenge is not only economic—it is also, and even mainly, cultural and sociopolitical, and in both cases, it reinforces quite different powers.

Fifth, can we assess the macroeconomic importance of a united ICULT and ICREA? Estimates are not lacking, but their bases of establishment are not concordant and are therefore debatable, as evidenced by the points below:

> Cultural and creative industries have become high-capacity engines for economic growth, representing 11.2% of all private enterprises and 7.5% of all employed persons (Creative Europe Programme).
>
> Made-in-France culture represents 84 billion euros of direct and indirect revenues throughout the country, more than the automobile or the luxury goods sectors.
>
> The value of goods and services represents 547 billion euros, or about 4% of gross domestic product of the European Union.

Even if these evaluations are sufficient (they concern both jobs, sales, percentage of gross domestic product, and value added directly or indirectly), many inaccuracies remain. Moreover, no method is known for evaluating evolving trends. On first glance, these calculations can be considered modest. This is a general conclusion, not my own, because indirect effects must be accounted for from a multitude of activities and productions. In any case, it is a diverse movement that now takes place across the planet.

References

Anderson C (2006) The long tail, why the future of business is selling less of more? New York: Hyperion

Bouquillion P, Combès Y (dir) (2012) Creative economy, creative industries. Paris: PUV

Bouquillion P, Miège B, Moeglin P (2013) L'industrialisation des biens symboliques – Les industries créatives en regard des industries culturelles. PUG, Grenoble

Caves RE (2000) Creative industries: contracts between art and commerce. Harvard University Press, Cambridge, MA

Collectif, (présentation: Bernard Miège), « La théorie des industries culturelles (et informationnelles), composante des SIC », Revue française des sciences de l'information et de la communication [Online], 1 | 2012, Online since 01 September 2012, connection on 27 April 2016. http://rfsic.revues.org/80

Florida R (2002) The rise of the creative class: and how it's transforming work, leisure, community and every day life. Basic Books, New York

Jenkins H (2006) Convergence culture: where old and new media collide. NYU Press, New York

Lash S, Lury C (2007) Global culture industry. Polity Press, Cambridge

Miège B (1989) The capitalization of cultural production. International General, New York/Bagnolet

Miège B (2011a) Theorizing the cultural industries: persistent specificities and reconsiderations. In: Wasko J, Murdock G, Sousa H (eds) The handbook of political economy of communication. Wiley-Blackwell, Chichester, pp 83–108

Miège B (2011b) Principal ongoing mutations of the cultural and informational industries. In: Winseck DR, Dal Jong J (eds) The political economies of media – the transformation of the global media industries. Bloomsbury Academic, London, pp 51–65

Miège B (2017) Les industries culturelles et créatives face à l'Ordre de l'Information et de la Communication. Grenoble: PUG, collection Communication en Plus

Miège B (2018) Cultural and creative industries and the political economy of communication. In: Deuze M, Prenger M (eds) Making media – production, practices and professions. Amsterdam University Press, Amsterdam, pp 69–80

Miguel de Bustos J-C (2017) GAFAM, Media and Entertainment Groups and Big Data. Les Enjeux de l'Information et de la Communication, 18(3A), 39–51, https://lesenjeux.univ-grenoble-alpes.fr/2017-supplementA/03-Miguel de Bustos/ Accessed 12 November 2018

Mosco V (1996) The political economy of communication. Sage, London
Rifkin J (2000) The age of access, the new culture of hypercapitalism where all of life is a paid-for experience. Putnam's Sons, New York
Throsby D (2001) Economics and culture. Cambridge University Press, Cambridge

Bernard Miège is an emeritus professor of information and communication sciences at the University Grenoble Alpes where he participates in the researches of the Gresec group. Among other research perspectives, he is also interested in cultural and creative industries.

Chapter 11
From Craft to Industry: Industrializing the Marginal Domains of Cultural Industries

Ilya Kiriya

Abstract For a long time, the basic underlying principle of cultural industries was the idea that the process of reproduction could be industrialized but not the creation itself. Over the course of a few dozers years, this idea determined the nonindustrial character of particular domains of culture, such as theater and performing arts, and some fields of education, maintaining them on the margins of the industrialization process. This chapter examines the complexity of the ongoing mediatization process, which brings such marginal domains into industrial logics, making them reproducible or partly reproducible. We can now see new schemes of the division of labor appearing in performing arts and other fields in which craft-based activity mainly consists of conceptualizing products, while the performances themselves become increasingly industrialized.

Keywords Craft economy · Cultural industries · Industrial logics · Performing arts

11.1 Introduction

For a long time, the basic underlying principle of cultural industries was the idea that the process of reproduction could be industrialized but the process of creation could not (Huet et al. 1978). Thus, the crucial function within any industrial field of culture was that of the so called "editor," a kind of gatekeeper who articulated creative functions within the reproduction and market distribution of cultural goods. The pivoting element was the technical reproduction (the mass production and wide-spread availability of cultural expression in space and time), which opened the door for the commodification of cultural goods on the basis of their mass circulation. Technical reproduction was the main element of the critical theory of the industrialization of culture approach put forward by Walter Benjamin (2008) and Teodor

I. Kiriya (✉)
National Research University Higher School of Economics, Moscow, Russia
e-mail: ikiria@hse.ru

I. Kiriya et al. (eds.), *The Industrialization of Creativity and Its Limits*, Science, Technology and Innovation Studies, https://doi.org/10.1007/978-3-030-53164-5_11

Adorno (Horkheimer and Adorno 2002) in the middle of XX century. Until the end of the century, the technical notion of reproducibility determined the nonindustrial character of various cultural domains, such as theater, performing arts, and education, maintaining them on the margin of the industrialization process. All such domains have been considered as unreproducible and, consequently, not proper cultural industries (which does not necessarily mean that they were noncommercial).

With the proliferation of digital technologies and the general process of commercialization, we can observe how marginalized cultural domains have progressively become mass oriented and better mediatized, factors that push them toward industrialization. Thus, theatrical performances are increasingly growing their audiences through festivals and movie–theater demonstrations, and education has gone online with the invention of Mass Open Online Courses (MOOCs) and distant learning technologies. Inside such domains, new forms of labor division have increased via the making of new strategic alliances with other, more classic, cultural industries, such as the audiovisual industry, the television industry, and the film industry. This chapter examines the complexity of the ongoing mediatization process, which brings such marginal domains into industrial logics, making them reproducible or partly reproducible.

We can now see new schemes of the division of labor in the performing arts and other fields appear in which the craft-based activity mainly consists of conceptualizing the product, while the performances themselves are becoming increasingly industrialized. This is the case of the musicals industry, in which the copyright system increasingly standardizes the performance itself, specifying music and other obligatory elements. The same thing happens in the comedy industry, in which the authorship of jokes is progressively separated from the production of the performance, making the case for joke writing as a phenomenon in the audiovisual industry. In the field of show business, we can see the proliferation of music festivals as a particular masses-oriented industry that is based on standardized rule, which are quite different from individually planned concerts and performances. In this chapter, we will analyze this process of industrialization using the cultural industry approach. As one might assume, a lot of activities that were previously unrelated to the cultural industries, such as education or the performing arts, are actually increasingly integrated into the cultural industries domain.

11.2 Cultural Industries and Their Theoretical Framework

The cultural industry theory has two major pillars. It relies on the critical approach of the Frankfurt School and the political economy of communication, which deals with the question of how limited communicative resources are unequally distributed across the world (Mosco 2009). For the early Frankfurt School scholars, the central point was technical reproducibility, which was already driving culture's transformation into an industrial good under market economy principles and laws, such as division of labor and standardization (Horkheimer and Adorno 2002). The political economy of communication became a generic approach to the issue in the cultural industry theories that emerged after the 1960s primarily in France and then in Britain.

Dialectics of the Enlightenment (1944) Horkheimer and Adorno's fundamental work, puts forward its main critical thesis concerning the loss of the transcendental character of art due to its commercialization and subordination to market logics. This thesis is based on Benjamin's (1936) idea of the reproducibility of art, which leads to a progressive loss of art's authentic aura and public orientation. While for Benjamin such a process was positive because it contributed to the emancipation of a large number of people, for Adorno and Horkheimer it led to the division of labor, the alienation from the result of the creative work, and the constant loss of the author's originality and free expression. Here, we can see the birth of the main peculiarity in the concept of industry. The notion of industry is not used to designate the particular branch of the economy (the modern usage of the term comes from the economic field) but to describe the mass mechanical reproduction of a product within the framework of labor division. From this point of view, industry is opposed to craft production. Such a notion and understanding of industry and industrialization is used in order to distinguish industrial culture from its opposite—the craft culture, which remains based on craft principles.

This theory of culture seems quite remote from the politico-economic concept of craft. According to Becker, craft is a collection of skills that can be used to produce useful objects or perform in a useful way as a high-class professional (Becker called it "virtuoso skill") (Becker 1978, 865). From this point of view, craft refers to the relationship between the craftsman and the entity defining the usefulness of his product, such as a client or employer. In opposition to craft, art rejects the idea of usefulness and perceives art as valuable in and of itself—as self-expression based on beauty. Such an understanding of art is quite close to Adorno's ideal. From the political economy point of view, craft refers to low-scale production that is mainly organized as a non-series production of goods and mainly without any division of labor. Usually, the craftsmen of the preindustrial period produced and distributed their products themselves.

However, such a politico-economic point of view has some commonality with the sociology-of-art approach, especially the notion of usefulness. When one has a need for shoes, one visits a cobbler and orders a pair; in such an instance, one is dealing with the category of usefulness. One of Adorno's central idea was the transformation of pure transcendental art into utilitarian art: a transformation of art that is somehow dependent on commercial demand into a craft. Yet, once we speak about a series production—a production not based on a particular command (an order) but on the mass production of stock—we find ourselves outside the realm of craftsmanship. We are then inside an industry in which the production is organized within the framework of the division of labor, specifically, the labor of the producers (makers) and that of the sellers (distributors). Now, when we need a pair of shoes, we go to a boutique and buy a standard pair produced in series. In today's industrialized world, the crafted reality represents a rather expensive value: that of crafted clothes, crafted shoes, or the crafted decoration of a house. Such services exploit the category of rarity, exclusivity, and the individual approach, differing from the general in-stock mass model produced for everyone. The uniqueness of craft production is often associated with art and beauty.

According to the theory of cultural industries that appeared in France in the late 1970s, the central element of cultural industries is the function of the "editor" (this word is used by French scholars while we perfectly understand that in English language it is probably not completely suitable to describe whole the range of gatekeepers in film, music, and other industries). This function is generally performed by companies that bring together the artistic and technical sides of a process based on technical reproduction and distribution (Huet et al. 1978). Generally, the creative (or artistic) process cannot be measured, and it is realized by creative teams mainly under craft principles, while the function of technical reproduction and distribution merely transforms a craft-produced concept into a product that can be sold on the market. In the case of the book industry, the editor could be a publisher. In the movie industry, the editor could be a production company. In the music business, the editor could be a record label. Generally, the concept—that is, the content of the cultural industry—is produced by compact creative teams with no particular division of labor and on the basis of a preorder. Therefore, major corporations must approve the idea of the film, for example, and order the entire film from the creative team. From this point of view, such a relationship is quite common to the craft principle (related to the making of an order of something). The work of the creative team is mainly based on the craft principle, but after the product is ready, it is technically reproduced and sometimes distributed across telecommunication networks via the means of a major corporation. This practice is fundamentally industrial.

The so-called French school appeared in the 1980s due to various industrial transformations of the media and communication sector in Europe in the second half of the twentieth century, including the increasing importance of such industries within the structure of contemporary economies, the deregulation of the audiovisual sector across Europe, and the intensification of transnational cultural exchanges. Thus, the research has been mainly oriented toward the analysis of the peculiarities of cultural industries as particular goods (Huet et al. 1978) and the politico-economical nature of the media as a public good (Murdock and Golding 1973).

The key element of the politico-economic feature of cultural industries is an individually taste-driven and unpredictable demand and the consumer value of cultural goods. Such an unpredictable character poses a problem to the price of cultural products, which is essentially accidental and does not rely on the cost of creative production. Such a creative part of production is considered as unmeasurable, and as a result, its cost is purely artificial. This constitutes a high risk for cultural production industries that are generally curbed through the non-salary based remuneration of creative workers according to the model of royalties related to a great extent to the commercial result of the final product (Huet et al. 1978; Herscovici 1994).

Despite some general principles, the cultural industries can be distinguished according to their potential to rely on different generic models of functioning and different types of products classified according to reproducibility, rareness, and other criteria. There are generally two main models of functioning, which are set out below.

The editorial model is mainly based on direct consumer payment for cultural goods that are generally materialized and represent a particular product, either a material one, such as a book, or an immaterial one supported by technology, such as digital music track.

The flow logics are mainly based on a model in which cultural production is not personally financed by the consumer but by a third party and the advertiser. The cultural good, in this case, is embodied in the service; it is therefore generally immaterial and has some continuity in space and time.

From these two generic models, we can see a lot of intermediary logics combining in different degrees. This generates a high diversity of forms for cultural products. Thus, we can speak about fully reproducible products relying on creative workers and semi-reproducible products, where the circulation is artificially limited in order to maintain rareness and high prices; we can also speak about social exchanges that are mainly organized by social media and search engines.

Over the last 20 years, this variety of products and logics of functioning has been largely driven by digital changes connected to the proliferation of mobile Internet telecommunication platforms and the growing diversity of consuming devices. All such changes allowed scholars to associate cultural industries with the larger segment of content industries and to find significant common ground between heterogeneous industrial and creative forms of product (Miège 2000; Benghozi 2011). The move toward a plethora of platforms and the broadening of the cultural industries field to that of the content industry has been accompanied by some corporate changes, particularly the financialization of the sector, which became one of the most powerful processes in the financial market as well (Bouquillion 2008).

This chapter follows the framework above and aims to introduce new fields to those preexisting, fields that have not yet been considered as industrially reproducible (and, as a result, have been excluded from the larger field).

11.3 Mediatized Performing Arts

Over the last 15 years, and especially after the implementation of some governmental programs in creative industries (Creative Britain: New Talents for the New Economy, report 2008), new massive forms of performance arts and theater have arisen. First, we have witnessed a dramatic growth in forms of mass theatrical activities, such as large theater festivals. In general, festivals in all fields of the performing arts (such as music and comedy) became increasingly visible and significant in terms of popularity. In the United Kingdom in 2016, the total audience for music festivals was estimated to a 3.9 million people (Wish You Were Here: The Contribution of the Live Music to the UK Economy, report 2017). Since the festival business does not rely on direct technical reproducibility because artists perform live at each iteration, it cannot be considered as entirely part of the cultural industries. However, the massification of festivals standardizes the performances and their format, and it starts to affect the creative part of the theatrical production; this suggests that there is indeed a progressive industrialization of performance. Moreover, we can observe more intense cross-sector collaboration aimed at reducing the costs of the production and at sharing the same location for different events.

Over the last 10 years, after the proliferation of high-speed data transmission and high-definition video, another trend has emerged that pushes theatrical production toward industrialization. This is the direct broadcasting of theatrical performances in movie theaters, which brings traditional theater inside the frameworks of technical reproducibility and the media industry. In 2015, 19% of the UK population watched live-to-digital arts content in cinemas, and 7% did so at home (Naylor et al. 2016). This contributes much more to a turnover for the movie industry than for theater; we can thus hypothesize that it also transforms the creative process inside theatrical production. Since performances should be attractive to the masses, both abroad and at the local level, their choices are highly driven by commercial logics. Performances and actors should be recognizable to wider publics, which could affect the choice of actors (which should be more recognizable in the movie industry rather than in theater itself).

Another rising field inside the performative arts that is intensely pushing the whole sector toward industrialization is international musicals. In the United Kingdom, for example, only about 15% of theatrical shows are musicals, but they deliver about 30% of total theatrical performances (Naylor et al. 2016). We consider musicals as semi-reproducible theatrical plays in which individual artistic performances (which remain the part of the unreproducible universe of the classic theater) coexist with a very standardized and commercialized way of production based on the mechanism of franchise. Within internationally recognizable franchises, such as Chicago and Mama Mia, the main property-rights holder specifies and standardizes all creative elements, such as music, choreography, visual profile of the artists. Such a standardization process makes the theatrical play reproducible and sets a borderline between the creator (the franchise owner) and the performer, who is now considered as more of a distributor. Moreover, such a distinction divides the labor and alienates the creator of the performance.

The division of labor more profoundly penetrates popular culture, especially in comedy. In the preindustrial period, comedy production was based entirely on the craft principle: the author of a joke was the main presenter during stand-up shows. However, the digital environment and multichannel television broadcasting have completely changed the landscape of comedy. The huge commercialization of the audiovisual sector and its orientation toward entertainment has turned it into a separate television genre. The proliferation of comedy television channels, such as Comedy Central, Laff, Sky Comedy have made the content supply question of paramount importance and transformed the sector.

In 2015, we studied this field in Russia and conducted 12 interviews with television producers. We found that within the television genres of satire and humor, a strong division of labor exists between those who write the jokes and those who present them. Moreover, the teams of joke writers migrated between different products across channels, while their presenters were much more linked to a single channel by relatively long-term contracts. Teams of joke writers considered themselves as relatively independent but poorly paid creative staff who were generally remunerated not under the wage system but according to the number of jokes they produced. Joke writers provisioned all the subgenres of television comedy. They wrote jokes for stand-up comedy shows. They may have been contracted for writing jokes for television series, and they were also commissioned to prepare jokes for parodies, television improvisation shows, and so on.

The building of the teams was also a process that went through a national television competition that has existed since the Soviet era: the so-called KVN (The club of funny and smart). KVN is a club in which teams representing young people affiliated with various institutions, companies, and universities can compete in different kinds of comedy tournaments. The best teams form the Premier League, and the league's competitions are aired by the state broadcaster. Almost all of Russia's best television comedy producers, such as the Comedy Club and Yellow, Black and White, rose to popularity through KVN. Moreover, since KVN is a former Soviet Union competition, KVN teams also make a good source of labor for national broadcasting industries in former Soviet countries. It is worth noting that, in 2019, ex-KVN actor and Ukrainian comedy producer Mikhail Zelensky was elected as president of Ukraine.

Here, we can see common logics relying on the model of Hollywood studios, which support several small, independent artistic teams, called "fish factories" by some cultural industries theorists (Miège 1984, 208), in order to have a perennial choice of free and flexible people to use in movie projects. The logics of interaction between joke writers and producers inside such teams are also based on industrial principles. Thus, producers who generally represent a television channel (its content policy and philosophy) regularly penetrate the creative production of jokes, thereby affecting the logics of said production.

11.4 Industrializing Education

In contrast to the fields mentioned above, the education sector started to be considered as a cultural industry some time ago, particularly by French media scholars, such as Pierre Moeglin. In his book Education Industries (2010), he studied industrialized forms of education, including textbook publishing, pedagogical informatics, and distance learning. For Moeglin, three main interconnected processes accompany the industrialization of education, namely the processes of technologization, rationalization, and ideologization. The first refers to the routinization and standardization of the processes of education as activity. The second deals with the organization of labor and management. The third concerns the ideology of progress and modernization that becomes the driver of the marketization, commercialization, new managerialism, and capitalist logics in education (Moeglin 2016).

This refers to the industrialization of education in terms of rationalization and the usage of reproducible media mainly as support for traditional education, such as distance video learning (used mainly to solve the problem of interconnection between campuses and the organization of cross-university activities) and textbook publishing (with which the industry has at least 200 years of history).

The central element of the similarities between the cultural and the creative industries is the general concern about property rights. In the era of digital platforms, this issue has become a central element for all content manufacturers. Since education is one of the most active sectors in the field of copyrights, some regulatory initiatives concern both cultural industries and the education sector (Combès 2007). Another important similarity resides in the rather conflicting nature of educational policies, as the sector faces the radical globalization, commercialization, and growth of cleavages between its public mission to educate and its mandate to be competitive, especially in a cross-national context (Readings 1996; Combès 2007).

All such studies were mainly focused on the general industrialization of education or some of its media products without essentially reexamining the fundamental relationship between the teacher and student, which, in most cases, remained unchanged. Our central argument is that today, with the proliferation of digital media platforms, this essential relationship is increasingly industrialized, making reproducible the core forms of higher education, such as lectures and seminars. The central element of such an industrialization process is MOOCs, which are video lectures and different forms of automated tests and peer assessment. Some universities, such as MIT, are structuring their entire curricula based on MOOCs. The implementation of MOOCs matches perfectly the ambitions of universities to be global players and to compete with each other for the best students from around the world. Universities have started to separate over different market segments, some of which are designed to attract global students and develop global competitiveness.

Persistent economic and social inequalities have also created the illusion that digital access to the world's best education via MOOCs can resolve the problems of developing countries by providing their populations with affordable education they can use to find a job or advance in the one they have (Friedman 2013). Meanwhile, digital platforms for MOOCs, such as EDX and Coursera, have been celebrated as the "next billion-dollar start-ups" (Adams 2018).

MOOCs are fundamentally changing the craft nature of teacher's and professor's labor. They transform the relationship between student and professor, which was previously based on interpersonal communication (either non-mediatized in the case of traditional lectures and seminars or mediatized interpersonal interactions in the case of textbooks or videoconferences), into a mass-communication-oriented practice aimed at a virtual and undefined public. This makes the fundamental relation that has been based on the individual performance of the professor (similar to the theater and other performing arts) reproducible on a particular medium and accessible to millions of people, which in turn makes online education a media product that functions according to the logics of digital media industries.

The first effect of this is the learnification of education (Van Dijk and Poell 2015) in which a division of education is based on relatively small and separately sold pieces of education activities (courses), which can be combined into entire curricula. In the more traditional concept of education, the outcomes represent a wholistic object and not the sum of isolated items, while in commercial logics, the consumer should have a choice between different elements. Another effect is the mediatization of education through digital platforms; this can be described as the uberization of education and the implementation of a mutual client-service assessment and ranking that contributes to the implementation of the neo-managerial practices in academia, such as key performance indicators for professors and academic units and the imposition of rank-dependent salaries. Together with digital bibliometrics and the big data system of evaluating academic performance, it oversimplifies representations of the quality of teachers' work.

Finally, another effect of making online education resembles the processes followed by cultural industries is the new division of labor. Professors remain the key figures of the new online education industry, but their creativity needs to be mechanically reproduced and made available to the public. This mechanical reproduction is ensured by the university (which grants facilities to shoot the video and support the work of the accompanying persons) and by the platform, which ensures distribution. In other words, the creation of online courses is similar to any cultural industry production process: the creative work is separated from the technical reproduction and marketing. Here, the business model is similar to any networked digital product and is mainly based on selling data about users to aggregators in the advertising sector. The model also implicates a large part of the digital labor (a high amount of unpaid work performed by users) (Fuchs 2015). Peer assessment, mentoring, and other methods of the self-organization of online course consumers are elements of such digital labor. Since platforms are responsible for the distribution, they format the professor's creative work and impose the format, such as the course duration and division of lectures into short pieces).

The digital education sector is under the control of big Internet oligopolies. Almost all the Big Five internet oligopolies provide online education services and hold assets within this segment. Microsoft controls its own platform of online courses and services for teachers developing digital skills at schools. Amazon is developing its AWS Educate platform providing teachers and students with access to cloud technologies. Google possesses G-suite, a platform of different services for trainers, teachers, and students based on collaborative technologies. Apple is currently developing Apple School, a platform for cloud managing accounts and devices within classes and schools. Finally, Facebook has developed Facebook Education, a set of educational tools for building e-learning communities. The Big Five control a significant amount of user data, which allows them to attract increasingly targeted advertisers. By providing massive education solutions, they have commercialized personal data and sell it to different advertisers.

In most cases, such educational solutions are based on user-generated content, which is shared by different education professionals. Most popular educational platforms (Udacity, Coursera, EdX) are created by universities or their consortiums. However, universities' participation in the capital of such platforms takes on a specific meaning at the level of their management, which has been confronted over the past 50 years with unprecedented growth in enrollment numbers. Online education allows universities to manage the scale of the problem by minimizing the cost of education, as it can now be reproduced without hiring large numbers of professors. From this point of view, online education will shift professors' contracts away from the tenure model toward less permanent forms of remuneration and, eventually, to a completely non-wage model.

11.5 Conclusion

In this chapter, we discussed how rich and diverse the reproduction of the marginal domains of the creative industries has become. This process is based on different forms of aggregation and the mediatization of theatrical performances, comedy, and forms of user-generated content. All such changes align with the strategies of industrial media corporations within the cultural field, which was previously independent of such concentration. Some of the activities, mainly in the performing arts, are not technically reproducible. They are not a result of the mechanical copying of creative content on a specific medium or digital network but they are based on the standardization of their production and the usage of rights' protections, such as the franchise model. For other activities, such as those in education ones or filmmaking, the new digital distribution environment has made them entirely reproducible. In all cases, a new division of labor between creative workers and the distribution of their labor is generating new business logics (see Table 11.1).

As can be seen, even the relatively low number of new sectors generates a high diversity of models. First, we can see that for some of these new industries, their

Table 11.1 New industrialized sectors of creative production and their features

	Performances			Education
	Musicals	Comedy	Broadcasting theatrical performances in movie theaters	Mass open online courses
Reproducibility	Based on standardization	Based on standardization	Based on technical reproducibility	Based on technical reproducibility
Changes in division of labor	Separation of performer and the author of the performance (rights owner)	Separation between author of joke and its performer	Addition of the broadcaster (movie chain) in traditional theatrical chain	Separation between authorship of course and its distribution (technically enabled)
Changes in business logics or model	Logics based on mass ticket sells and mass marketing of the franchise	No huge changes	No huge changes	Model of "freemium" based on user data sells and user-generated content

reproduction remains far from technical reproducibility, which is the classic idea of the cultural industries. Second, we should stress that no new sectors generate a new model of functioning (business logics) and are just exploiting the new field without creating some new form of business. For example, the comedy sector generates a new industrial market but does not really affect the business logics of the sector, which remain on tickets sales or advertising. The same is applies to the movie-theater broadcasts theatrical performances, which create a new mass market for the performances but still correspond to the classic editorial model of the cinema. The division of labor is either based on the addition of a new stage in the production chain (the new means of distributing theatrical performances in movie theaters) or the classic separation of a previously wholistic task to different tasks performed by different actors.

With the ongoing mediatization of new sectors of the economy driven by the development of digital platforms, we must expect an increase in similarities between sectors previously unincluded cultural industries and their logics of functioning. Indeed, we can examine transportation, which is increasingly dependent on big data and digital networking, and amateur sports, which are very much oriented toward the usage of self-tracking and social media technologies, because such have become increasingly involved in production of media content, such as networked communication between users of public transportation.

Appendix: The New Production Chain in Gag and Humor Production on Television

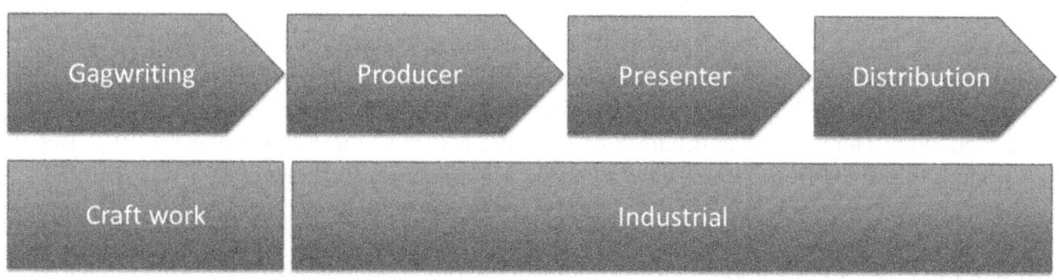

References

Adams S (2018) This company could be your next teacher: Coursera plots a massive future for online education. Forbes, 16 Oct. 2018, Available from: https://www.forbes.com/sites/susanadams/2018/10/16/this-company-could-be-your-next-teacher-coursera-plots-a-massive-future-for-online-education/#56714ea52a39

Becker H (1978) Arts and crafts. Am J Sociol 83(4):862–889

Benghozi P-J (2011) Économie Numérique et Industries de Contenu: un Nouveau Paradigme pour les Réseaux. Hermès, La Revue 59(1):31–37
Benjamin W (2008) The work of art in the age of mechanical reproduction. Penguin, London
Bouquillion P (2008) Les industries de la culture et de la communication: les stratégies du capitalisme. Presses universitaires de Grenoble, Grenoble
Combès Y (2007) Quelles Perspectives Possibles entre Industrialisation de la Formation et Industries Culturelles? In Colloque AIERI. Paris: Unesco. Available from: https://hal.archives-ouvertes.fr/hal-01387613. Accessed: 5 May 2019
Creative Britain. New Talents for the New Economy (2008) London. Retrieved from https://webarchive.nationalarchives.gov.uk/+/http:/www.culture.gov.uk/images/publications/CEPFeb2008.pdf
Dijk, J. van, & Poell, T. (2015). Higher education in a networked world: European Responses to U.S. MOOCs. Int J Commun 9, 2674–2692. Retrieved from https://ijoc.org/index.php/ijoc/article/view/3398/1448
Friedman TL (2013, January 27) Revolution Hits the Universities. New York Times, p. SR 1
Fuchs C (2015) Social media: a critical introduction. Sage, London
Herscovici A (1994) Economie de la Culture et de la Communication: Éléments pour une Analyse Socio-Économique de la Culture dans le Capitalisme Avancé. l'Harmattan, Paris
Horkheimer M, Adorno TW (2002) Dialectic of enlightenment, philosophical fragments. In Schmid Noerr G (ed). Stanford: Stanford University Press
Huet A, Ion J, Lefèbvre A, Miège B, Peron R (1978) Capitalisme et Industries Culturelles. Presses Universitaires de Grenoble, Grenoble
Moeglin P (2010) Les Industries Éducatives. Presses universitaires de France, Paris
Moeglin P (2016) Industrialiser L'éducation: Anthologie Commentée (1913–2012). Presses universitaires de Vincennes, Saint-Denis
Miège Bernard (1984) Postface à la 2e édition (p. 199–214). In Huet, Armel; Ion, Jacques; Lefebvre, Alain; Miège, Bernard; Péron, René, Capitalisme et Industries Culturelles. 2e édition, Grenoble: Presses universitaires de Grenoble
Miège B (2000) Les industries du Contenu: Face à L'ordre Informationnel. Presses universitaires de Grenoble, Grenoble
Mosco V (2009) The political economy of communication. Sage, London
Murdock G, Golding P (1973) For a political economy of mass communications. Socialist Register 10(10):205–234
Naylor R, Lewis B, Branzanti C (2016) Arts council England analysis of theatre in England credits written and prepared by Photo credits for section covers. London: Arts Council England, Retrieved from https://www.artscouncil.org.uk/sites/default/files/download-file/Analysis of Theatre in England – Final Report.pdf
Readings B (1996) The University in Ruins. Harvard University Press, Cambridge, MA
Wish You Were Here. The Contribution of the Live Music to the UK Economy (2017) Report. London. Retrieved from https://www.ukmusic.org/assets/general/Report_WYWH_17.pdf

Ilya Kiriya holds a PhD in journalism from the Moscow State University and PhD in communication studies from Grenoble University (France). He was an assistant professor at Moscow State University (Faculty of journalism). Since 2007 is a full professor in the National research university "Higher School of Economics" where he is a chair of the School of Media. Ilya Kiriya's main scientific interests are in field of political economy of communication and media in post-soviet countries. His works are published in the International Journal of Communication, Russian Politics, and Hermes Communication Journal.

Chapter 12
Intellectual Property Rights and the Production of Value in a "Creative Economy"

Vincent Bullich

Abstract Very early on, the heralds of the "creative industries" emphasised on the imperative of a legal framework based on strong intellectual property to ensure their growth. In a context of intense international competition, intellectual property rights appeared to allow guaranteeing the "singularity" of local products and thus extricate them from untenable price-based competition. However, the excessive bolstering of those rights is likely to modify how they operate and, therefore, make them an obstacle to the development of a "creative economy".

Keywords Creative industries · Intellectual property · Economy of singularities · Commodification · International competition

The idea of "creative industries" was first mentioned in speeches, mainly Anglophone, in the political, economic or even academic spheres. It referred to a series of activities grouped together according to one main characteristic: the central role of "creativity" in their production and valorisation processes, presented as the ability to have "original ideas" (Howkins 2001), meaning acting according to symbols and senses. To this apparently tautological minimal definition—since industries are "creative" when they offer "creativity"—is often added a second characteristic, that more specifically designates the methods used to monetize production. Therefore, as of 1998, the United Kingdom's *Creative Industries Task Force of the Department for Culture, Media and Sport* defined the creative industries by emphasising on the "creative" dimension of the activities that they cover as well as their economic development specificities based on the "creation and exploitation

V. Bullich (✉)
GRESEC (Groupe de Recherche Sur les Enjeux de la Communication—Research Group on the Challenges of Communication), Université Grenoble Alpes, Grenoble, France
e-mail: vincent.bullich@univ-grenoble-alpes.fr

I. Kiriya et al. (eds.), *The Industrialization of Creativity and Its Limits*, Science, Technology and Innovation Studies, https://doi.org/10.1007/978-3-030-53164-5_12

of intellectual property rights".[1] For his part, John Howkins, the inventor of the notion of "creative economy", considers that "*Intellectual property is the currency in the new economy*" (Howkins 2005: 5). Subsequently, a report from the United Nations Conference on trade and development defined "creative industries" as a range of (relatively) homogeneous economic activities, considering that *All these activities are intensive in creative skills and can generate income through trade and intellectual property rights* (UNCTAD 2008: IV).

It is not a matter here of piling on examples but simply of showing that what is at stake is clearly identified and demonstrated: the development of a growing range of economic activities grouped together under the "creative industries" umbrella seems to fundamentally depend on such rights. Over and above the production of ideas, the "creative economy" therefore has an overriding need for a specific legal framework allowing for "ideas" to be converted into "cash" (Howkins 2001) or *outputs* (Bilton 2007). This process is nevertheless a "black box" in the speeches mentioned above and intellectual property rights in this context appear to be a kind of latter-day philosopher's stone that is capable of changing ideas into gold. It is this process that we are going to examine in the following pages. To do so, we put forward the following proposition: the essential function of intellectual property rights is to include and maintain "creative" products and services in an "economy of singularities" (Karpik 2007), i.e. in markets based on competition for quality, free of any axiology, and in which price, quality and production cost are disconnected from each other in the valorisation process.

It is through them that most "creative industries" produce wealth in a highly competitive international context; nevertheless, owing to their decisive strategic importance, they have, for some years, been subject to continuous reinforcement, hence evolving towards a state of hypertrophy that is likely to threaten the development of a "creative economy" as a whole.

This chapter, therefore, aims to open the "black box", shed light on its contents and thus clarify certain motivations that can be attributed to the "creative economy". This combines an institutionalist approach to trade that can be found in recent currents of economic sociology (Steiner and Vatin 2009), and a critical approach to communicational phenomena drawing for instance from political economy of communication (Wasco et al. 2011).

In the first part, we will briefly explain certain characteristics that are unique to the production of creative industries and suggest a contribution stemming from intellectual property rights to understand the process of "singularisation" that increasingly shapes the economy of "creative" products and services. In the second part, we will assess the scope of this process according to these products' means of valuation.

[1] According to the Creative Industries Task Force, the scope of the "creative industries" is thus made up of "activities which have their origin in individual creativity, skill and talent and which have a potential for wealth and job creation through the generation and exploitation of intellectual property" (CITF/DCMS 1998: 3).

12.1 The Production of "Singularity": Definition and Guarantee of "Protection"

12.1.1 "Creative" Industries, Products and Services: Activities and Products with Specific Properties

What differentiates "creative" firms (industrial or otherwise) from those operating in other sectors or branches of activity is their ability to incorporate symbolic components in their products, in variable proportions, however, i.e. meanings, expressive, aesthetic or sensitive values.[2] It indeed appears that, despite being very unevenly delineated, its semiotic or symbolic dimensions are generally put forth in both institutional and academic discourses[3] in order to construct the very heterogeneous category of "creative industries". From this point of view, creativity is mainly praised for its ability to produce original and new meanings. These are integrated into the various products and are decisive components in their valuing, these symbolic and sensory dimensions of the products and services are considered at least as important in the eyes of the consumer as their strictly "functional" dimensions.[4] Therefore, their qualities cannot be reduced to "objectivable" technical or economic criteria that may or may not encourage buying. On the contrary, it is largely related to subjective motivations and criteria appraisal based on the individual's personal relationship with these symbolic/sensory elements.

Thus, what is at stake for industrial policies and the "creative" producers is to come up with sufficiently attractive symbolic components in order to avoid competition based on price or material properties and moreover weaken the potential to substitute their products with others. It is precisely that component that provides the foundation for the entire "differentiation" strategy and this is precisely where intellectual property rights[5] are decisive. Through them, it is possible to render abstract a growing share of products and services from the common means of competition based on price to put them back into an "economy of singularities" (Karpik 2007). Indeed, unlike product differentiation theories (Chamberlin 1933; Lancaster 1966) that include multiple product qualities but postulate their comparability according to a common value scale (an "objectivable" utility), L. Karpik develops a theory in which products are designated as singular according to three

[2]For example, it is on this "sensitive" value (i.e. fundamentally linked to sensory perception) that deli food markets are built.

[3]On this topic, refer, for instance, to O'Connor (2007).

[4]We should further point out that various authors insist on the fact that products from the creative industries share a common consumption characteristic: indeed, these products are generally "*experience goods*" (Nelson 1970). We also come across the idea that we are faced with an "*experience economy*" (Hartley 2013): the value of the products proposed can only be appraised by the consumer after the fact, i.e. in the very act of consumption; but this characteristic is fundamentally linked to their symbolic/sensitive dimension (Flew 2012; Hartley 2013).

[5]More especially, the brands, the *design* and the literary and artistic property, see *infra*.

interdependent criteria: (1) Their "multidimensionality" (each product is the aggregate of an "indivisible" set of characteristics), (2) Their "incommensurability" (as comparison is impossible, what this means for the consumer is moving on from the "economic decision"—computation—to the "judgement") and (3) The uncertainty that affects their value resulting from the first two properties.

If singularities exist "as such" in economy (e.g. a masterpiece) according to Karpik (2007), the majority of "singularities" stemming from industries that have freshly been qualified as "creative" have been so by virtue of institutions (*lato* sensu) that define them and "protect" them as such, such as intellectual property rights. Making this proposition implies studying two aspects. The first concerns the role of the legal institution in the construction of that "singularity". This approach implies imagining "singularisation" to a greater extent than "singularity", the process more than the data, and thus refraining from a substantialist vision that would define "singularity" solely as an intrinsic, "natural" property of the item under consideration. The second concerns the preservation of the "singular" nature of the product and the ways in which it is valued. This then means looking, on the one hand, at the mechanisms that guarantee the item's uniqueness and, on the other hand, at the transformation of the institutionally recognised "singular" into a monopoly granted to operators, a process which is one of the very points of laws of intellectual property.

12.1.2 Judicial Production of the Singular

One of the great contributions of the approach in terms of social constructivism is to have revealed the fact that the fundamental function of institutions is one of denominating and classifying individuals as objects and that, in so doing, they participate in the definition of social reality. Since the seminal works of Berger and Luckmann (1966), this perspective has spread far beyond the sociological context and been borrowed and confirmed by authors from very different backgrounds like Searle (1995), Douglas (1986) and Descombes (2005). All of them emphasis on institutions' function in "typifying" and how the ideas that they convey are performative in being a production factor of the social world. Institutions (*lato* sensu) appear to impose rules, to a greater or lesser extent, on the social actors, by adjusting their conduct and configurating their cognitive schemes. From this point of view, intellectual property rights are a form of institution of a particular kind since, as a legal rule, they are backed by the State and, as such, supposedly have compelling power of enforcement.

As an institution, intellectual property rights are therefore involved in the joint qualification of an object, the particularity of which is to be immaterial and that upon completion of an eligibility procedure, may, or may not, be endowed with a property that "singularises" it and an individual or legal entity which, upon completion of the procedure, may, or may not, be designated as the author and/or owner of the object in question.

Mainly, such eligibility procedures test the newness (or "originality"[6]) of the object and, to a lesser extent its scope (technical and industrial—aesthetic and symbolic). When applicable, it is assigned with a particular status: "the author" (*lato* sensu), "the inventor", the "creator" and is thus identified, "singularised", in the eyes of the law.

Those objects, in the majority of the legal systems in democratic countries, correspond to the market economy, of four kinds of laws that we refer to collectively under the expression "intellectual property":

- The law on artistic property (or copyright) that qualifies expressions in original works.
- The law on patents that identifies technical inventions.
- The law on trademarks that identifies the name of a product or a legal entity.
- The law on designs and models that singularises the visual aspects of an industrial product.

We should mention here that, to become properties, these objects must be "expressions" or concrete forms (drawings, designs, sound or visual recordings, texts, etc.) produced on the basis of ideas and not ideas themselves (which remain intangible in legal terms).

The legal moment devoted to the "rise in singularity"[7] of "creative" products and services thus ideally occurs according to two simultaneous qualification procedures: the first considers the qualities of the object and constitutes it, when applicable, as property, and the second identifies the "owner of the object".

Apart from the proprietary aspects related to it (consequences of the temporary authorisation of a monopoly) which we will examine next, this designation of the owner plays a major role in the valuation of production of creative industries in that it constitutes information for potential consumers on the quality of the products and the services offered. The name of an artist, a designer, a product or a firm thus functions both as a cognitive resource conducive to trade and as an engine driving the impulse to buy. It is also the very property that lies behind the establishment of a counterfeiting industry. It is therefore of primary importance for the creative industries that the identity of their products be "protected", for it is that on which their "incommensurable" character depends on, and that lifts competition on price and/or technical specifications.

---

[6]"Originality" is an indispensable condition for the legal existence of a "work of the intellect" in the legislation of all member states of the World Intellectual Property Organization (WIPO). Although considerable differences can be found in the doctrines of those countries, originality is generally assessed in terms of "newness", to which we can add the manifestation of the "author's mark" and the author's awareness in making a work of art through his very activity (in the continental European tradition), or else through the manifestation of a "minimal degree of creativity" found in the object (in the tradition of *copyright* and *Common Law*).

[7]We are borrowing this concept from Heinich (1998) in order to characterise the assertion of uniqueness and the non-substitutable nature of the products under consideration.

12.1.3 Protection of Identity

For this "rise in legal singularity"—recognition of the object's uniqueness (the concrete expression of the idea) as well as its owner(s)—to have an economic scope, it must go hand in hand with mechanisms that guarantee the non-substitutability of the products linked to it. To achieve this, the law grants an operating monopoly. This need for recognition and institutional protection of the identity of products is all the greater in that the objects in question—expression, knowledge, information, name, etc.—are immaterial and, as such, easily appropriable by others as they are "naturally" non-rival and non-excludable.[8] Therefore, with contributing to the qualification of the "singularity" of creative industries' products, intellectual property rights have the function of guaranteeing their uniqueness in different markets. Faced with the growth in the production and trade of counterfeits,[9] that protection has been reinforced over the last three decades by expanding the "legal arsenal" on the one hand and by increasing the number of actors overseeing its application on the other.

We thus observe a dual movement of intensification in the production and overwriting of legislative texts at a supranational level (the WTO's TRIPS agreements,[10] WIPO treaties[11] and the ACTA agreement[12]), a regional level (e.g. European directives on the harmonisation of copyright and similar rights) and a national level,[13] all intended to foster optimal protection of "singularity" on the majority of the global markets. This dual movement was driven by actors both state and private, principally from the Triad nations (Sell 2003; May and Sell 2006), which have managed to impose their vision within the supranational bodies (WTO,

---

[8]In economic sciences, those two characteristics were laid down as the result of by Arrow's (1962) analysis of the economic properties or information (although he does not use these terms himself). Non-rivalry characterises the fact that an individual's consumption of a piece of information (or an idea) does not prevent another individual from consuming that same piece of information; non-excludability refers to the fact that it is impossible (or extremely complicated) to prevent the consumption of a piece of information (or the idea) from such time as it becomes public.

[9]The Organisation for Economic Co-operation and Development (OECD) estimates that the global market in tangible fake goods, which accounted for more than 250 billion dollars in 2007, increased by 250% over the period 2001–2007; the market in pirated digital goods, on the other hand, is not valued for want of reliable indicators (OECD 2009a, b). We should point out, however, that these figures should be taken with a pinch of salt in that they usually come from firms working for the industries affected by counterfeiting and not from independent observatories.

[10]Agreements on those aspects of intellectual property rights, that impinge upon trade from the World Trade Organization drafted in 1994, came into force in the following year.

[11]World Intellectual Property Organization that administrates 24 international treaties, the majority of which have been ratified and/or revised over the last 30 years.

[12]Anti-Counterfeiting Trade Agreement on which multilateral negotiations began in 2007 and currently applies to eight countries, including the United States and Canada.

[13]For example, in the United States in 2009, there were no less than 52 amendments to the general revision of the 1976 law on copyright whereas only 36 amendments were enacted in the general revision of the 1909 law (more than a third of which between 1965 and 1974).

WIPO and UNESCO). It is accompanied by greater involvement on the part of those state actors, as well as the same bodies in charge of administrating and overseeing the application of these laws[14] on the world's primary markets (Bullich 2011b). Therefore, the extension of the "singularity regime" that has occurred with the development of "creative industries" is done within the framework of the geopolitics of intellectual property rights indubitably dominated by the interests of the Triad nations, which thus have a tool at their disposal that is capable of slowing down opportunities for substitute products and therefore price-driven international competition, which becomes impossible for them. To this trend, we can add the more recent one of "judicial stacking"—overwriting laws on the same subject[15]—which is increasingly prevalent in the "creative economy" and inevitably heightens tensions between intellectual property rights and the other forms of rights (freedom of speech, right to information, competition law, etc.; in this kind of legal contest, we generally see the prevalence of intellectual property rights). Finally, the use of the syntagma "intellectual property rights" is generally metonymic: it refers to a "system" made up of domestic law texts, international bi- and multilateral agreements, various contractual, regulatory and administrative clauses, material and administrative organisations and social representations which drive its development (Bullich 2011b). It is precisely this system that has been spectacularly reinforced on a worldwide level, concomitant with the emergence and development of a "creative sector".

12.2 The Construction of Value

We have stated that the creative industries were first and foremost characterised by the integration of intellectual resources (generally significant or sensitive) on which the economically valuable dimensions of their products rest predominantly. We have just seen in the previous point that, in codifying such integration, intellectual property laws constitute one of the stages in the "singularisation" of products, identifying and guaranteeing the relation between an immaterial object and its author/producer. We are now going to look at the role of intellectual property rights in the process of "social construction"[16] of the value of products and services from the creative industries. To do this, we will first differentiate the "alienable resources"

[14]This supervisory mission has been conducted by international interprofessional associations (but generally driven by American industrial concerns), the most active of which, as far as the "creative sector" is concerned, are the *International Intellectual Property Alliance* (IIPA), the *Business Software Agency* (BSA), the *Motion Picture Association* (MPA), the *International Federation of the Phonographic Industry* (IFPI) and the *Business Action to Stop Counterfeiting and Piracy* (BASCAP).

[15]We can add, for example intellectual property rights—artistic and trademark property—to contractual clauses that are very stringent for the consumer.

[16]By opposing or complementing a "substance value", i.e. a value that is considered to reside solely in the "permanent" characteristics of the object (Orléan 2011).

methodologically from the "attached resources"[17] (Lampel 2011) at the disposal of such industries: intellectual property rights are at once the objects of the transaction ("alienable resources"), and a "market device" (Callon et al. 2007) that identifies producers and products ("attached resources").

Creative industries are thus particular in that they (practically) systematically produce two types of products that can be traded on two different but interdependent markets:

- Products and services that present a strong "symbolic" component (anthropological point of view, etymologically that "unite and explain, express meaning") and an "original" component (legal characterisation).
- Rights on concrete expressions or forms of "ideas" (as understood by Howkins 2001).

This particularity implies that we look at three aspects that constitute this value construction to which intellectual property rights contribute: (1) The use value of such rights, (2) Their exchange value and (3) The market values of the products and services to which they refer.

12.2.1 Use Value of Intellectual Property Rights

Fundamentally, intellectual property rights constitute a bundle of rights (Ostrom and Schlager 1992), the use value of which resides in the control of others' actions they can provide, thus endowing ideas, whether expressions or manifestations, with an exchange value. We have just explained that these rights are part and parcel of the transformation of products and services into "singularities": that "singularity" is not therefore defined solely by the properties of the products under consideration but also by their legal treatment; in a fair number of cases, the "singular" nature is assessed rather by the difference in degree than by the difference in nature, and intellectual property rights reinforce this distinction (as illustrated, for example by the now dominant role of trademarks in the textile industry or design in the luxury goods industry).

What is considered "singular" is therefore partly constructed by the law. It is so, on the one hand, in the context of a qualification test that recognises or refutes uniqueness, because of the newness or "originality" of the immaterial object, resulting from "creativity" on which the considered firms' production is based. On the other hand, it also temporarily guarantees, by means of different bodies and

[17] Joseph Lampel defines "attached resources" as "resources that cannot be separated from the identity of the actors that hold them" (2011: 335). He defines "alienable resources" as resources that are "controlled but not embedded in the identity of the actor in such a way as to prevent transfer of control or ownership to others" (Ibid.).

procedures, the operating monopoly of that object to those same firms.[18] In doing so, the law contributes to an economic model that is founded on an idea of artificial rarity. It is indeed these laws' fundamental ability to prevent[19] others from using a "protected" object, applying conditions to such use (which usually implies recognition in the form of a fee or royalty) which is the source of their value. This excludability can be observed on three levels:

- In terms of direct competition between producers.
- In terms of related sectors (i.e. sectors in which the actors are likely to use immaterial objects on markets that are nonetheless distinct from those of the original producers, like, for example the spin-off product economy in the film industry).
- In terms of consumption (constraining certain uses, particularly in the context of artistic property).

This aspect was initially revealed by Garnham (1986) in a study focusing on the economic operation of the cultural industries. It is nonetheless also relevant to the "creative" sectors, the idea of artificial rarity through intellectual property rights providing a response to two major aims: that of protecting the "creative" product and service markets from any practices likely to impair them, and increasing the scope of the commodification process by progressively including senses that may be assimilated (and therefore be negotiated upon) to these products and services.

12.2.2 The Construction of Exchange Values

Through a mechanism of exclusion or conditional use, intellectual property rights transform an idea (or rather its expression) into a commodity. It is described as followed by two eminent legal specialists see it: these "rights, as understood by justice, do not apply to a pre-existing value; rather they create that value by allowing the immaterial object to become an object of exchange" (Vivant and Bruguière 2009: 6). Such rights are thus the medium—neither unique nor necessary, but socio-historically situated—through which the idea as such enters the field of economic exchange. This means that intellectual property rights constitute an institutional frame that provides a deep-reaching structure to the means of production and consumption of cultural/creative products and services. However, as suggested by certain authors, led by Howkins (2001), we cannot assume that "the creative economy *needs*" such rights to develop: indeed, various studies show that "creative"

[18]We should emphasise here that the concept of "singularity" cannot be reduced to the concept of "monopoly" owing to the symbolic, signifying and sensitive dimension attached to the object under consideration (its "indivisible multidimensionality" (Karpik 2007) whence the pre-eminence of the attention given here to artistic property rights, trademark rights and design rights and the lesser consideration given to patent law.

[19]"Exclusivism" is a founding attribute of property law (Munzer 2001).

industrial activities can fully develop without this legal framework (see, for example the study of the phonographic sector in India by Manuel 1993). Rather, intellectual property rights appear to be an effective, rather than necessary, condition for the process of idea commodifying (Bullich 2011a). They function as a mechanism that transforms "authority resources into allocation resources" (according to the categories of Giddens 1984): they grant the rightful owners relative control over the activities of others[20] and subordinate a part of them to monetary influx (such is the principle of the "licence": user licence, right to broadcast, etc. granted in return for a fee). For this reason, intellectual property rights are they themselves objects of transaction and therefore have their own exchange value. The markets for these different rights—which also operate according to the "singularity" regime—are particularly difficult to quantify: though certain transactions are widely publicised and commented upon (e.g. the takeover in 2012 of Lucasfilm by Disney for a record sum in excess of four billion dollars, aiming mainly at getting hold of the *Star Wars* franchise), the majority of the international reports and studies insist on the fact that the valuations of the total sum of such transactions are risky (Netanel 2009). However difficult it may be to quote exact figures, everyone agrees on the recently acquired importance of these right markets (ibid.).

12.2.3 The Ambivalent Role of Intellectual Property Rights on "Creative" Products and Services Markets

As explained in the second part, property rights guarantee information for potential consumers as to the quality of the offered products and services: the "social" identity, "protected" by intellectual property rights (like the name of an artist, a designer, a product or a firm), functions both as a cognitive resource that fosters exchange and a driver of the impulse to buy.[21] However, a number of industries in the "creative" sector (particularly the cultural industries that form its core), include an internal contradiction that is capable of impairing their effectiveness as a source of wealth. Indeed, as stated above, property rights institutionally reinforce the rarity of what are considered to be "singular" or "singularised" products. Such products then present the particularity of being "incommensurable": their respective qualities cannot be assessed based on "objectivable" technical or economic criteria—like, for example their price—but, because they operate on a symbolic level, they are to a large extent linked to motivations and criteria that are subjectively or intersubjectively assessed and that appear, as such, to be deeply dependent—"entrenched"—on their

[20]As ownership is characterised not as the sway of will over an object but as a triadic relationship that associates an object and two social statuses: the owner and the non-owner (see Hegel 2003 and, more recently, Descombes 2005).

[21]On the "authenticity" guaranteed by the brand and/or signature and the impulse to buy on the art markets, see, for example Edelman and Heinich (2002).

socio-historical context of emergence. The use value of products from the "creative" sector is thus essentially constructed *by and in* the social interaction that both contribute to determining meaning and quality to the sensitive dimension. No Doubt, to an even greater extent than for "functional" products, the value of symbolic products cannot be assessed in terms of "substance value", i.e. value that may be found in the relation between the subject and the object. As taught by anthropology and sociology of culture, the value given to symbolic products is collectively decided upon.[22] Particularly in the case of artistic property, a fundamental tension, inherent to the process of commodification of "products of the intellect" can, therefore, be identified. There is, on the one hand, a need for publicisation, which is the basis for the constitution of products and services' use value, and, on the other hand, a need for the control of such publicisation, i.e. the production of rarity, whereby the exchange value of both the rights and the products they cover is created.

A second ambivalence as to the role of intellectual property rights in the production of value in "creative" products and services has recently been put forward by the apologists of the "creative economy" themselves. Indeed, those authors—led by Howkins (2006)—now consider that intellectual property rights that are too strong ("*strong IP*") may impair the development of all of this economy's businesses. In so doing, they follow in the footsteps of those whose critiques are increasingly more distinct, particularly in academia.[23] They challenge how effective these rights' incentives are and consider them as a tool that serves a limited number of private interests to the detriment of the general interest.[24] The "creative industries" partisans thus generally emphasise two aspects of the current laws, which they consider particularly harmful. The first concerns the duration of such rights. This critique was initially expressed by 17 renowned economists[25] who, in their capacity of "friends of the court" (*amici curiae*), put their name to a report lodged with the Supreme Court of the United States in 2002. Among other things, that report denounces the extension of the duration of *copyright* insofar as the measure will have no other impact than to accentuate monopoly rents and therefore inflate royalty fees, therefore impinging on the consumer and on any individual wishing to produce a reissue of works. That extension seems even more incongruous in that, apart from the few works that are most demanded, the shelf-life of the large majority of products from the cultural/creative industries is particularly brief (Akerlof et al. 2002). This

[22]On the criticism of "substance value" in economics and its replacement by value originating not in the object or relationship of the individual to the object but in the social relations produced by the object, see Orléan (2011); on the anthropological criticism of the dominant economic value model, see Hénaff (2002).

[23]For a brief summary, see Bullich (2013).

[24]For example, the 1998 amendment increasing the duration of *copyright* in the United States was given the nickname "*Mickey Mouse Protection Act*", *lobbying* from the Disney Group having been so insistent.

[25]Among them, we find the Nobel Prize winners, K. Arrow, R. Coase and M. Friedman, who join in with their colleagues in protesting against the extension of the duration of *copyright*.

observation of a "less than optimal use" of these resources, in the context of an economy in which exclusivity rights are far too frequent, forms the basis of the second category of critiques which are especially prevalent in the comments promoting the "creative economy". Intellectual property rights, as currently codified in the countries that have ratified the principal supranational treaties (WIPO agreements and TRIPS agreements) therefore arise as obstacles to access, which is difficult to overcome for the weakest financial actors. In general, these rights tend to contribute to the reduction of the offer: (1) Through the overexploitation of dedicated works and less investment in innovation, (2) Through the non-re-publication of works with limited commercial potential and—moreover—(3) Through their fostering of a significant rise in the costs allowing productive adaptations and reuse (Gowers 2006). As things stand, these property rights, therefore, appear to counter the development of a healthy "ecosystem" for the "creative economy", which is why numerous voices have called for them to be "relaxed". Therefore, apart from those academics who consider the new policies on intellectual property rights as "excessive" (e.g. Flew 2012), policy consultants and specialists have recently adopted a stance that contrasts with the dominant doctrine of law reinforcement. As already mentioned, since 2006 J. Howkins has been arguing in favour of laws that "adapted" to the "new economy"; also mentioned are A. Gowers and I. Hargreaves, both appointed by the Cabinet of the British Prime Minister's office to produce reports on intellectual property. These were respectively published in 2006 and 2011, and they both recommended a relaxation of the laws in order to be in line with changes in the technical and economic environment. This stance is also shared by the OECD (Peters et al. 2009: 81 *et seq.*).

12.3 Conclusion

This chapter started with suggesting that the emergence of "creative" industries and the "creative" economy is the symptom of a wish (both industrial and political) to see the "singularisation" of production backed-up by intellectual property rights. But firstly, it would of course be impossible to reduce the phenomenon to that aspect, especially as such rights are only one of the forms according to which products are "endorsed" or "qualified". This fosters the dismantling of the price-quality-production cost equation and guarantees their non-substitutability (alongside territorial endorsement labels, for example production quality labels). They nonetheless appear to be the most successful form of endorsement labelling as they generate value in and of themselves and, what is more, are negotiable.

Furthermore, although we undeniably see the adaptation of an organisational and economic model that has already been tried and tested in the context of cultural in a growing number of sectors, the effects of this process on the production of value are ambiguous. Therefore, the path taken over the last decade by the majority of OECD countries' governments, making intellectual property rights an economic tool supposed to relieve the pressure off of international competition, may also result in a "gridlock economy" (in the words of Heller 2008), because of these rights' hypertrophying effect and the fact that the idea of artificial rarity takes precedence over all other considerations.

Finally, the recent insistence on intellectual property rights reveals a major phenomenon in the understanding of contemporary capitalism: the central role of institutions—and therefore of politics—in the configuration of the markets.

References

Akerlof G, Arrow K, Bresnahan T, Buchanan J, Coase R, Cohen L et al (2002) The copyright term extension act of 1998: an economic analysis. Supreme Court of the USA, Washington, DC

Arrow K (1962) Economic welfare and the allocation of resources to invention. In: Nelson R (ed) The rate and direction of economic activity. Princeton University Press, New York, pp 609–626

Berger P, Luckmann T (1966) The social construction of reality. A treatise in the sociology of knowledge. Random House, New York

Bilton C (2007) Management and creativity. Blackwell Publishing, London

Bullich V (2011a) Le Droit d'auteur en Regard de la Théorie des Industries Culturelles. Les Enjeux de l'information et de la Communication. https://lesenjeux.univ-grenoble-alpes.fr/2011/Bullich/index.html. Accessed 17 Sept 2018

Bullich V (2011b) Le Dispositif Diplomatique des États-Unis contre le Piratage de Biens Culturels. In: Mattelart T (ed) Piratages audiovisuels. Les réseaux souterrains de la mondialisation culturelle. INA Editions, Paris, pp 53–74

Bullich V (2013) Perspectives Critiques sur la Propriété Artistique. Les Enjeux de l'Information et de la Communication.https://lesenjeux.univ-grenoble-alpes.fr/2013-supplement/07Bullich/index.html. Accessed 17 Sept 2018

Callon M, Millo Y, Muniesa F (2007) Market devices. Blackwell Publishing, Hoboken

Chamberlin E (1933) Theory of monopolistic competition: a re-orientation of the theory of value. Harvard University Press, Cambridge

Creative Industries Task Force/Department for Culture Media and Sport (1998) Creative industries mapping document. Report for the Department for Culture Media and Sport of the United Kingdom, London

Descombes V (2005) Les Institutions du Sens. Éditions de Minuit, Paris

Douglas M (1986) How institutions think. Syracuse University Press, Syracuse

Edelman B, Heinich N (2002) L'Art en Conflits. La Découverte, Paris

Flew T (2012) The creative industries. Sage, London

Garnham N (1986) Contribution to a political economy of mass-communication. In: Collins R, Curran J, Garnham N, Scannel P, Schlesinger P, Sparks C (eds) Media culture and society. A critical reader. Sage, London, pp 9–32

Giddens A (1984) The constitution of society: outline of the theory of structuration. University of California Press, Berkeley

Gowers A (2006) Gowers review of intellectual property. The Stationery Office, London

Hartley J (2013) Creative industries. In: Hartley J (ed) Creative industries. Blackwell Publishing, London, pp 1–40

Hegel G (2003/1820) Principes de la Philosophie du Droit. Paris: Presses universitaires de France

Heinich N (1998) Ce que l'Art Fait à la Sociologie. Éditions de Minuit, Paris

Heller M (2008) The gridlock economy. Basic Books, New York

Henaff M (2002) Le Prix de la Vérité. Le Seuil, Paris

Howkins J (2001) The creative economy. Penguin Books, London

Howkins J (2005) The creative economy. knowledge-driven economic growth. In: International conference: Asia-Pacific creative communities: a strategy for the 21st century. India, Jodhpur.

http://www.unescobkk.org/fileadmin/user_upload/culture/Cultural_Industries/presentations/Session_Two_-_John_Howkins.pdf. Accessed 17 Sept 2018
Howkins J (2006) The mayor's commission on the creative industries. In: Hartley J (ed) Creative industries. Blackwell Publishing, London, pp 117–125
Karpik L (2007) L'économie des singularités. Gallimard, Paris
Lampel J (2011) Converting values into others values: fairs and festivals as resource valuation and trading events. In: Moeran B, Pedersen J (eds) Negociating values in the creative industries. Cambridge University Press, Cambridge, pp 334–347
Lancaster K (1966) A new approach to consumer theory. J Polit Econ 74(2):132–157
Manuel P (1993) Cassette culture: popular music and Technology in North India. University of Chicago Press, Chicago
May C, Sell S (2006) Intellectual property rights. A critical history. Lynne Rienner Publishers, London
Munzer S (2001) Property as social relations. In: Munzer S (ed) New essays in the legal and political theory of property. Cambridge University Press, Cambridge, pp 36–75
Nelson P (1970) Information and consumer behavior. J Polit Econ 78(2):311–329
Netanel N (2009) The development agenda. Global intellectual property and developing countries. Oxford University Press, Oxford
O'Connor J (2007) The cultural and creative industries: a review of the literature. A report for creative partnerships. School of Performance and Cultural industries—The University of Leeds, Leeds
Orléan A (2011) L'empire de la valeur. Seuil, Paris
Ostrom E, Schlager E (1992) Property-rights regimes and natural resources: a conceptual analysis. Land Econ 68(3):249–262
Peters M, Marginson S, Murphy P (2009) Creativity and the global knowledge economy. Peter Lang, London
Searle J (1995) The construction of social reality. Simon and Schuster, New York
Sell S (2003) Private power, public law. The globalization of intellectual property rights. Cambridge University Press, Cambridge
Steiner P, Vatin F (Dir) (2009) Traité de sociologie économique. Presses universitaires de France, Paris
The Organisation for Economic Co-operation and Development (OECD) (2009a) Magnitude of counterfeiting and piracy of tangible products: an update, Paris
The Organisation for Economic Co-operation and Development (OECD) (2009b) Piracy of digital content, Paris
United Nations Conference on Trade and Development (UNCTAD) (2008) The creative economy—report 2008. http://www.unctad.org/en/docs/ditc20082cer_en.pdf. Accessed 17 Sept 2018
Vivant M, Bruguière J-M (2009) Droit d'auteur. Dalloz, Paris
Wasco J, Murdock G, Sousa H (eds) (2011) The handbook of political economy of communication. Wiley-Blackwell Publishing, Oxford

Vincent Bullich is an Associate Professor in Communication Sciences at the University of Grenoble Alpes, a member of the Gresec (research group on the challenges of communication). His work focuses mainly on the socioeconomic analysis of the cultural and communication industries as well as the political economy of intellectual property.

Chapter 13
Innovation and Media: Googlization and Limited Creativity

Patrick-Yves Badillo and Dominique Bourgeois

Abstract In many countries, media are facing severe crises. This chapter examines how media companies have undertaken a process of innovation that has nevertheless been accompanied by limited creativity. First, a literature review will recall the fundamental definitions of innovation and present various works on media innovation. Second, we will show that the ongoing innovation process is mainly based on a new media model, which we have called "the media Googlization model." Media Googlization focuses on a new digital management process that aims to take advantage of digital data, traffic, and advertising. This process represents a strong shift for media companies. Third, we will show that this innovation is a process of creative destruction with limited creativity. Indeed, media Googlization induces a destruction of media's traditional economic model, with, of course, new features. However, this innovation is accompanied by limited creativity because the priority has not been to fuel creativity in the production of quality informational and cultural media products. We will show that digital development tends to lead less to new forms of quality creative content than to a new form of industrial system driven by Internet platforms and media Googlization. We will draw on the Swiss press to illustrate our analysis.

Keywords Creativity · Creative destruction · Innovation · Googlization · Media

---

P.-Y. Badillo (✉)
University of Geneva, Geneva, Switzerland
e-mail: Patrick.Badillo@unige.ch

D. Bourgeois
University of Fribourg, Fribourg, Switzerland

I. Kiriya et al. (eds.), *The Industrialization of Creativity and Its Limits*, Science, Technology and Innovation Studies, https://doi.org/10.1007/978-3-030-53164-5_13

13.1 Introduction

In many countries, media are facing severe crises. Revenues, particularly those of daily newspapers, have dramatically declined, while traditional radio and television have had to evolve in a new technological and economic context. At the same time, an innovation process can be observed with the development of online media, the participation of users (in the form of, for example, user-generated content), and changes in organizations and journalistic work, such as that created by integrated newsrooms. Furthermore, the media is generally included in both cultural and creative industries because it is seen as dependent on a creativity from which it derives value [see, for example, UNESCO's (United Nations Educational, Scientific and Cultural Organization) 2013 classification of cultural and creative industries, which includes cinema, radio, and television]. Have changes to the media favored creativity? This chapter examines how a process of innovation has been underway in the media. We show that a new economic and managerial model, which we have called "the media Googlization model," is emerging but is accompanied by limited creativity.

First, we will conduct a literature review on innovation and media. Then, we will propose the media Googlization model as a new economic and managerial media model. Finally, the third section revisits innovation as a form of creative destruction and analyzes the limits of creativity in the media. We will draw on the Swiss press to illustrate our analysis.

13.2 Innovation and Media

13.2.1 Main Theories of Innovation

Let us recall the main theoretical approaches of innovation (Badillo 2013). Schumpeter is the key author of the technology push model. For him, innovation "consists in carrying out New Combinations" (Schumpeter 1939: 84). He considers five types of innovation and a general process of creative destruction: "The fundamental impulse that sets and keeps the capitalist engine in motion comes from the new consumers' goods, the new methods of production or transportation, the new markets, the new forms of industrial organization that capitalist enterprise creates . . . This process of Creative Destruction is the essential fact about capitalism" (Schumpeter 1942: 82–83).

Today, innovations in the media cannot only be explained by the technology push model. Other theories have shown that other elements may be important, such as the market (the demand pull or market pull innovation model) or organizational networks. In the open innovation model (Chesbrough 2003), new ideas come from both outside and inside the firm. Moreover, the disruptive innovation model (Christensen et al. 2015) can explain the rise of some new media. Von Hippel (2005) demonstrated the importance of users in the innovation process. Various communication theories, particularly recent approaches to media use, have led to a better understanding of the way users appropriate technology or even divert innovation by adapting innovation to new uses.

Rogers illustrated how the analysis of the logic of innovation evolved. His works moved from diffusionism to a process in which the user plays an important role. Indeed, in the third edition of his book (Rogers 1995), Rogers introduced the term "re-invention," which was defined as "the degree to which an innovation is changed or modified by a user in the process of its adoption and implementation" (1995: 174). According to Denning and Dunham (2010), "Innovation is the adoption of new practice in a community ... Success at innovation lies in the intersection among the innovator's domain expertise, social interaction skills, and ability to recognize and move into opportunities (realizable possibilities)" (6, 23). These authors highlighted the role of Google as a new information ecosystem that "through its infrastructure 'platform," (300) interacts with and supports the work of four groups. The first group is that of "content providers," i.e., media companies and individuals who create information. Advertisers are the second group. The third group is made up of consumers who "are the hundreds of millions of people who visit Google every day. Their searches reveal their interests ... They ... contribute ideas for improvements" (300). And the fourth group is that of innovators who work through the Google platform and who "constitute a rich and diverse product development network and attract many users who want to try new products. They generate revenue and expand the value of Google tools and technology." (Denning and Dunham 2010: 300).

According to us, this ecosystem has been so successful that it may be a model for other companies that develop their activities through digital platforms. Finally, we argue that the communication and social dimensions of innovation are essential. We showed that new digital re-innovation processes can be set up by promoting human relationships and social creativity (Badillo 2013).

13.2.2 Innovation in the Media

> Today, innovation is the buzzword in the news media industry. Strategies and initiatives are formulated and implemented by institutions and companies to cope with the developments, the new demands and requirements in the news media industry. Governments are also developing policies to support innovation activities. (Van Kranenburg 2015: 6).

In recent years, the word "innovation" has regularly appeared in the media and in the spheres of media professionals (e.g., WAN-IFRA 2018). Media stakeholders are aware of the challenges their organizations are facing. Innovation is perceived as a necessity and a matter of daily hard work: "'Innovation is not an event. It's not a lab. It's not the perfect day once a year. It's something that's happening 365 throughout your organization and it's a really hard process,' says Niddal Salah-Eldin, Director of Digital Innovation at WELT [a daily newspaper owned by Axel Springer]"

(Flueckiger 2018). The issues are generally approached from managerial and journalistic points of view.

Thus, it seems clear that innovation theories can be very useful in understanding changes in the media. However, according to Bleyen et al. (2014), "innovation in media is not well understood; it seems to be ill defined and poorly captured by statistics." (29). Content-related innovation, in particular, is generally not taken into account. Without being exhaustive, we can sum up some recent approaches specifically centered around media innovation. Storsul and Krumsvik (2013) recalled various approaches of innovation literature that have helped define the concept of media innovation, and they emphasized two dimensions of change: what is changing and the degree of novelty. Concerning the degree of novelty, the distinction between incremental and radical innovations is obvious: in the media, most innovations have been incremental; but radical or disruptive (Christensen 1997) innovations are now challenging the industry. Concerning the kinds of change, Storsul and Krumsvik (2013) applied Francis and Bessant's (2005) four Ps of innovation (product, process, position, and paradigmatic innovation), and they added a fifth type: social innovation, which is defined by Mulgan et al. (2007) as "new ideas that work to meet pressing unmet needs and improve peoples' lives" (Mulgan et al. 2007: 7).

Bleyen et al. (2014) proposed another typology of media innovations that include various aspects of content innovation; the five categories of innovation are business model innovation, production and distribution innovation, inner form innovation ["a new stylistic feature" (35)], core innovation ["a new theme or message" (35)], and consumption and media innovation ["a new way of consuming a content, or a related service" (35)]. That typology "takes as a starting point the standard distinction between product and process innovation, which is also reflected in the distinction made by Handke (2010) between creative and humdrum innovations" (Bleyen et al. 2014: 34). Process innovation is indeed divided into production and distribution innovation and business model innovation, while core and inner form innovations are two categories that characterize product, i.e., content innovation. Bleyen et al. (2014: 35) situated the fifth category—consumption and media innovation—between process and product innovation. According to Bleyen et al. (2014), "from the media industries' point of view" (28) the most important innovations concern the product, notably the core (for example, new types of TV shows), and business model categories, while the other types are driven more by external players, mainly information and communication technology and technology companies.

The impact of digitalization on media, particularly on news media, has been widely studied recently. From an innovation and management perspective, Küng (2015) analyzed five media outlets in the United States and the United Kingdom: *The Guardian*, *The New York Times*, *Quartz*, *BuzzFeed*, and *Vice Media*. As she underlined, the theoretical basis is the theory of disruptive innovation: "The news industry is facing a classic case of disruptive innovation. The effect the invention of the internet has had on the print newspaper is similar to the effect the launch of the railways had on horse-drawn transportation" (Küng 2015: 5). Other studies are centered around changes in newsrooms and journalistic work (Paulussen 2016). Some authors consider that innovation may emerge in the media thanks to journalists who are leading the process of newsroom change (García-Avilés et al. 2018). Moreover, according to Bruns (2014), innovation in media practices, driven by professional media practitioners, but also by users of media, "will prove to have the more immediate impact on the further evolution of the contemporary media ecology" (23).

In particular, media professionals must adapt their content and marketing practices to the Internet, as search engines drive a great amount of traffic to news websites. Search engine optimization (SEO) has thus become a tool used by media professionals in order to increase traffic. Giomelakis and Veglis (2016) showed that, in the case of Greece, media websites with the most traffic also have the largest proportion of SEO practices and that there was a clear correlation between traffic and various SEO factors. Moreover, search engines, and more particularly Google, which is a quasi-monopoly in many countries, have a significant effect on the web traffic of media websites and more generally on news gathering, news production, distribution, and, thus, journalism.

There are lengthy debates about big Internet companies, their digital platforms, and their influence on economic, political, and social activities. Beyond the innovative aspects of digital platforms, recent studies have critically examined the economic and social consequences of the use of digital platforms. In particular, according to Plantin and Punathambekar (2019), such digital platforms have reached "the scale, indispensability, and level of use typically achieved previously by infrastructures. Google and Facebook are perhaps the most compelling examples of this infrastructural evolution of digital platforms. They are both Internet companies that first leveraged the properties of platforms to increase their market power, yet they have been increasingly developing capacities that are typically understood as infrastructures" (169). Van Dijck et al. (2018) described the three processes of datafication, commodification, and selection that are developing on digital platforms, and they questioned the compatibility of private interests and public values.

Dogruel (2013) described some of the limits of the dominant approaches to media innovations by considering that three different concepts of it can be found in media economics and management research traditions:

> One approach discusses media innovation as an 'external,' mainly technical product or process innovation that 'demands' change in media organisations—applying a more or less implicit techno-deterministic position. A second field of study analyses new technological devices as new media consumer products, predominantly focusing on adoption and diffusion theory. Here, media economics scholars focus on media technologies (cf. interactive television, Internet, smartphones) but also on new media standards such as DVD . . . or broadband . . . In line with the literature on creative/cultural industries . . . a third set of research considers new media content (media formats, single media titles) as media innovation—often related to marketing-oriented approaches (32).

Dogruel (2013) then proposed to approach innovation from a "creative/cultural industries perspective" (33). and an "economic and sociological perspectives." (35). Concerning the creative/cultural industries perspective, she quoted Stoneman (2010), who introduced the notion of 'soft innovation': "Soft innovation is innovation in goods and services that primarily impacts upon aesthetic or intellectual appeal rather than functional performance" (Stoneman 2010: 22). Dogruel also recalled Handke (2010) research on the record industry, which recognized that the industry is both a high-tech manufacturing and cultural industry.

13.3 The Media Googlization Model

We argue that the ongoing innovation process in the media may be explained by a new media economic and managerial model. Of course, that does not mean that various innovations, particularly incremental innovations, are not developing concerning the contents of media products or new media uses. However, we consider that the main changes in the media ecosystem are linked to the emergence of a new media economic and managerial model. We will now summarize this new model (for first drafts, see Badillo and Bourgeois 2016a, 2017b).

Media companies are now seeking markets or market segments that are mainly interesting from the point of view of Internet audiences. Advertising is not the unique goal; media companies now try to get more traffic and, at the same time, data about visitors to their online platforms. As mentioned by Bell et al. (2017), "The influence of social media platforms and technology companies is having a greater effect on American journalism than even the shift from print to digital" (9). Moreover, "The influence of social platforms shapes the journalism itself. By offering incentives to news organizations for particular types of content, such as live video, or by dictating publisher activity through design standards, the platforms are explicitly editorial" (10). We introduced the "media Googlization model" (Badillo and Bourgeois 2015) to have a new understanding of the mutation of the media correlated to the influence of platforms. Thus, what we call "the advertising-traffic-data model" or "the media Googlization model" is emerging (see Fig. 13.1). We use the term "Googlization" to focus on the importance of online platforms and the new digital management processes they have created.

The "media Googlization model" is a new media economic and managerial model. It differs from the traditional model that has long been considered the economic and managerial basis of the media. The traditional model is a two-sided model: advertising and payments by consumers are the two sources of revenue for media. In the traditional model the content is defined by an editorial concept in order to attract readers. And, obviously, Web traffic was not taken into account in the traditional model. The media Googlization model has the following specific characteristics.

- It is a multi-sided model; a company offers various products and/or services that can attract advertising resources and specific audiences, including various informational and non-informational services and commercial products (e-commerce of events, etc.).
- Advertising and traffic are essentially the prerequisite of editorial concepts; a company has to adapt its editorial concepts to what we call advertising-traffic-

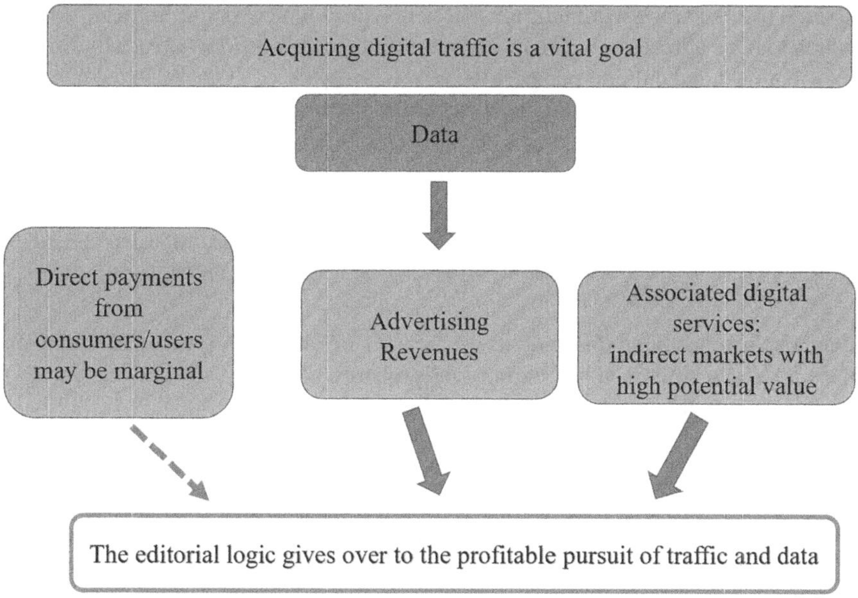

Fig. 13.1 The media googlization model

data. Thanks to digital flexibility, media are now able to define and change editorial concepts in order to get traffic.

- In this new framework, media activities must be understood from the general perspective that the new Holy Grail is traffic and data. If one gets a lot of traffic, one can likely obtain high advertising revenues, and in the near future, one will be able to propose new services and/or sell data. New services will be linked to geolocation and information about visitors. Media could become a central means of knowing consumer preferences and uses for many kinds of commercial and noncommercial fields of interest. For example, if one knows the people interested in specific health questions, one can advertise specific services. In other words, information is a means of creating traffic, and traffic allows the development of advertising and the acquisition of high-value data.

The innovation process at the heart of the growth of the media Googlization model is mainly focused on a new management process in a digital context. This process leads to a kind of destruction of the traditional media economic model while creating, of course, new features of the industry. Indeed, print journalism is facing a major crisis in many countries, with a decline of traditional resources, i.e., paying readers and advertising resources. Other media, such as television, are also concerned, especially in relation to the development of streaming services. The search for online traffic and data is becoming the core of the media ecosystem, but it does not push for quality content. In the media Googlization model, editorial logic gives over to the profitable pursuit of traffic and data. Moreover, it is reasonable to assume that the Googlization of the media may lead to new online content, some of which may be attractive to audiences, but of limited cost and low creativity from an informational and cultural perspective.

While our analysis of the impact of media platforms is largely convergent with the approach of Bell et al., let us indicate an important difference. Bell et al. (2017) stated:

> Platforms rely on algorithms to sort and target content. They have not wanted to invest in human editing, to avoid both cost and the perception that humans would be biased. However, the nuances of journalism require editorial judgment, so platforms will need to reconsider their approach (10).

Our conclusion is quite different, as we are not sure all the platforms will reconsider their approach. Media Googlization will probably contribute to the weakening of journalism and the limiting of creativity.

13.4 Creative Destruction and Limited Creativity

The process of creative destruction can be clearly observed today in the media industries, particularly in the process of digitalization, which changes the methods of production, the products (online content, free content), the forms of industrial organization and the markets (geographic and those linked to various social media). Let us deepen the theoretical approach of innovation in creative industries with an exploration of creative destruction.

13.4.1 Revisiting Innovation as Creative Destruction

In Schumpeter's innovation approach, the "process of Creative Destruction is the essential fact about capitalism" (Schumpeter op.cit.). In this fundamental analysis, the process of innovation relies on both destruction and creation. One component of innovation is destruction aimed at improving performance and increasing profit. In this case, innovation is related to the management of human resources or the betterment of procedures and technologies. Additionally, the model includes a creative component, which means that the innovation process has an undisputable human dimension, which appears in the activities of managers, researchers, engineers, designers, etc.

Recent changes in the creative industries can be analyzed by considering the process of creative destruction. Creative industries, such as the media, largely rely on a human dimension; they are based on the work of artists, designers, journalists, and, more generally, human creation, which can be partially personalized and partially depersonalized. The human dimension of creation is key in media innovation, especially content innovation, but destruction is also at work and may have considerable human impacts. We have shown that the media's innovation process is mainly focused on a new digital management process, which represents a kind of destruction that brings with it some new features, but the creative process does not necessarily prioritize the human aspect of innovation.

13.4.2 Creative Industries: Which Content Innovations?

There are various possible approaches to the changes in the creative industries, in particular the media. We will not analyze the issue from the point of view of the arts or entertainment. We will not view it solely from a management perspective, although this is important for media companies and media management literature. Let us recall, as stated by Dwyer (2016), that "there is no consensus on what creativity actually is. Simply put, there is no theory of creativity" and "there is surely no agreed theory of managing creativity" (343–344). Our approach based on the literature on cultural and creative industries is focused on innovation, as a creative destruction. It is applied to the production of information, especially on news, by media.

Since the first studies in the United Kingdom 20 years ago, many governments have recognized the concept of "the creative industries": for example, the UK Creative Industries Council was created in 2011 and a campaign "Creative France" was launched in October 2015 in France. More recently, the wider idea of the creative economy has emerged, defined by UNCTAD (United Nations Conference on Trade and Development) as "an evolving concept which builds on the interplay between human creativity and ideas and intellectual property, knowledge and technology" (UNCTAD2020). However, there are various definitions of the creative industries, and it is not easy to measure a creative economy (e.g., O'Connor 2010; Bouquillon et al. 2013). Beyond the debates among researchers about definitions and measurement, the reference to creativity is inserted in the power relationship between industry actors, and it contributes to challenge and transform public policy (Bouquillon et al. 2015).

Thus, a creative perspective can be useful in understanding some of the significant stakes in media changes. Jones et al. (2015) considered four primary drivers of change in creative products and creative industries: demand, public policy, technology, and globalization. They also identified "four primary types of change in the creative industries—Preserve, Ideate, Transform and Recreate—as particular combinations of change in semiotic codes and material base" (Jones et al. 2015: 4). Miège (2017) developed a critical approach to cultural and creative industries; in particular, he analyzed the arrival of content industries: the content industries will increasingly provide information and cultural content for communication industries.

Beyond various categories of innovation that can be applied to the cultural and creative industries, it seems possible to distinguish between new technological, managerial, and economic characteristics and what constitutes creativity with impacts on the informational and cultural field. Setting up digital platforms has been obviously innovation for traditional newspaper companies: many newspapers have now digital-first offerings, such as reportages designed to be consumed online. Undoubtedly innovation processes are going on from the technological point of view: streaming and podcast offerings, access every time, everywhere... New processes of management, production, dissemination, and journalistic work are developing. Some digital newspaper leaders like *The New York Times* are offering a diversity of narrative content with high quality. Does that mean that we assist to a generalized process of creativity from the point of view of the quality and the diversity of content? In fact, form and content should not be confused: there is a large diversity of new narrative formats, such as short, ludic, and dynamic videos; but that does not mean that content is generally based on in-depth investigation. As regards new media products, creativity concerns mainly technologies and formats. But content is often impoverished and the diversity of content is decreasing since many newspapers closed and fewer journalists are working. Journalistic creativity has to be supported by a large number of journalists, which permits a diversity of opinions, and also by in-depth analyses guaranteed by the professionalism and independence of journalists. Let us give some numbers to show the impoverishment of journalism. In the United States, there were 74′410 newsroom employees in the newspaper sector in 2006 and only 37′900 in 2018 (Pew Research Center 2019). If there is less investment on information professionals (journalists), it is obvious that the diversity and the quality of content are in danger. Of course, there are other information sources than the media on the Web. But, as shown by various studies, "dis-information," "mis-information," and "mal-information" (Wardle and Derakhshan 2017: 20) are spreading on the Web. The need for quality information is all the more strongly that the difficulty to spread truth on the Web was demonstrated by an authoritative study: "Falsehood diffused significantly farther, faster, deeper and more broadly than the truth in all categories of information" (Vosoughi et al. 2018). We argue that creativity in the field of media production, particularly in news production, is limited because it is not mainly oriented towards hierarchized, checked, and deep information. Therefore, according to us, the core issues in the new media ecosystem are the following ones:

- To what extent does the media Googlization model explain the destruction of the old media system and the development of a new media system?
- And to what extent is the new media system accompanied by true journalistic creativity, beyond new economic and managerial characteristics? For us, creativity and innovation in this field should mean checked, hierarchized and deep information. In particular, do content innovations that appear in the new system favor informational and cultural quality?

The Googlization of the media is indisputably a trend toward a new economic and managerial system, with the associated destruction of the old system, but creativity to produce quality information is limited.

13.5 The Swiss Press

The Swiss press is very illustrative of the rise of the media Googlization model. It has a long-standing tradition of quality information, diversity, and high newspaper readership. Above all, it is essential to democracy since regular "votations" are organized and information is at the core of the political Swiss model. The media, in particular newspapers, enlighten debates with relevant information. But the Swiss media system is challenged in terms of economic issues and, in particular, the Swiss paid for press is facing a crisis.

At first glance, the Swiss media situation may not appear so bad if one considers that uses of media are developing, particularly uses of new media by young generations. Nevertheless, the economic dynamics are detrimental to traditional media. In a previous study (Badillo and Bourgeois 2016a), we showed that the financial resources of Switzerland's main traditional media (press, radio, and television) are lower than those of the country's telecommunications sector (fixed and mobile telecommunications, Internet, and cable companies). Traditional media are poor, and furthermore, the dynamics of their financial resources are negative. The telecommunications sector benefits from a much higher level of financial resources, and these resources have progressed over time. But, the telecommunications sector develops information technology and does not produce content.

Moreover, the Swiss media's economic system is itself challenged by the development of online content and services. In Switzerland, the media system has long been based on print journalism and public television. However, the print industry is losing resources, and the public broadcaster is facing a decline of its public resources, due to political decisions. Correlatively, print and television have both been developing strategies to produce online content. We analyze the press because it is the main media industry that has faced a large crisis. In this context new business models and creation of new content—including audiovisual entertainment—are developing. The Swiss press is increasingly shaped by the digital transformation that we have modelized in term of media Googlization.

In the Swiss press, especially the daily press for which people have traditionally paid, both sales and advertising revenues have indeed dramatically declined. The main press companies have introduced various measures to diminish costs, such as integrated newsrooms and layoffs. The first integrated newsroom in Switzerland was created by Ringier in 2010: the editorial offices of the German-speaking newspapers *Blick*, *Sonntagsblick*, *Blick am Abend* and *Blick.ch*, together with Web-TV, were joined together. Since then, other integrated newsrooms were created by the press companies and the main strategies have favored online news. For example, in 2018, the print edition of *Blick am Abend* was abolished. The end of *L'Hebdo* in 2017, a magazine in the French-speaking part of Switzerland, may have been considered as the beginning of a trend toward the disappearance of many newspapers, even well-known, quality newspapers.

Unquestionably, destruction is affecting Swiss media. Innovation has developed through the free press—free print newspapers since the beginning of the years 2000, and, of course, free online press—the rise of news and communication on the Internet, new sources of revenue for media firms, new content, and new organizational structures.

The understanding of the media Googlization model could be clarified by analyzing the strategies of the two main Swiss press companies, Ringier and TX Group—TX Group was previously called Tamedia; at the end of 2019 Tamedia decided to change its name to TX Group and the name "Tamedia" was given only to the TX Group's paid media sector. We presented detailed case studies related to TX Group and Ringier (Badillo and Bourgeois 2017a). Let us update some main elements. These companies are indeed examples of the new online media model that is radically changing the production of news. TX Group and Ringier have tried to resist destruction by developing digital strategies with scale and scope economies at the heart of their new activities. Both companies have expanded digital news platforms with, of course, digital advertising. They have also increasingly developed other digital services, with many online platforms. Their new digital activities, such as classifieds platforms and many e-commerce platforms, are, in general, profitable. In 2019, TX Group's digital offerings represented 51% of its total revenue and 77% of its EBITDA (Earnings before interest, taxes, depreciation, and amortization); the upward trend towards digital is strong, since in 2014 the figures were respectively 24.5% and around 33%. Furthermore, the EBIT margin (Earnings before interest and taxes/Revenue), which gives an indication of profitability, is low for TX Group's paid media activities—less than 3% in 2019—while it is high for "classifieds" online activities—48.7% in 2019—such as *homegate.ch*, *ImmoStreet.ch*, which are real estate portals. Concerning Ringier, digital businesses represented 46% of Ringier's total 2018 revenue and contributed some 71% to its 2018 EBITDA. The global Ringier's EBITDA margin (EBITDA/Revenue) was equal to 11.3% in 2018. Marc Walder, Chief Executive Officer of Ringier, emphasized that "The Ringier Group has successfully transformed itself from a classic publishing house into a modern and diversified media corporation over the past few years" (Ringier 2019: 155).

Of course, for Swiss media companies, the development of digital activities is accompanied by the creation of new content, even if the focus is increasingly on digital services rather than information. Further, the issue of quality journalism remains important, as underlined by Pietro Supino, chairman of TX Group's Board of Directors: "We will endeavor to create lasting added value through quality journalism, attractive advertising opportunities and innovative digital offers" (Tamedia 2017: 5). It must be noted that, for example, TX Group has launched its own quality monitoring program. Moreover, companies such as TX Group could at any time reinvest in the information sector and produce quality information, as they generate significant profits from their digital services.

Even if the two main Swiss press companies are successful in their digital transformation, two main issues have to be recalled. A process of concentration is going on in the Swiss press, as we demonstrated in other contributions (Badillo and Bourgeois 2016b, 2017a). Concentration implies a decline in pluralism. Moreover, the core business of the two main Swiss press companies is less and less the production of information and more and more the deployment of various digital services through online platforms. We can conclude that creativity from the managerial point of view is satisfying, since these companies are flourishing in some digital segments. But, from another hand, creativity relying on the capacity of the whole Swiss press to produce fundamental and quality information is questioned.

13.6 Conclusion

To understand recent changes in the media, we have focused our analysis on innovation and creativity. Innovation has to be analyzed as creative destruction. We have proposed "the media Googlization model." We have shown that the innovation at the heart of the media Googlization model is mainly focused on a new management process in a digital context with an underlying objective of improving profit. Let us note that we have analyzed the limits of "media Googlization," but we are fully aware of the importance and success of innovations supported by Google itself. The main issue for us is the incidence of "media Googlization" on the production of information by media. The Swiss press illustrates the Googlization of the media.

Beyond new economic and managerial characteristics, will the new media system lead to a development of creativity that will favor informational and cultural quality? The Googlization model is so strong that it is now increasingly adopted and integrated into the media model. Getting traffic, audience, and data is becoming a dominant activity of the media. We have proposed a new economic and managerial model that clarifies the ongoing strong shift—a mutation of the media. Is the new press an industry dominated by the goal of producing information or developing traffic and data? We hope our contribution will foster debate. In fact, the true challenge for media and society is to fuel creativity to produce information and cultural products and to enhance the quality of information and media products.

Acknowledgments We thank the reviewers for their comments and suggestions.

References

Badillo P-Y (2013) Les théories de l'innovation revisitées: une lecture communicationnelle et interdisciplinaire de l'innovation—Du modèle « émetteur » au modèle communicationnel. Les Enjeux de l'information et de la communication 14(1):19–34. https://lesenjeux.univ-grenoble-alpes.fr/2013/Badillo/index.html. Accessed 28 Apr 2018

Badillo P-Y, Bourgeois D (2015) Media "googlization": the case of the Swiss media model and the press. In: Communication to the International Media Management Academic Association (IMMAA) Conference, Moscow, 17–18 Sept 2015

Badillo P-Y, Bourgeois D (2016a) Les médias publics: concentration ou concurrence « numérique » exacerbée? Chapter 1. In: Badillo P-Y (Coord), Bourgeois D, Deltenre I, Marchand G (eds) Médias publics et société numérique. L'heure du grand débat. Slatkine, Geneva, pp 17–69

Badillo P-Y, Bourgeois D (2016b) Media concentration in Switzerland, chapter 14. In: Noam EM, The International Media Concentration Collaboration (eds) Who owns the World's media? Media concentration and ownership around the world. Oxford University Press, New York, NY, pp 357–379

Badillo PY, Bourgeois D (2017a) The Swiss press model. Democracy, concentration and digital diversification. Recherches en communication 44:9–30. http://sites.uclouvain.be/rec/index.php/rec/article/viewFile/10423/7983. Accessed 7 May 2019

Badillo P-Y, Bourgeois D (2017b) Media crisis: innovation without creativity? The case of the Swiss media. In: Communication to the international conference "The industrialization of creativity and its limits: value, self-expression and the economy of culture in times of crisis", Saint Petersburg, 23–24 Jun 2017

Bell EJ, Owen T, with Brown PD, Hauka C, Rashidian N (2017) The platform press: how Silicon Valley reengineered journalism. Tow Center for Digital Journalism, Columbia Journalism School, Columbia University. https://academiccommons.columbia.edu/doi/10.7916/D8R216ZZ. Accessed 8 May 2019

Bleyen V-A, Lindmark S, Ranaivoson H, Ballon P (2014) A typology of media innovations: insights from an exploratory study. J Media Innov 1(1):28–51

Bouquillon P, Miège B, Moeglin P (2013) L'industrialisation des biens symboliques: les industries créatives en regard des industries culturelles. PUG, Grenoble

Bouquillon P, Miège B, Moeglin P (2015) Industries du contenu et industries de la communication. Contribution à une déconstruction de la notion de créativité. Les Enjeux de l'Information et de la Communication 16(3B):17–26. http://lesenjeux.u-grenoble3.fr/2015-supplementB/01-Bouquillon-Miege-Moeglin/index.html. Accessed 10 Jan 2018

Bruns A (2014) Media innovations, user innovations, societal innovations. J Media Innov 1 (1):13–27

Chesbrough H (2003) Open innovation: the new imperative for creating and profiting from technology. Harvard Business School Press, Boston, MA

Christensen CM (1997) The Innovator's dilemma. HarperCollins, New York, NY

Christensen CM, Raynor ME, McDonald R (2015) What is disruptive innovation? Harv Bus Rev 93 (12):44–53

Denning P, Dunham R (2010) The innovator's way: essential practices for successful innovation. MIT Press, Cambridge, MA

Dogruel L (2013) Opening the black box. The Conceptualising of media innovation, chapter 2. In: Storsul T, Krumsvik AH (eds) Media innovations. A multidisciplinary study of change. Göteborg, Nordicom, University of Gothenburg, pp 29–43

Dwyer P (2016) Managing creativity in media Organisations, chapter 20. In: Lowe GF, Charles CB (eds) Managing media firms and industries: What's so special about media management? Springer International Publishing Switzerland, Switzerland, pp 343–365

Flueckiger S (2018) How Axel Springer's WELT avoids 'glitter pony' innovation. World News Publishing Focus, Blog of WAN IFRA. https://blog.wan-ifra.org/2018/11/05/how-axel-springer-s-welt-avoids-glitter-pony-innovation (On-line article, Posted 2018-11-05, 11:11). Accessed 20 Nov 2018

Francis D, Bessant J (2005) Targeting innovation and implications for capability development. Technovation 25(3):171–183

García-Avilés JA, Carvajal-Prieto M, Arias-Robles F, De Lara-González A (2018) Journalists' views on innovating in the newsroom: proposing a model of the diffusion of innovations in media outlets. J Media Innov. https://www.journals.uio.no/index.php/TJMI/issue/view/589 (On-line First). Accessed 12 Dec 2018

Giomelakis D, Veglis A (2016) Investigating search engine optimization factors in media websites: the case of Greece. Digit J 4(3):379–400

Handke C (2010) The creative destruction of copyright—innovation in the record industry and digital copying. PhD thesis, Erasmus University Rotterdam, Rotterdam

Jones C, Lorenzen M, Sapsed J (2015) Creative industries: a typology of change. In: Jones C, Lorenzen M, Sapsed J (eds) The Oxford handbook of creative industries. Oxford University Press, Oxford, pp 4–30

Küng L (2015) Innovators in digital news. I.B. Tauris & Co. Ltd (In Association with the Reuters Institute for the Study of Journalism, University of Oxford), London

Miège B (2017) Les industries culturelles et créatives face à l'ordre de l'information et de la communication. Presses Universitaires de Grenoble, Grenoble

Mulgan G, Tucker S, Ali R, Sanders B (2007) Social innovation: what it is, why it matters and how it can be accelerated. Working paper, Skoll Centre for Social Entrepreneurship, Oxford, Saïd Business School, University of Oxford. http://eureka.sbs.ox.ac.uk/761/1/Social_Innovation.pdf. Accessed 12 May 2019

O'Connor J (2010) The cultural and creative industries: a literature review. Newcastle upon Tyne: creativity, culture and education series, November 2010. http://www.creativitycultureeducation.org/wp-content/uploads/CCE-lit-review-creative-cultural-industries-257.pdf. Accessed 10 May 2017

Paulussen S (2016) Innovation in the newsroom, chapter 13. In: Witschge T, Anderson CW, Domingo D, Hermida A (eds) The SAGE handbook of digital journalism. SAGE, Los Angeles—London, pp 192–206

Pew Research Center (2019) Newspapers fact sheet, 9 Jul 2019. https://www.journalism.org/fact-sheet/newspapers/. Accessed 16 Mar 2020

Plantin J-C, Punathambekar A (2019) Digital media infrastructures: pipes, platforms, and politics. Media Cult Soc 41(2):163–174

Ringier (2019) Ringier annual report 2018. Ringier AG, Zurich. https://www.ringier.com/en/media/annual-reports/annual-report-2018 (Published March 2019). Accessed 17 Mar 2020

Rogers E (1995) Diffusion of innovations, 4th edn. Free Press, New York

Schumpeter JA (1939) Business cycles. A theoretical, historical and statistical analysis of the capitalist process, 1st edn. McGraw-Hill Book Company, New York, Toronto, London (Abridged version used in this chapter: document produced in digital version by Didier Lagrange, in the framework of "Les classiques des sciences sociales", Chicoutimi). http://classiques.uqac.ca/classiques/Schumpeter_joseph/business_cycles/schumpeter_business_cycles.pdf. Accessed 14 Mar 2020

Schumpeter JA (1942) Capitalism, socialism, and democracy, 1st edn. Harper & Row, New York. (Edition used in this chapter: George Allen & Unwin Ltd., 1976)

Stoneman P (2010) Soft innovation. Economics, product aesthetics, and the creative industries. Oxford University Press, Oxford

Storsul T, Krumsvik AH (2013) What is media innovation? In: Storsul T, Krumsvik AH (eds) Media innovations. A multidisciplinary study of change. Nordicom, University of Gothenburg, Göteborg, pp 13–26

Tamedia (2017) Annual Report 2017 Tamedia. https://tx.group/tl_files/content/Group/Investor%20Relations/Englisch/2017_geschaeftsbericht_en.pdf. Accessed 14 Mar 2020

UNCTAD (2020) Creative Economy Programme Webpage. http://unctad.org/en/Pages/DITC/CreativeEconomy/Creative-Economy-Programme.aspx. Accessed 15 Mar 2020

UNESCO (2013) Creative economy report, 2013 special edition. United Nations Development Programme (UNDP), The United Nations Educational, Scientific and Cultural Organization (UNESCO), New York, Paris

Van Dijck J, Poell T, de Waal M (2018) The platform society. Oxford University Press, New York

Van Kranenburg H (ed) (2015) A European comparison of innovation policies to trigger innovation in journalism and news media (January). Radboud University and Het Stimuleringsfonds voor de Journalistiek, Nijmegen. http://www.parlementairemonitor.nl/9353000/1/j4nvgs5kjg27kof_j9vvij5epmj1ey0/vjugg24lpox0/f=/blg521377.pdf. Accessed 25 May 2017

Von Hippel E (2005) Democratizing innovation. MIT Press, Cambridge, MA

Vosoughi S, Roy D, Aral S (2018) The spread of true and false news online. Science 359 (6380):1146–1151

WAN-IFRA [World Association of Newspapers and News Publishers] (2018) Innovation in news media world report 2018. Innovation International Media Consulting Group, London

Wardle C, Derakhshan H (2017) Information disorder: toward an interdisciplinary framework for research and policy making. In: Council of Europe Report DGI(2017)09. Council of Europe, Strasbourg

Christensen CM (1997) The innovator's dilemma. HarperCollins, New York, NY, USA

Patrick-Yves Badillo is a Professor at Geneva University, and Director-founder of Medi@LAB-Genève, a research institute on innovation, media, and communication science. He is working on innovation, digital change, media concentration and social media, influence through the Web, health communication, and digital divide. He published nine books and more than 200 publications and researches (https://archive-ouverte.unige.ch/authors/view/29736; http://patrickbadillo.com/). He is head of the Master program in "Médias et communication digitale." Expert: European Research Council (2015), French National Board of Universities (CNU 2011–2014), Swiss, Belgian, and Canadian National Science Foundations. Head of the project "Innovation and Social Networks" (Swiss National Science Foundation), in collaboration with the Luxembourg Institute of Science and Technology, and the University of Technology, Sydney. Following his success at the National French University "Concours d'agrégation" he was Professor at Aix-Marseille University. Then he served as director (1997–2008) of the "École de Journalisme et de Communication d'Aix-Marseille", as director (2008–2011) of the IRSIC Laboratory, and responsible for the ANR Digital Economy and Society Prospective think tank and President for the main Colloquium in Science and Information Technologies (French National Research Agency-ANR 2008–2012). He obtained his PhD in the field of innovation and information technology at Paris I Panthéon Sorbonne University, and a post-master diploma in telecommunications and media management, Paris-Dauphine. He first worked at France Telecom, National Center for Telecommunications Studies (CNET), as head of studies in economic and technological fields related to the development of satellite, cable, optical fiber, and attached to the General Director of the CNET.

Dominique Bourgeois was Professor and holder of the Chair in Communication and Media Science at the University of Fribourg, Switzerland, from 2009 to 2019. She created in 2010 and was head of the Master's program in "Business Communication." As Professor Emeritus, University of Fribourg, she is developing a research project on new media uses, media innovation, and health communication, in collaboration with Geneva University. She is also co-author of the MOOC "Innovation, media and digital transformation," Geneva University (available in 2020 on the Coursera platform). She is working on digital innovation, business and digital communication, media economics, e-Learning, social media, uses of information, and communication technology (see her publications http://dominiquebourgeois.eu/). She is an expert for the Swiss National Science Foundation and the Swiss Association of Communication and Media Research. She was a member of the jury Television of the Swiss Press Award (Reinhardt-von Graffenried foundation). She obtained a first PhD in International Economics and a second PhD in Economics/Econometrics, Aix-Marseille University. After her success in the National French University "Concours d'agrégation," she became Professor in economics, Angers University, then Aix-Marseille University, France. She produced several official reports for various institutions and ministries, especially in the field of econometric forecasting, prospective, and strategic analysis. She has also carried out various researches and publications on media and new media, innovation, and digital issues. She had responsibilities in several international research projects (e-Learning and information technology, European Commission; communication and digital strategies in the context of a major crisis, European Commission). She was also in charge of researches dedicated to the Swiss, French, and European part of a major study on media concentration (project led by Columbia University); she is co-author of three chapters in the book: E.M. Noam, and *The International Media Concentration Collaboration. Who Owns the World's Media? Media Concentration and Ownership around the World*. New York, NY: Oxford University Press USA.

Afterword: Emphasizing the Limits

From an economic standpoint, creativity is related to promises put forward by new developmental policies appearing in different countries in recent decades. That is why there is a general expectation from creative industries to improve the quality of life by foregrounding tolerance, inclusivity, and self-expression. The editors and authors of this volume have questioned this framework by focusing on the limits of creativity and its industrialization, including unfulfilled promises and unrealized potential that may contrast with what is envisioned by policy makers, optimists, and experts in the field. The contributions gathered in this volume point to issues related to the inequalities around creative work, the rise of the new oligopolistic strategies of global corporations in the creative field, and the domination of purely economic, competitive, and productivist logics and ideologies, among other elements. These processes pose limitations to genuine self-fulfillment, self-expression, and the development of open, democratic societies as creativity becomes a part of industrializing, rationalizing, and optimizing mindsets that constitute the core of contemporary cultural capitalism. Hence, this volume foregrounds the idea that the social technology of creativity in policy and discourse is inseparable from questions of class, social inequality, and exclusion. To gauge the political economy of creativity in relation to the current situation, we suggested exploring the shifts and transformations of creative imaginaries, practices, and business models taking shape as a result of political circumstances at the micro and macro levels.

This volume opened with an exploration of sustainability concerns regarding the perspectives of growth and work practices. The chapter by Mark Banks and Paula Serafini discussed the allegedly sustainable character of the creative economy that is usually positively assessed and often characterized as environmentally friendly. Their contribution demonstrates how this view fosters a rather depoliticized way of thinking about the idea of sustainability, one in which creative industries are somehow imagined as potentially green and transformative. The limits of sustainability, however, are evident when one considers the extractivist dimension that capitalism constantly intensifies. The creative and cultural industries are also dependent on the extraction of resources, just like all other economic sectors. Banks and

I. Kiriya et al. (eds.), *The Industrialization of Creativity and Its Limits*, Science, Technology and Innovation Studies, https://doi.org/10.1007/978-3-030-53164-5

Serafini's chapter unlocks the kinds of questions that this volume is concerned with, probing readers to rethink the structural and ideological dimensions of positive assessments of the creative economy and the creativity hype. If we think of the creative field in terms of labor sustainability, the integration and mediation of economic activities in all aspects of social life produces labor outcasts that exist in a limited and liminal space in terms of career prospects. Yet, these petty producers, rather than acting autonomously and beyond the system, are integrated in the mandates of compulsory creativity and innovation that often strip their cultural production from meaningful politicization (Larsen 2014: 161).

For Arvidsson, the limits of the industrious economy (that is to say, informal economic activities) brought forth by waves of capitalist restructuring moves entrepreneurship beyond the scope of economic rationalities, transforming it into what he discusses as "actorpreneurship", a phenomenon through which industriousness becomes an existential project and "a way of coping and surviving" (Arvidsson 2019: 56). In this regard, the chapter by Jaka Primorac, Valerija Barada, and Edgar Buršić provided a detailed empirical account of average Croatian creative workers who also rely on family and community to make ends meet while perceiving themselves as members of an elite group. Thus, other than being the driver of a new social sustainability model, as often conceived by industrial think tanks and politicians, creative economy, in the late capitalist context, reproduces societal inequalities.

Likewise, Margarita Kuleva brought such concerns to the Russian post-transitional paradigm. According to her ethnographic study, the creative workers of new and so-called creative spaces in Moscow are merging a Westernized work culture and aesthetics (that may resemble those of the Tate and Guggenheim) with old Soviet practices related to the heroization of work that magnifies levels of self-oppression. Further, by studying the reception of creative writing programs in Italy, Guidotti showed how such programs can be regarded as regulating the inclusion/exclusion process of an industrially intensified literary field.

This volume's contributions have also considered the broader political context in which creativity is today encoded with positive meaning and the crises relating to it, such as the above-mentioned ecological one. As a case in point, the economic crisis in Europe and the world brought about a post-2010 rearrangement not only of economic priorities but also political governance. The rise of an internally antagonistic yet global new right, or alt-right, expressed in the election of strongmen such as Donald Trump in the United States, Jair Bolsonaro in Brazil, and Viktor Orbán in Hungary, among others, entails a readjustment (or in some cases outright rejection) of the openness and tolerance of the initial creative economy promoted by ex-socially democratic, third way governments. The wholehearted entrepreneurial and unapologetically market-oriented imaginary of this new right mobilizes a creativity even more stripped off its prior social democratic context and undertones.

In this sense, Panos Kompatsiaris and Nada Endrissat discussed how contemporary art events initially oriented toward the attraction of anti-capitalist activism may run the danger of becoming entertaining spectacles. A similar aestheticization of politics, as Yiannis Mylonas showed, emerged as an ideological paradigm during the Greek economic crisis and was meant to produce consensus over the allegedly self-inflicted nature of a national debt crisis and drive individualized energies toward risky entrepreneurial ventures in the grim realities of a neoliberal restructuring framework. This ideological mandate of creativity as a nation-developing framework seemed to transform aspirations of self-expression and art into biopolitics.

Tatiana Romashko further pursued such reflections in considering the Russian case by describing how, within a 10-year time frame, the country's cultural policy has been colonized by geopolitical discourses and notions of a Russian world along with concerns regarding the protection of national sovereignty. In turn, Evangelos Chrysagis showed how DIY cultural producers attempt to resist the full commercialization of their activities and ideological co-optation by creative capitalism. The manifestos that Chrysagis described inform the moral standpoints of practitioners and their DIY ethos harvests transformative cultural strategies.

Finally, Part III of this volume reexamined the industrial model of creative industries by putting emphasis on technology and the market mechanisms related to this industrialization. Bernard Miège introduced the ambivalent character of the notion of creative industries as a concept and also demonstrated their heterogeneity in contrast to the well-conceptualized notion of cultural industries. In his contribution, Ilya Kiriya showed how the new domains of culture previously considered as non-industrialized have become increasingly standardized, mass-oriented, and commodified. Domains such as online education, musicals, theatrical performances, or comedy television have become progressively dominated by the commercial logics of reproducible cultural industrial forms. Vincent Bullich further explained how the intellectual-property-rights framework and its massive implications in the field of creative industries is used to create the artificial singularity of creative products and disconnect them from the notion of quality. Thus, intellectual property rights, instead of protecting authors and making publicly available the content of cultural industries, are mainly used to limit competition for the benefit of big commercial players. The book concluded with a chapter of Patrick-Yves Badillo and Dominique Bourgeois in which they analyzed the media's model of creative development, which they call "Googlization," by looking at the Swiss media. From the perspective of creative-destruction, the authors argued that the Googlization model reduces innovation and compromises quality while augmenting profit.

The interdisciplinary contributions included in this volume addressed the current economic, political, and sociocultural dimensions of creativity in the context of the increasingly globalizing, or colonizing, drives of the cultural and creative industries (Lash and Lury 2007). They navigate the limits of creativity in the ideological configurations and the political operationalization of creative practices under the pretext of development, as creativity becomes an ideological dispositif for the various instrumentalist needs of commerce and state policy.

References

Arvidsson A (2019) Changemakers: the industrious future of the digital economy. Polity, London
Larsen SN (2014) Compulsory creativity. Cult Unbound 6:159–177
Lash S, Lury C (2007) Global culture industry. Polity Press, Cambridge

The manufacturer's authorised representative in the EU is Springer Nature Customer Service Centre GmbH, Europaplatz 3, 69115 Heidelberg, Germany. If you have any concerns regarding our products, please contact ProductSafety@springernature.com

Printed and bound by CPI Group (UK) Ltd, Croydon, CR0 4YY
30/09/2026
02225460-0014